Possessed Women, Haunted States

Possessed Women, Haunted States

Cultural Tensions in Exorcism Cinema

Christopher J. Olson and
CarrieLynn D. Reinhard

LEXINGTON BOOKS
Lanham • Boulder • New York • London

Published by Lexington Books
An imprint of The Rowman & Littlefield Publishing Group, Inc.
4501 Forbes Boulevard, Suite 200, Lanham, Maryland 20706
www.rowman.com

Unit A, Whitacre Mews, 26-34 Stannary Street, London SE11 4AB

British Library Cataloguing in Publication Information Available

Library of Congress Cataloging-in-Publication Data Available

ISBN 978-1-4985-1908-3 (cloth : alk. paper)
ISBN 978-1-4985-1909-0 (electronic)

∞™ The paper used in this publication meets the minimum requirements of American National Standard for Information Sciences Permanence of Paper for Printed Library Materials, ANSI/NISO Z39.48-1992.

Printed in the United States of America

This book is dedicated to all the feminists in our lives fighting for equality for everyone every day.

Contents

Acknowledgments   ix

1   Introduction: The Politics of Possession   1

2   The One That Started It All: Feminist Tensions in *The
    Exorcist*   21

3   Rip-offs and Homages of the 1970s: Spotlighting
    Exploitation with *Abby* and *Şeytan*   43

4   Revisiting *The Exorcist*: Challenging and Extending the
    Traditional Exorcism Narrative   67

5   Keeping the Devil at Bay: Slashers, Parodies, and Satirizing
    Religion   87

6   Dangerous Boys and Rebellious Priests: *Possessed* and the
    Real Story of *The Exorcist*   107

7   True Stories and Found Footage: The Exorcism Cinema
    Resurgence   125

8   From Reaffirming to Challenging Tradition: *The Last
    Exorcism* and *The Last Exorcism Part II*   149

9   Conclusion: The Resiliency of Tradition   167

Filmography   185
Bibliography   189
Index   197
About the Authors   205

Acknowledgments

The authors would like to thank the following people for their help in completing this book:

Clelia Sweeney
Jennifer Dunn
Kathleen Turner
Lara Stache
Jimmy Manning
Brendan M. Leonard
Daniel Stamm
Father Richard Woods
Lindsey Porambo
Nick Johns
Rolph Picler
The writers and directors of all the
exorcism movies discussed in this book

ONE

Introduction

The Politics of Possession

A girl on the cusp of womanhood becomes increasingly disobedient and uninhibited, and no longer behaves like the proverbial "good little girl." Fearing that the girl has become possessed by a malevolent force, her distant but loving parent seeks the aid of a holy man dealing with his own spiritual crisis. After an internal existential struggle, the holy man regains his sense of purpose and battles the invading entity for control of the girl's soul.

This story—presented here in admittedly broad strokes—will likely sound familiar to anyone who has seen director William Friedkin's classic horror film, *The Exorcist* (1973). In this instance, however, we refer to Michal Waszynski's Yiddish-language film *Der Dibuk* (aka *The Dybbuk*, 1937), which follows a similar narrative trajectory that recurs throughout the horror subgenre we term "exorcism cinema." The above plot synopsis—with only minor variations—could easily apply to *Abby* (1973, William Girdler), *Repossessed* (1990, Bob Logan), *The Exorcism of Emily Rose* (2005, Scott Derrickson), *The Unborn* (2009, David S. Goyer), *Grace: The Possession* (2014, Jeff Chan), and dozens of other films that depict the exorcism of a possessed individual, most commonly a girl or young woman. These films tackle similar material from various religious viewpoints, and appear to have emerged in two key historical periods: the 1970s and the 2010s. In fact, only a handful of exorcism films were produced prior to the 1970s,[1] with *Der Dibuk* representing perhaps the most notable example.

In *Der Dibuk*, Sender (Mojzesz Lipman) and Nisan (Gerszon Lemberger), two young men living in a Polish shtetl, pledge to one day wed their two unborn children, despite an enigmatic stranger's warning that they

1

should not make promises regarding the lives of future generations. Later, Sender's wife dies giving birth to his daughter, and Nisan drowns while traveling home to his own wife, who has borne a son. Eighteen years later, the now-grown children, Lea (Lili Liliana) and Chanan (Leon Liebgold), meet and fall in love, ignorant of their fathers' pledge. Unaware of Chanan's true parentage, Sender arranges for Lea to marry the nervous and effeminate Menasze (M. Messinger). Infuriated by this turn of events, Chanan implores malevolent forces to help him win Lea's hand, but dies under mysterious circumstances.

On her wedding day, Lea visits the local graveyard to invite the souls of her mother and grandparents to the celebration, but summons Chanan's soul instead. That evening, during the ceremony, Lea rejects her new husband and speaks with a deep, almost manly voice. The mysterious stranger reappears and declares that the young bride has become possessed by Chanan's soul, now an evil spirit known as a dybbuk. The elderly rabbi Ezeriel ben Hodos (Abram Morewski) agrees to exorcize the girl, but only after wrestling with his own crisis of faith. After successfully banishing the wicked spirit, the rabbi departs with Sender to prepare the wedding ceremony anew. As soon as the men leave, however, Lea senses Chanan's spirit lingering in the room; she confides that she still loves him, and then commits suicide so they may be reunited in death.

Nearly forty years later, *The Exorcist* covered similar thematic ground, becoming a pop culture phenomenon in the process. In that film's climactic exorcism sequence, young Regan MacNeil (Linda Blair) lies in bed with her hands and feet lashed to the bedposts. A pair of priests, one younger and the other older, loom over her; both men appear exhausted and afraid as they stare down at Regan, but the flame of righteousness burns behind their eyes. Speaking in a guttural, almost masculine growl, Regan spits curses at them as she thrashes about violently, her body twisting and contorting in unnatural ways. The priests endure her words, even as she damns them and all the people they love to an eternity of torment in the deepest pits of hell. Regan spews a stream of bright green vomit onto the older man, who wipes it away and holds his cross high as he chants "The Power of Christ compels you!" in his efforts to drive the demon from the poor child.

The Exorcist entered the collective pop culture consciousness in a way few movies have before or since, and the harrowing imagery described above has greatly influenced how people everywhere think about exorcism. At the same time, these images and the terror they stirred in audiences inspired filmmakers from around the world to produce their own exorcism films, a trend that continues to this day. Indeed, over the past forty years, whether attempting to capitalize on *The Exorcist*'s success or to push the boundaries of horror cinema, numerous other writers, directors, and producers have put their own cinematic spin on the dual experiences of demonic possession and exorcism rituals. In fact, *The Exorcist*'s highly successful (i.e., financially lucrative) formula now effectively serves as the narrative blueprint for the entire exorcism cinema subgenre.

Remarkably, exorcism films produced in different cultural and/or historical contexts appear to share several common themes. In this book, we discuss how the "traditional exorcism narrative" established by *The Exorcist* allegorically explores the oppression of various marginalized groups (mainly women, people of color, and the non-heteronormative). The repeated use of this plot structure requires analysis because it routinely portrays a girl or young woman as both a threat to those around her and a victim of forces beyond her control. These narratives commonly situate the possessed girl or woman as some dreadful thing that a male savior (e.g., priest, rabbi) must dispel or repress, thereby restoring so-called normal (e.g., patriarchal, heteronormative, colonial) life. At the same time, however, such films also position the possessed girl as a passive figure incapable of freeing herself from demonic influence, and therefore entirely reliant upon the heroic priest savior's efforts. Thus, exorcism films simultaneously portray the possessed girl or woman as both the monster and the damsel in distress.

We contend that nearly all exorcism films that appeared after *The Exorcist* function as metaphors for the empowerment and subsequent disempowerment of traditionally marginalized individuals. We have identified 127 exorcism films produced primarily in two main historical periods, and the majority appear to involve the tensions and struggles outlined above, which manifest onscreen in the clashes between the possessed individual (usually a woman) and the holy person (most often a man) sent to battle this emerging threat to normalcy and order. While such films do not explicitly endorse or advance any sort of anti-feminist, misogynistic, racist, or homophobic ideologies, they nevertheless reflect the tensions and struggles that occur at a societal level between countercultural forces and traditional modes of thinking. As a means of unpacking the various themes regarding the treatment of non-dominant groups, this book considers how the exorcism cinema subgenre embodies a number of sociocultural tensions and struggles, and whether or not those representations have changed over time.

ON THE NATURE OF HORROR

Horror's roots extend back to the earliest days of human civilization.[2] Much of folkloric tradition consists of frightening tales involving ghosts, witches, vampires, and other supernatural creatures, all designed to teach the reader or listener a lesson regarding morality and normality. Contemporary horror stories also explore more realistic psychological or sociocultural anxieties—often using the aforementioned monsters to stand in for real world fears—and this tendency to explore actual fears can help audiences recognize and cope with terrors they face in the real world.

Horror's ability to reflect and reveal actual anxieties might explain why the genre has endured and remained popular for so long. As with all genres, horror contains repetitions of particular tropes or conventions (i.e., monsters, nighttime, shadows, death, etc.) that serve to classify a text as belonging to that genre. Such conventions create a system of shared expectations; the presence of these tropes helps an audience to make sense of the text and its meaning,[3] and filmmakers can use these conventions to reach particular audiences. Moreover, filmmakers can recombine tropes and conventions however they wish and still produce a film classifiable as horror. At the same time, horror films sometimes contain anomalous content that may not explicitly reference specific tropes, but audiences nevertheless recognize them as "horror" because they include other tropes associated with the genre or its various subgenres.[4]

In either case, genre films function as a "social ritual" designed to "portray our culture in a stable and invariable ideological position."[5] Horror texts achieve this function by reflecting, representing, and even challenging aspects of the sociocultural context from which they emerge: as Andrew Tudor notes, they represent "an 'embedded' feature of social life, as simultaneously both symptom *and* cause, reflection *and* articulation, language of ideological production *and* reproduction."[6] Thus, beyond simply providing audiences with emotional and physical reactions of revulsion and disgust or fear and anxiety, horror film tropes also provide for more complex and intellectual reactions as viewers consider the monster's presence in relation to the true evils that exist in the real world.[7] Indeed, as Douglas E. Cowan observes, horror can often "demonstrate those aspects of ourselves we would far rather forget."[8] In other words, horror texts often hold a mirror up to a given society or culture, and the reflection reveals what that society deems evil, disgusting, horrible, and so on.

Many theorists have used the theoretical lens of psychoanalysis to explore how horror films manifest these evils. For instance, Noël Carroll argues that monsters propel the vast majority of horror films because they embody contradictions, routinely manifesting as the "abnormal, as disturbances of the natural order."[9] Monsters exemplify the impure, the unclean, and the threatening, and both film and literature regularly present them as "categorically interstitial, categorically contradictory, incomplete, or formless."[10] Monsters represent opposing binaries because they embody features, themes, and metaphors that simultaneously connote either good or bad qualities. For instance, vampires and zombies occupy a liminal space between the living and the dead, while werewolves inhabit the space between humans and animals. Other examples include aliens (physical unknowns), giant insects (the miniscule made large), and the possessed individual (human yet demonic). Horror stories position fear and disgust as the natural reactions to the monster's abnormality, and audiences become conditioned to react with "horror" to these unnatural manifestations. Viewers learn to consider misshapen or deviant things as immoral, evil, dangerous, and harmful, and this perception relates to the idea that when something inhabits a dual state it therefore exists outside the normal order. Thus, horror movies inspire fear primarily because they contain monsters that "are not only physically threatening; they are cognitively threatening. They are threats to common knowledge."[11] In essence, viewers experience dread because they have learned to fear the illogic that the monster represents.

Like Carroll, Barbara Creed argues that horror movies reflect Julia Kristeva's concept of abjection because they portray dualistic images.[12] Abjection occurs when something transgresses the boundary separating the human from the non-human or the normal from the abnormal, which in turn reveals such traditional boundaries as porous and fragile.[13] Such images inspire fear or revulsion because they occupy the human and inhuman realms at the same time, and audiences often find these images pleasurable and repellent in equal measure. Creed asserts that monsters frighten because they cross the borders between opposing states such as good/bad, desirable/undesirable, alive/dead, clean/dirty, human/beast, and man/woman. A viewer experiences abjection when something onscreen crosses or threatens to violate the boundaries separating these binary states, because these transgressions frequently generate conflict between symbolic order (e.g., patriarchal authority and paternal law) and the chaos that threatens to undo its stability (e.g., women and other marginalized peoples becoming empowered). Horror film audiences derive pleasure from abjection because they experience these transgressions from a safe distance, confident that the onscreen hero will ultimately dispel the threat and end the transgression. In the context of the horror film, the hero's triumph over evil serves to remove the abjection and thus ends the threat it poses to society.[14]

Creed notes that throughout history, religion has been used to purify the abject, "to re-draw the boundaries between the human and the non-human,"[15] and thereby restore stability to a society or culture. That same purification now occurs through encounters with art. Texts such as horror films explore the relationship between the physical and the metaphysical, and manifest the intangible as a physical threat the protagonist must confront and defeat.[16] Furthermore, these intangibles often reflect prevailing sociocultural tensions, such as those between feminism and patriarchal authority.[17] Perhaps this explains why Creed and other psychoanalysts examine horror films;[18] they seek to uncover how the genre uses abjections and monsters to convey themes regarding the repression or oppression of undesirable morality and to explore how these films express and deal with "universal fears or historically determined cultural anxieties."[19] Indeed, horror is a highly malleable and adaptable genre, and authors and filmmakers frequently use metaphorical horrors to explore actual fears, tensions, and anxieties.[20] Thus, horror films function as a venue through which to explore sociocultural tensions regarding sexuality, gender, class, and more.

The physical confrontations depicted in horror films often reflect viewers' psychological struggles with their own fears and larger, more abstract sociocultural anxieties. Thus, the hero's clash with the abject can function as a learning experience for viewers. Cowan refers to a "metataxis of horror" or the feeling of dread that arises from the realization that the known social order can rapidly unravel, and he contends that horror films push audiences to confront such possibilities and their outcomes.[21] Yet, horror films routinely depict individuals overcoming monsters and restoring normalcy, and this might explain why the genre remains so popular with audiences. Indeed, Rick Pieto contends while some critics dismiss the entire genre as disreputable, horror endures precisely because of its capacity to reflect real world concerns.[22] Horror's attractiveness stems from its tendency to depict the monster as a horrifying Other, either through appearance or voice (such as the demonic voices of the possessed), which in turn serves to reinforce the differences between the viewer and the monster. According to Robin Wood, "Otherness" reflects that which a dominant ideology "cannot recognize or accept but must deal with . . . either by rejecting and if possible annihilating it, or by rendering it safe and assimilating it."[23] When the hero does finally vanquish the monster (along with the threat it represents), this victory normalizes the ideological boundaries regarding the "correct" way to live, thereby strengthening convention.

Stephen King asserts that monsters fascinate largely because audiences desire to see them vanquished.[24] He claims viewers do not fear the monster's physical or mental aberrations, but rather the lack of order they imply. Thus, horror stories and films do not frighten because they depict abject imagery, but rather because they portray abject ideas that challenge the status quo. The monster's defeat signals the restoration of order, and audiences flock to horror primarily because they feel the need to restore "feelings of essential normality."[25] All horror basically reflects the struggle between order (the Apollonian) and chaos (the Dionysian), and the terror only ends once "the Dionysian forces have been repelled and the Apollonian order restored again."[26] Likewise, Wood argues that horror's central theme involves the relationship of the Other (i.e., the monster) to normal society or culture.[27] Tudor puts forth a similar argument when he observes that horror films often conform to a three-part "seek and destroy" narrative structure: "a monstrous threat is introduced into a stable situation; the monster rampages in the face of attempts to combat it; the monster is (perhaps) destroyed and order (perhaps) restored."[28] *The Exorcist* exemplifies this struggle between order and chaos, or stability and instability, because the supernatural elements occur in a familiar suburban setting; when the heroes repulse the evil and restore equilibrium, the return to normality feels like a relief.[29]

Sometimes, though, a question remains regarding whether or not the hero has in fact vanquished the monster's evil. Such ambiguities can leave the audience wondering if the restored status quo represents the "correct" way to live, and this uncertainty creates a sense of paranoia regarding life's fundamental stability. Horror movies accomplish this not because they depict brutality and gore, but rather because they reflect larger sociocultural anxieties and allow viewers to confront their own subconscious fears.[30] Effective horror tackles larger sociocultural fears that might otherwise remain unspoken, and allows the audience to confront those fears directly. Viewers enjoy horror because it allows them to focus on make-believe horrors rather than the real, often uncontrollable horrors they face in their everyday lives. Horror films can render these everyday horrors manageable by comparison.[31] In other words, buying into a horror film's constructed reality during the viewing experience can help viewers cope with anxieties they encounter on a daily basis.[32] Thus, like dreams, horror films allow people to express and perhaps even master otherwise uncertain feelings of fear and terror.[33] Furthermore, horror's allegorical nature allows viewers to indulge thoughts and emotions that society and culture term deviant but may in fact encompass the very thoughts and feelings individuals must entertain if they hope to cope with reality.[34]

As much as they operate on an individual level to process fears, horror films can also function as cultural nightmares, allowing a community to process tensions both "attractive and repellent."[35] Thomas Fahy explains that the feelings generated during the engagement with a horror text—anxiety and fear during the engagement, relief, and mastery afterward—not only explain why people derive pleasure from horror, but also inform how they view and interact with the world around them.[36] Fahy contends that horror frequently inspires viewers to ask important questions regarding the complex interplay between violence, justice, suffering, and morality, and to consider how these concepts ultimately impact their own lives.

For these reasons and others, the horror genre remains popular with audiences, and has for well over two hundred years.[37] During the early part of the twenty-first century, despite a widespread perception among both fans and critics that the genre has reached a creative nadir, the horror film thrives as Hollywood continues to produce mid-budget films for a willing horror audience.[38] More importantly, while critics and scholars have traditionally positioned horror as a male genre,[39] women currently comprise a substantial percentage of horror's fanbase,[40] likely because horror films often contain surreptitious depictions of female empowerment.[41] Given this demographic information, we believe it becomes even more important to consider how horror films—particularly those depicting possession and exorcism—frequently portray girls and young women as both monsters and damsels in distress rather than as heroic or empowered individuals.

DEFINING THE EXORCISM CINEMA SUBGENRE

Possession films comprise one of horror cinema's most common and enduring subgenres. In such films, an individual or object becomes possessed, and while the cause of this possession varies from film to film, it nevertheless threatens the established order. According to Tudor, the idea of possession, "whether by demonic invasion, reincarnation, or witchcraft, is a particularly distinctive threat since it postulates a highly personal attack upon our being."[42] Tudor observes that in supernatural horror films, the devil seeks either world domination or the destruction of the family or community, and these two thematic threads frighten mainly because they inspire both terror and identification in the viewer.[43] Kevin J. Wetmore, meanwhile, argues that religious horror films in general and exorcism films in particular frighten primarily because they play on people's fears that demons and devils actually exist, and must be expunged from the world.[44] The construction of such monsters promotes a collective identity among the religious and conveys morality lessons that limit the expression of undesirable thoughts, feelings, and actions.[45] In fact, questions regarding religion or spirituality, and thus matters of life and death, routinely provide content for horror films.[46] As discussed above, others assert that horror films unsettle both believers and nonbelievers alike because they use religious themes to reflect and address widespread sociocultural anxieties. Whatever the case, the possession subgenre's longevity and popularity seem to indicate the audience's desire to confront spiritual, social, and cultural matters.

From this possession subgenre come the occasional films that also feature exorcisms. Carol J. Clover applies the term "occult film" to those films that depict possession, and sometimes involve exorcism.[47] Carrol Fry similarly discusses occult films as a subset of horror films, but she further divides this subgenre by distinguishing films that in some way depict satanic content.[48] She counts stories that focus primarily on exorcism among these satanic films. In this book, we use the term "exorcism cinema" to refer to any feature length film (regardless of the medium through which it premieres) that depicts both a possession and a subsequent exorcism ritual. We prefer the label exorcism cinema over "occult film" and "satanic film" because we find these previous labels too broad and believe they could describe any film that includes satanic or other occult content. This study focused only on films that include an onscreen depiction of an exorcism ritual to end a possession, and this ritual could obey the rules of an established religion, a modified religious rite, a spiritual or metaphysical activity, or a more pragmatic activity such as hypnosis or violence. These possessions can result from demons, ghosts, dybbuks, or other spirits or non-corporeal entities invading and taking control of a living human being. Meanwhile, regardless of whether they succeed or fail, the exorcism rituals reflect a variety of spiritual or religious beliefs. Thus, the term "exorcism cinema" allows us to narrow the scope of this study, and to consider films that may not have received much attention but nevertheless share common themes that are worthy of analysis.

At this point, we should clarify that in this book we examine ideology rather than ritual. In other words, we do not consider exorcism films as faithful representations of religious beliefs, but rather as allegories for the sociocultural tensions of various historical periods. Nevertheless, our examination of the exorcism cinema subgenre hinges on at least a cursory understanding of why people believe in and practice exorcism, because such rituals and beliefs heavily inform the narrative structures of such films. For example, *The Exorcist* offers a moderately accurate depiction of the Catholic rite of exorcism,[49] and since this film established the conventions of what we term the traditional exorcism narrative, we must therefore briefly consider the historical and sociocultural implications of the practice of exorcism. Furthermore, while stories of possession and exorcism rituals occur in many religions and cultures (including Islamic, Hindi, and Shinto religions), Hollywood tends to focus on the Judeo-Christian approach, and therefore we focus primarily on this approach as well.

According to Father Richard Woods, Christian and Jewish exorcists appear in the Gospels and the Acts of the Apostles.[50] Similarly, Richard Deutch notes that the Bible includes references to Jewish exorcists performing rites without invoking the figure of the Christ.[51] Examples of demonic possession also appear in the New Testament, which notes that Jesus Christ performed exorcisms and passed this ability on to his apostles,[52] thereby establishing the foundation for the exorcism rituals later used by the Catholic Church.[53] For instance, Paul supposedly drove a spirit out of a young woman whose masters profited from her soothsaying abilities.[54] This exorcism—performed on a girl who gained power through her possession—closely resembles cinematic portrayals of possession and exorcism. Additionally, early Christians performed exorcisms, including on pagans, using Christ's name and the sign of the cross to banish unclean spirits.[55] They also laid hands, read passages of scripture, and commanded the demon to depart, actions that recur throughout the exorcism cinema subgenre. In writing about *The Exorcist*, Woods argues that possession, cinematic or otherwise, primarily serves to either prove to the skeptical world that God exists, or to help Satan recruit followers; possession can convince people to follow Satan, while exorcism can inspire people to follow God.[56] Thus, possession and exorcism demonstrate in microcosm the battle for human souls that occurs between the forces of good and evil; allegorically, then, these two diametrically opposed acts function as stories about a given society's or culture's attempt to determine the boundaries of appropriate moral behavior.

Concerns over viewers' moral lives abound in horror films, and thus they consciously or unconsciously reflect a particular religious approach to matters of life and death, good and evil, and the supernatural.[57] Pieto notes that contemporary horror films (particularly those produced in Western cultures) routinely feature Catholic iconography.[58] Furthermore, one of Catholicism's central concerns regards the battle between good and evil, as represented by the eternal struggle between God and Satan, and this could explain why horror often appropriates Catholic imagery. For instance, vampires fear crosses, zombies often rise from Christian burial grounds, and exorcisms usually conform to Catholic rituals. Similarly, horror films frequently depict a conflict between good and evil, which manifests onscreen as a clash between virtuous heroes and unnatural things that threaten the symbolic order. Therefore, the Catholic discourse internalized by both religious and non-religious viewers can potentially impact how they interpret the imagery in horror films, especially those that utilize Catholic images and narratives. At this point, Catholicism, or at least the Western approach to it, has become intertwined with popular culture, resulting in the legitimization of Christian theology through its repetitive use in horror films.[59]

Alexandra Heller-Nicholas argues that the narrative similarities between horror and Catholicism such as those noted above become most apparent when examining *The Exorcist* and other films that reflect, exploit, or rip-off its plot and tone.[60] She contends that exorcism films all share in the "moral spectacle" of possession and exorcism. Even if they do not depict Catholic rituals, exorcism films nevertheless share a common "cultural imagination,"[61] which leads to a sort of standardized depiction of the melodramatic struggle between good and evil. The evil manifests as a malevolent force (e.g., demon, spirit, entity, etc.) that possesses a virtuous individual (most commonly a girl or young woman) and impels them to act in dangerous and destructive ways that threaten both the individual and the larger society. The good takes the form of a spiritual force, often personified by a religious figure (most commonly a man) knowledgeable in the (typically Judeo-Christian) rites of exorcism who must confront and drive out the invading entity. Yet, cinematic representations of exorcism are less about theological realism and more about the ritual's melodramatic impact on the viewers. According to Heller-Nicholas, this melodramatic impact renders the "exorcism trope so endearing,"[62] and therefore requires further analysis to understand what makes the ritual so impactful in these films.

In recent years much scholarship has been devoted to the various subgenres of horror cinema, particularly slasher films, torture porn, vampires, and zombies. Yet, films depicting possession and exorcism have not received the same amount of scholarly attention outside of that devoted to the critical examination of *The Exorcist*. This book attempts to address this lack of scholarship by considering the historical trajectory of the exorcism cinema subgenre by analyzing how the characters, narratives, and themes of such films reflect and comment on the prevailing ideologies of the sociohistorical periods during which they were produced and received

POSSESSED WOMEN, HAUNTED STATES: AN OVERVIEW

Ideology refers to a way of thinking about or understanding the world.[63] Ideology shapes and is in turn shaped by social relations and practices, creating a sense of what is "normal" or "natural" at any given point in history for a society or culture.[64] Furthermore, all individuals, cultures, and societies conform to one ideology or another, and multiple ideologies often clash in an attempt to gain dominance. The characters, stories, and themes in a film represent various ideologies,[65] and demonstrate that cinema does not simply reflect reality but ultimately constructs it to align with a particular ideological perspective.[66]

This book seeks to examine the ideological messages found in the films that encompass the exorcism cinema subgenre. By ideological messages, we refer to the beliefs and values that become embedded, either intentionally or unintentionally, in any given film. These beliefs and values can result in informal or incidental learning, and thereby inform and influence how audiences make sense of reality. This understanding of incidental learning draws on media effects studies, such as the encoding/decoding model,[67] cultivation theory,[68] social cognitive theory,[69] and perceived reality.[70] These theories describe how mediated messages often contain specific, ideologically-informed content, and how constant and consistent exposure to such media depictions can impact the way people make sense of not only themselves, but also of others and the world around them. Thus, mediated ideological messages can allow people to "'experience' themselves in ways which do not fully correspond with their real situation,"[71] and thus potentially affect their values and conceptions of reality.

Horror texts contain such unreal situations, and they routinely have immediate and lasting impacts on people. In the case of horror films, audience and reception studies demonstrate how the depictions they contain often linger in viewers' memories[72] and convey notions regarding specific social and cultural values.[73] For example, research suggests horror viewers prefer the traditional ending of horror films, in which the hero vanquishes the threat and good triumphs over evil.[74] Given the impact such films can have, we want to understand how they maintain or challenge the prevailing sociocultural ideologies of the historical periods in which they were produced and received. Moreover, we want to determine if the ideological messages contained in such films eventually make the transition from reactionary to revolutionary, as Wetmore contends.[75]

Possessed Women, Haunted States consists of three sections that examine the main historical periods during which the majority of exorcism films were produced: the 1970s, the 1980s–1990s, and the 2000s–2010s. We argue that these films function as social allegories, able to honestly depict and possibly critique "the relationship of the Other to the heteronormative, the bourgeois family, 'normal' community life, and/or 'functional' society under capital."[76] Such movies allow for an examination of the tensions that exist in society during various sociohistorical periods. Yet, despite their potential for critique and revolution, the common structure of horror movies typically results in the suppression of that which is different, a paradox particularly evident in exorcism cinema.

Like horror films in general, exorcism films concern themselves with the repression and oppression of sociocultural undesirables. Wood argues that repression occurs when the mind becomes unable to access particular thoughts or feelings, which then re-emerge through dreams or desires.[77] Meanwhile, oppression occurs when an external force seeks to keep an individual or group out of power. Wood argues that the two concepts are connected as repression represents a form of "fully internalized oppression," suggesting that when a person becomes suppressed they might internalize this oppression and subsequently repress the desire to hold power or be treated equally.[78] Thus, this book considers how depictions of possession and exorcism reflect the various sociocultural tensions that often lead to the oppression, suppression, and repression of non-traditional beliefs, behaviors, and identities. We contend that the cinematic construction of possession uses women, people of color, and non-heteronormative individuals to create an Other who represents a threat to established order and normality. We accomplish this by analyzing these films through a variety of critical theoretical approaches.

First, we explore them through the lens of feminist theory, which we employ to understand how patriarchal structures enable male and masculine domination over women, and how the oppression of feminine characteristics impacts the lives of women. David Allyn notes that a sexual double standard rooted in Victorian era attitudes regarding female cleanliness and purity serves to emphasize male pleasure over female pleasure and thereby reinforces men's continued dominance over women.[79] Indeed, under the auspices of patriarchy,[80] masculinity and the heterosexual male body function as the default for normality, while anything associated with the feminine or female body becomes marginalized. While the influence of male domination and thus the practices and ideological messages of "the patriarchy" varies across time, cultures, and geographical locations, the elevation of masculinity and the suppression of femininity tend to remain constant.[81] This suppression occurs particularly with regard to how women can properly express their sexuality within a patriarchal society.[82] Wood argues that the internalization of such ideology renders female sexuality as one of the primary locations for repression in Western civilization.[83]

Second, we explore issues of racism by considering exorcism films from a colonialist perspective, in an effort to understand how the ideological messages contained in such films reflect the conquest and control of cultures and nations by imperial forces, such as the British Empire.[84] People living under such conditions—most commonly people of color or other non-European ethnic or racial minorities—become impacted by a host of economic, political, cultural, and social changes.[85] A colonized group enters a postcolonial state in one of two ways: either the colonizing force leaves and thereby returns self-governance to the people, or the people have in some way attempted to resist the colonizing forces.[86] This theoretical perspective considers how members of a non-dominant culture respond to the influence of a dominant culture.[87] Such response can emerge through the wholesale adoption of the dominant culture's values and norms, the outright rejection of these beliefs and activities, or through some process of negotiating the appropriation of these beliefs, adjusted to better align with their pre-existing cultural values and norms. As with the oppression of female sexuality, Western civilization often deprives other cultures of their distinctive characteristics, and this represents another form of repression.[88]

Third, we use queer theory to explore concerns regarding homophobia. Queer theory informs our understanding of how the act of possession serves to disrupt, transgress, and transcend a binary notion of sexuality that relies on heteronormative assumptions. Heteronormativity positions heterosexual monogamy as "something biological and medically necessary," and thus as "normal" behavior.[89] Moreover, any variation from this conventional default, such as homosexuality, subsequently becomes positioned as abnormal.[90] Queer theorists challenge the idea of homosexuality as a biological necessity, and argue that so-called normative behavior actually represents a sociocultural construct. As Harry M. Benshoff notes, queer theory critiques "social constructions of gender and sexuality and race" in an effort to move beyond considering those identities in purely binary terms.[91] Thus, the term "queer" and queer theory have been applied to anyone who self-identities as something outside of traditional binaries and heteronormativity.[92] Wood further discusses how deviations from mainstream sexual norms represent another area of repression and oppression.[93]

All of these theoretical approaches seek to understand how power becomes constructed, maintained, and circulated within a society and culture. Michel Foucault describes power as both decentralized and relational, meaning that power alternately resides in the hands of the authority or the populace at different times throughout history.[94] As such, power can manifest in the form of the sociocultural codes that shape norms and ideas of normality, but those who resist such attempts at normalization can also hold power. Indeed, exorcism cinema appears to illustrate this circulation of power, because it depicts traditionally marginalized individuals gaining the power to resist their oppression, but ultimately becoming oppressed once more by those in authority positions (i.e., white, heterosexual males in Western societies[95]).

Foucault also argues that the process of normalization serves to regulate the body and an individual's behavior by labelling some bodies and behaviors as deviant and unnatural.[96] This becomes significant when considering that possession and exorcism focus primarily on the body, which contorts unnaturally during possession and undergoes physical discipline during exorcism. Such acts indicate how power can regulate, discipline, and normalize an individual's behavior. Thus, the analyses in this book consider how patriarchy oppresses women, how colonial and imperial powers oppress people of color, and how heteronormativity oppresses queer identities. In horror films, anything that does not conform to the rationalized, masculine norms of Western civilization consistently becomes positioned as monstrous;[97] thus exorcism cinema positions feminist ideologies,[98] homosexuality,[99] and other non-white, non-heterosexual, and non-Christian male identities[100] as threats to the established order.

We argue that within the framework of exorcism cinema, possession consistently grants women, people of color, and queer individuals the power to resist their oppression, while exorcism returns them to a marginalized position within a society or culture. Moreover, the possessed individual sometimes exists at the intersection of these various identities, thereby furthering their marginalized and oppressed state. Of course, exorcism films do not directly address these struggles, but rather they metaphorically depict them in a way that stimulates the viewer's desire to see these newly empowered individuals become suppressed once more. Thus, this book analyzes how systems of oppression manifest in stories of possession and exorcism, which frequently position the possessed person as an Other and a threat to mainstream society. More importantly, these ideological messages of oppression manifest repeatedly throughout the periods in which exorcism cinema has occurred.

In this book, we conducted close textual analyses of 18 of the 127 exorcism films produced thus far to understand how the ideological messages described above have manifested onscreen since the release of *The Exorcist* in 1973. We conducted in-depth analyses of these specific fictional movies because of their historical and/or cultural importance, and because possession and exorcism are central to each film's story line. Furthermore, these films illustrate both the expansive application of the traditional exorcism narrative as well as its concentration through the repeated use of the subgenre's tropes. In addition to these close reads, we watched a total of sixty-one films, and thoroughly researched the remaining sixty-six films identified in the filmography. Each analysis chapter in this book focuses on a specific time period, and accounts for as many of the films pertinent to that period as possible. We recognize that not every film receives an equitable level of analysis in this book, but we hope the in-depth analysis and discussion of the films included in each chapter prompts others to take this research further than is possible here.

The chapters in the book's first section focus on the 1970s, beginning with a discussion of how *The Exorcist*'s success spawned numerous foreign rip-offs and exploitation films. Chapter 2 argues that despite the handful of exorcism films released prior to the 1970s, *The Exorcist* truly established the conventions of the exorcism cinema subgenre, and functioned as the template for all subsequent exorcism films produced during the following four decades. Chapter 3 examines how international producers attempted to capitalize on *The Exorcist*'s phenomenal success either by copying its narrative directly or by altering the content or marketing of existing films to more closely reflect the conventions it established. This chapter also considers how the films *Abby* (1974, William Girdler) and *Şeytan* (1974, Metin Erksan) depict the oppression of both women and people of color and thus align with the traditional exorcism narrative. Chapter 4 explores *The Exorcist*'s sequels and prequels, which attempt to bring other marginalized groups into the traditional exorcism narrative, but ultimately return the focus to women.

The chapters in the next section focus on the 1980s–1990s and consider why this period produced relatively few exorcism films. Chapter 5 considers how the rise of sociocultural anxieties regarding teen sexuality, rampant drug use, and the AIDS epidemic created a prevailing sociocultural narrative that allowed for the rise of the slasher subgenre and the simultaneous decline of the exorcism cinema subgenre into parody; thus, this chapter analyzes two such parodies with *Repossessed* and *Teenage Exorcist* (1991, Grant Austin Waldman). Chapter 6 analyzes *Possessed* (2000, Steven E. de Souza) in an effort to understand how the exorcism cinema subgenre shifted toward focusing on "real stories" of exorcism, while also considering how other films produced during this period—notably *Amityville II: The Possession* (1982, Damiano Damiani) and *Stigmata* (1999, Rupert Wainwright)—challenge the traditional exorcism narrative, even though the possessed individuals still embody deviance in some form.

The chapters in the final section consider how the socially conservative environment that emerged after the events of September 11, 2001, helped usher in the exorcism cinema subgenre's resurgence, which has thus far resulted in the production of eighty-two exorcism films. Chapter 7 argues that the theatrical rerelease of *The Exorcist* in 2000 and the terrorist attacks of 9/11 led to a new wave of exorcism films, many of which either claim a basis in actual events or employ a documentary aesthetic to create a sense of authenticity. This chapter analyzes two examples of each type of realistic storytelling approach to understand how they produce stories that support patriarchal authority. Chapter 8 considers how *The Last Exorcism* (2010, Daniel Stamm) conforms to the traditional exorcism narrative, while *The Last Exorcism Part II* (2013, Ed Gass-Donnelly) directly challenges the power dynamics that emphasize the suppression of feminine sexuality and agency. The final chapter considers the historical trajectory of the exorcism cinema subgenre and examines how these films continue to depict the traditional exorcism narrative and reinforce the privileged and oppressive assumptions inherent to that narrative.

Through an in-depth analysis of 18 exorcism films, and a consideration of the remaining 108, our project uncovers how the tropes and themes that comprise the traditional exorcism narrative render these films as allegories for the oppression of marginalized peoples. We have listed all the films that conform to our definition of the exorcism cinema subgenre chronologically in the filmography. Because this book represents one of the first comprehensive attempts to examine the exorcism cinema subgenre as a whole, we hope it inspires others to use our analyses as a foundation for their own research on the other films in this subgenre, particularly those that have received little or no scholarly consideration thus far.

NOTES

1. In addition to *Der Dibuk*, other notable pre-*Exorcist* exorcism films include *Naked Evil* (aka *Exorcism at Midnight*; 1966, Stanley Goulder and Steven Jacobson), *The Devils* (1971, Ken Russell), and *Las melancólicas* (aka *Exorcism's Daughter*; 1971, Rafael Moreno Alba). We discuss these films further in chapter 2.
2. Rosemary Jackson, *Fantasy: The Literature of Subversion* (London: Methuen, 1981), 53–55, 68–69.
3. Thomas Schatz, "Film Genre and the Genre Film," in *Film Theory and Criticism* (6th Ed.), eds. Leo Braudy and Marshall Cohen (New York: Oxford University Press, 2004), 691.
4. Douglas E. Cowan, "Religion and Cinema Horror," in *Understanding Religion and Popular Culture: Theories, Themes, Products and Practices*, eds. Terry Ray Clark and Dan W. Clanton, Jr. (New York: Routledge, 2012), 61.
5. Schatz, "Film Genre," 700.
6. Andrew Tudor, *Monsters and Mad Scientists: A Cultural History of the Horror Movie* (Cambridge: Basil Blackwell Ltd., 1991), 5. Italics in original.
7. Cynthia A. Freeland, *The Naked and the Undead: Evil and the Appeal of Horror* (Boulder: Westview Press, 2000), 273–74.
8. Douglas E. Cowan, "Horror and the Demonic," in *The Routledge Companion to Religion and Film*, ed. John Lyden (New York: Routledge, 2009), 403.
9. Noël Carroll, *The Philosophy of Horror, Or, Paradoxes of the Heart* (New York: Routledge, 1990), 16.
10. Ibid., 32.
11. Ibid., 34.

12. Barbara Creed, "Horror and the Monstrous-Feminine: An Imaginary Abjection," in *Feminist Film Theory: A Reader,* ed. Sue Thornham (Edinburgh: Edinburgh University Press, 1999), 251–66.

13. Barbara Creed, *The Monstrous-Feminine: Film, Feminism, and Psychoanalysis* (New York: Routledge, 1993), 8–11.

14. Barbara Creed, "Kristeva, Femininity, Abjection," in *The Horror Reader,* ed. Ken Gelder (New York: Routledge, 2000), 64–65.

15. Creed, "Horror and the Monstrous-Feminine," 258.

16. Peter Falconer, "Fresh Meat? Dissecting the Horror Movie Virgin," in *Virgin Territory: Representing Sexual Inexperience in Film,* ed. Tamar Jeffers McDonald (Detroit: Wayne State University Press, 2010), 123–37.

17. R. W. Connell and James W. Messerschmidt (2005) define patriarchy as "the long-term structure of the subordination of women" (839).

18. Chris Dumas (2014) justifies the psychoanalytic approach to horror thusly: "You may or may not be convinced of the veracity of Freud's theories, but when you talk about horror cinema, you really cannot avoid them—and if you try, you miss the very heart of the genre itself. Perhaps one reason for this is that when you invoke ideas like 'anxiety' or 'desire,' you are already in the realm of the psychoanalytic, and horror cinema is all about anxiety and desire—indeed, these are the bases of the entire genre" (23).

19. Barry Keith Grant (ed.), "Introduction," in *The Dread of Difference: Gender and the Horror Film* (Austin: University of Texas Press, 1996), 7.

20. Stephen King, *Danse Macabre* (New York: Pocket Books, 1982/2010), 146.

21. Cowan, "Religion and Cinema Horror," 63.

22. Rick Pieto, "'The Devil Made Me Do It': Catholicism, Verisimilitude and the Reception of Horror Films," in *Roman Catholicism in Fantastic Film: Essays on Belief, Spectacle, Ritual and Imagery,* ed. Regina Hansen (Jefferson: McFarland & Company, Inc., 2011), 52–64.

23. Robin Wood, "The American Nightmare: Horror in the 70s," in *Horror, The Film Reader,* ed. Mark Jancovich (New York: Routledge, 2002), 27.

24. King, *Danse,* 41.

25. Ibid., 185.

26. Ibid., 422.

27. Robin Wood. *Hollywood from Vietnam to Reagan . . . and Beyond* (2003, New York: Columbia University Press), 71.

28. Tudor, *Monsters,* 81.

29. King, *Danse,* 422.

30. Ibid., xiii.

31. Ibid.

32. Ibid., 13

33. Isabel Pinedo, "Recreational Terror: Postmodern Elements of the Contemporary Horror Film," *Journal of Film and Video* 48, no. 1/2 (1996): 26.

34. King, *Danse,* 32.

35. Pinedo, "Recreational Terror," 26.

36. Thomas Fahy (ed.), "Introduction," in *The Philosophy of Horror* (Lexington: The University of Kentucky Press, 2010), 1–13.

37. According to *Encyclopedia Britannica,* the horror genre "was invented by Horace Walpole, whose *Castle of Otranto* (1765) may be said to have founded the horror story as a legitimate literary form." For more, see http://www.britannica.com/art/horror-story, accessed June 7, 2015.

38. Steffan Hantke, "Academic Film Criticism, the Rhetoric of Crisis, and the Current State of American Horror Cinema: Thoughts on Canonicity and Academic Anxiety," *College Literature* 34, no. 4 (2007): 191.

39. Grant, "Introduction," 1–12.

40. Christine Spines, "Horror Films . . . and the Women Who Love Them!" *Entertainment Weekly,* July 31, 2009.

41. Ibid., 33.

42. Tudor, *Monsters*, 63.

43. Ibid., 75.

44. Kevin J. Wetmore, *Post-9/11 Horror in American Cinema* (New York: Continuum, 2012), 140.

45. Jason C. Bivins, "By Demons Driven: Religious Teratologies," in *Speaking of Monsters: A Teratological Anthology*, eds. Caroline Joan S. Picart and John Edgar Browning (New York: Palgrave-MacMillan, 2012), 107.

46. Cowan, "Horror and the Demonic," 405.

47. Carol J. Clover, *Men, Women, and Chain Saws: Gender in the Modern Horror Film* (Princeton, NJ: Princeton University Press, 1992), 66.

48. Carrol L. Fry, *Cinema of the Occult: New Age, Satanism, Wicca and Spirituality in Film* (Bethlehem: Lehigh University Press, 2000), 92-93.

49. "'The Exorcist' Fairly Close to the Mark," *National Catholic Reporter*, Sept. 1, 2000.

50. Richard Woods, *The Devil* (Merrimack: The Thomas More Press, 1973), 69.

51. Richard Deutch, *Exorcism: Possession or Obsession?* (London: Bachman & Turner, 1975), 40.

52. Juan B. Cortés and Florence M. Gatti, "Demonology and Witchcraft," in *The Case Against Possessions and Exorcisms: A Historical, Biblical, and Psychological Analysis of Demons, Devils, and Demoniacs* (New York: Vantage Press, 1975), 23–45.

53. Woods, *Devil*, 83.

54. This incident occurs in Paul 16:16–18.

55. Cortés and Gatti, "Demonology," 27.

56. Woods, *Devil*, 28, 112.

57. Bryan Stone, "The Sanctification of Fear: Images of the Religious in Horror Films," *The Journal of Religion and Film* 5, no. 2 (2001): Online.

58. Pieto, "Devil Made Me Do It," 52–64.

59. Bivins, "Religious Teratologies," 109.

60. Alexandra Heller-Nicholas, "'The Power of Christ Compels You': Moral Spectacle and The Exorcist Universe," in *Roman Catholicism in Fantastic Film: Essays on Belief, Spectacle, Ritual and Imagery*, ed. Regina Hansen (Jefferson: McFarland & Company, Inc., 2011), 65–80.

61. Ibid., 67.

62. Alexandra Heller-Nicholas, *Found Footage Horror Films: Fear and the Appearance of Reality*, (Jefferson: McFarland & Company, Inc., 2014), 154.

63. Ania Loomba, *Colonialism/Postcolonialism* (New York: Routledge, 1998), 31.

64. Davina Cooper, *Power in Struggle: Feminism, Sexuality and the State* (Buckingham: Open University Press, 1995), 21.

65. Jill Dolan, "Ideology in Performance: Looking Through the Male Gaze," in *The Feminist Spectator as Critic* (Ann Arbor: UMI Research Press, 1988), 41–58.

66. Anneke Smelik, "Feminist Film Theory," in *The Cinema Book* (3rd Ed.), ed. Pam Cook (London: British Film Institute, 2007), 491.

67. Stuart Hall, "Encoding, Decoding," in *The Cultural Studies Reader*, ed. Simon During (New York City: Routledge, 1993), 90–103.

68. George Gerbner, Larry Gross, Michael Morgan, Nancy Signorielli, and James Shanahan, "Growing Up with Television: Cultivation Processes," in *Media Effects: Advances in Theory and Research* (2nd Ed.), eds. Jennings Bryant and Dolf Zillmann (Hillsdale: Lawrence Erlbaum Associates, 2002), 43–66.

69. Albert Bandura, "Social Cognitive Theory of Mass Communication," in *Media Effects: Advances in Theory and Research* (2nd Ed.), eds. Jennings Bryant and Dolf Zillmann (Hillsdale: Lawrence Erlbaum Associates, 2002), 121–53.

70. W. James Potter, "Perceived Reality in Television Effects Research," *Journal of Broadcasting and Electronic Media* 32, no. 1. (1988): 23–41.

71. Stuart Hall, "Culture, the Media, and the 'Ideological Effect,'" in *Mass Communication and Society*, eds. James Curran, Michael Gurevitch, and Janet Woollacott (London: Edward Arnold, 1977), 315–47.

72. For more, see Joanne Cantor's research on fright reactions to horror, such as: Joanne Cantor, "Fright Reactions to Mass Media," in *Media Effects: Advances in Theory and Research*, eds. Jennings Bryant and Dolf Zillman (Hillsdale: Lawrence Erlbaum Associates, 1994), 213–41; Kristen Harisson and Joanne Cantor, "Tales from the Screen: Enduring Fright Reactions to Scary Media," *Media Psychology* 1, no. 2 (1999): 97–116; and Joanne Cantor, "'I'll Never Have a Clown in My House'—Why Movie Horror Lives On," *Poetics Today* 25, no. 2 (2004): 283–304.

73. For more on this argument, see Barry Brummett's rhetorical analysis of horror films in Barry Brummett, "What Popular Films Teach Us About Values: Locked Inside with the Rage Virus," *Journal of Popular Film and Television*, 41, no 2 (2013): 61–67.

74. Cynthia M. King and Nora Hourani, "Don't Tease Me: Effects of Ending Type on Horror Film Enjoyment," *Media Psychology* 9, no. 3 (2007): 473–92.

75. Wetmore, *Post-9/11 Horror*, 1–22.

76. Christopher Sharrett, "The Horror Film as Social Allegory (and How It Comes Undone)," in *A Companion to the Horror Film*, ed. Harry M. Benshoff (Malden: John Wiley & Sons, Inc., 2014), 56.

77. Wood, *Hollywood*, 64.

78. Ibid.

79. David Allyn, "Single Girls, Double Standard," in *Make Love, Not War: The Sexual Revolution, an Unfettered History* (Boston: Little, Brown, 2000), 10–22.

80. We acknowledge that the term patriarchy represents a problematic and altogether simplistic designation in and of itself, and thus we must briefly explicate our use of the term throughout this book. As Seemin Qayum and Raka Ray (2010) observe, the term patriarchy now functions primarily as a "loose descriptor rather than as a useful analytic frame" and that "the conceptualization of patriarchy as a unitary universal phenomenon obscures more than it reveals" (112). At the same time, however, we contend the term invokes notions of systemic sociocultural attitudes regarding masculine domination normalized and reinforced via representations in mass culture texts, such as horror films. Thus, terms like patriarchy or patriarchal institutions represent useful foundational concepts for our discussion of exorcism cinema films.

81. Loomba, *Colonialism*, 18.

82. Juliet Mitchell, *Psychoanalysis and Feminism* (New York: Vintage Books, 1974), xvi–xvii.

83. Wood, *Hollywood*, 66.

84. Loomba, *Colonialism*, 2.

85. Ibid., 4.

86. Ibid., 7.

87. Ibid., 12.

88. Wood, *Hollywood*, 67.

89. Niall Richardson, Clarissa Smith, and Angela Werndly, *Studying Sexualities: Theories, Representations, Cultures* (New York: Palgrave Macmillan, 2013), 44–45.

90. Ibid.

91. Harry M. Benshoff, *Monsters in the Closet: Homosexuality and the Horror Film* (New York: Manchester University Press, 1997), 255.

92. According to Harry M. Benshoff (1997), this "includes people who might also self-identify as gay and/or lesbian, bisexual, transsexual, transvestite, drag queen, leather daddy, lipstick lesbian, pansy, fair, dyke, butch, femme, feminist, asexual, and so on" (5).

93. Wood, *Hollywood*, 67.

94. Michel Foucault, *The History of Sexuality: An Introduction (Vol. 1)* (New York: Random House, 1978), 92–102.

95. Cooper, *Power in Struggle*, 9.

96. Justin D. Edwards and Rune Graulund, *Grotesque*, (New York: Routledge, 2013), 26.

97. Chris Dumas, "Horror and Psychoanalysis: An Introductory Primer," in *A Companion to the Horror Film*, ed. Harry M. Benshoff. (Malden: John Wiley & Sons, Inc., 2014), 30.

98. Sharrett, "The Horror Film," 57.

99. Benshoff, *Monsters*, 2.

100. Ibid., 4 and Wood, "American Nightmare," 28.

TWO

The One That Started It All

Feminist Tensions in The Exorcist

Mark Kermode observes that *The Exorcist* emerged during a time of great social and religious upheaval, when prevailing ideas about sexuality, family dynamics, the Church, and even the American Dream itself were in a state of extreme flux.[1] He argues that the film dominated the 1970s cultural landscape partly because it tapped into several of the decade's most prevalent anxieties, such as the generation gap, the rise of second-wave feminism (which appeared to threaten traditional conceptualizations of the family and the home), and religion's role within a contemporary scientific and technological society. *The Exorcist* reflects all of these fears, and this could explain why it had such a profound impact on North American audiences of the time.

The Exorcist premiered on December 26, 1973, roughly one year after Pope Paul VI delivered a well-publicized speech urging renewed vigilance against the devil's power and influence.[2] The pope's declaration seemed to confirm secular beliefs that the Catholic Church had become an archaic, ineffective, and altogether irrelevant institution in the context of the seemingly more enlightened twentieth century. Religious belief—particularly regarding the devil's existence—represents a fundamental aspect of American identity and society, even as many Americans harbor a deep mistrust of organized religion and the clergy (a stance that perhaps reflects the counterculture's extreme wariness of authority during the late 1960s and early 1970s).[3] Nonetheless, Vatican II's decision to conduct mass in contemporary languages rather than Latin likely rekindled public interest in the Church, because it offered more transparency and insight into the institution's inner workings and history as once mysterious rituals (such as exorcism) became more accessible to lay people.

21

At the same time, however, the 1970s experienced a renewed interest in all things occult, including possession, witchcraft, and Satanism.[4] While this interest did not necessarily lead to a widespread resurgence in the belief and practice of demonology, it nevertheless had a noticeable effect on the popular culture produced during this period, much of which dealt explicitly with supernatural topics. The film adaptation of William Peter Blatty's 1971 novel *The Exorcist* capitalized on the social, cultural, and spiritual confusion of the time because it rode this wave of interest in the supernatural. At the same time, it offered viewers a sense of hope, because it positioned Roman Catholic beliefs as the antidote to the creeping secularism that threatened to overtake society.

While Kermode notes that director William Friedkin did not intend for *The Exorcist* to include such social and/or cultural commentary,[5] critics note that the film's narrative nevertheless reflected a number of prevalent sociocultural tensions—such as the sexual revolution, the generation gap, the conflict between science and religion, and more—and this likely contributed to its phenomenal success.[6] Stephen King, for instance, observes that *The Exorcist* "is a film about explosive social change, a finely honed focusing point for that entire youth explosion that took place in the late sixties and early seventies."[7] Yet, mainstream society did not readily embrace this newly emerging youth culture, and in many ways rejected it outright. As Vivian Sobchack observes, mainstream popular culture of the time responded to the youth explosion and its attendant generational crisis by frequently depicting children as abject creatures that victimized the stability of middle-class households, and thereby upset the natural order.[8] Robert F. Willson Jr.'s 1974 review of *The Exorcist* echoes this idea, particularly when he describes how the beautiful and innocent young Regan transforms into a snarling, foul-mouthed beast.[9] Willson's observation recalls the prevailing discourse surrounding the generation gap, as parents came face-to-face with unruly children. By situating a rebellious preteen girl on the verge of adolescence at the center of its narrative, *The Exorcist* played on the fears and anxieties that plagued an audience already exhausted from confronting the oncoming obsolescence of their own deeply held values and beliefs.

Barbara Creed, however, contends that *The Exorcist* frightens primarily because it exploits emerging fears regarding female empowerment, uninhibited feminine sexuality, and changing gender dynamics in the workforce and political arena. She claims that the film's shocks arise primarily from its "exploration of female monstrousness and the inability of the male order to control the woman whose perversity is expressed through her rebellious body."[10] This idea echoes Carol J. Clover's observation that occult films routinely depict imagery that worries, troubles, and questions masculinity,[11] which in turn recalls Peter Hutchings' assertion that horror films tend to explore masculine fears and anxieties.[12] *The Exorcist* premiered around the same time as the emergence of second-wave feminism and the women's liberation movement, and contemporary American audiences no doubt internalized the onscreen horrors because they reflected prevailing concerns regarding women's changing social roles. Thus, by depicting not only a rebellious young girl but also her independent, agnostic, and sexually enlightened mother, *The Exorcist* explicitly targets and exploits two of the 1970s most widespread and recognizable sociocultural anxieties.

At the same time, the film includes a number of themes that directly tackle other sociocultural anxieties of the period, including those regarding urban decay, the emergence of the gay rights movement,[13] the decline of religious morality and perceived ethical corruption of society, and the dissolution of the traditional family. *The Exorcist* likely resonated with audiences of the period because many viewers no doubt felt powerless to halt the oncoming social and cultural disruption from occurring, and they turned to the movies for some small measure of relief. The film comforts the audience because it offers images of heroic individuals battling and defeating an unnatural force that threatens to upset or obliterate the natural social order.[14]

This chapter explores the common scholarly readings and critiques of *The Exorcist*, which provide the foundation for our own understanding of the film and its themes. Of all the films that comprise the exorcism cinema subgenre, *The Exorcist* has received the most academic scrutiny; critics have deconstructed and critiqued the film using psychoanalysis and feminist film theory for years, and much has been written about its narrative, characters, and underlying themes. In this chapter we argue that because of its phenomenal success, *The Exorcist* provided the narrative tropes and metaphors that would inform subsequent exorcism films. We term these narrative tropes and metaphors the "traditional exorcism narrative" and consider how its two key components—that is, the possessed individual (usually a woman) and the holy person (usually a man)—reflect the tensions and struggles that societies and cultures often face with regard to issues of women's empowerment.

CRITICAL READINGS OF *THE EXORCIST*

The Exorcist opens with Father Lankester Merrin (Max von Sydow), an aged Catholic priest, overseeing an archaeological dig in the deserts of Northern Iraq. Merrin uncovers pieces of an amulet that once bore the image of Pazuzu,[15] an Assyrian wind demon he battled and defeated years ago while exorcising a young African boy. Shaken by this discovery, Merrin arranges to return home to the United States, but not before he visits a statue of Pazuzu in the ruins outside the archaeological site.

Meanwhile, in the idyllic Washington, DC, suburb of Georgetown, well-known actress Chris MacNeil (Ellen Burstyn) lives with her precocious preteen daughter Regan (Linda Blair). After playing with an Ouija board she found in a closet, Regan becomes increasingly disobedient and inhumanly strong. Fearing for her child (and her own physical and mental well-being), Chris consults psychologists and physicians, but they can find nothing medically wrong with the girl. Nevertheless, Regan's unusual behavior continues to escalate, until one night she kills her mother's lover by throwing him out of her bedroom window.

At a loss to explain Regan's unruly and destructive behavior, the doctors suggest an exorcism as a final recourse. Though skeptical, Chris meets with Jesuit priest and board certified psychiatrist, Father Damien Karras (Jason Miller), who struggles with his own sense of guilt over his mother's recent hospitalization and subsequent death. At first, Karras also dismisses the idea that Regan has become possessed, and refuses to seek permission to exorcise her. However, after listening to a recording of the girl speaking in reverse and watching as the words "HELP ME" appear in the flesh on her stomach, Karras finally agrees to perform the exorcism with Father Merrin's assistance.

Regan's bedroom becomes a battleground as the two priests attempt to cast out Pazuzu, who delights in toying with them. Karras, in particular, must endure the demon's taunts about his mother's soul burning in the fires of hell. Eventually, the two men tire, and they retreat into the hall to gather their strength. Unbeknownst to Karras, Father Merrin returns to complete the ritual on his own. Shortly thereafter, Karras enters the room and finds Merrin dead from a heart attack, leaving the younger priest to confront the demon alone. After a brief but violent physical confrontation with the possessed Regan, Pazuzu departs from the girl's body and possesses Karras, who leaps out the window to his death before the demon can compel him to further harm the girl. A few days later, Regan—who does not remember her ordeal—moves to Los Angeles with her mother.

According to various feminist critiques, *The Exorcist* uses a young female body to explore conflicts between good and evil, right and wrong, chaos and order. The film depicts female rebellion as both monstrous and appealing, and thus highlights abjection's most ambiguous aspect: the monster entices even as it threatens the symbolic patriarchal order. This dual positioning allows viewers to experience the pleasure that comes from violating taboos, while reassuring them that order will eventually be restored.[16] Creed describes abjection as that which threatens to destroy life, but at the same time reaffirms the boundaries of normality.[17] Thus, in exorcism films, a male patriarchal figure—and by proxy the audience—must confront the abject, and subsequently reaffirm normality.

Expelling or excluding the abject constitutes a vital step in facilitating the proper creation of self, and this might explain why individuals in the process of constructing or negotiating their identity—for example, those entering a new phase of life, like Regan—tend to succumb to possession onscreen more than those who have settled comfortably into their roles as prescribed by the symbolic order. In other words, possession suggests a form of liberating identity negotiation, allowing young people to explore the boundaries of convention and normality, while exorcism seems to suggest a form of oppression for people who must align their identities with this symbolic order. Many psychoanalytic and feminist critiques of the film argue that these abjections and metaphors deal with the empowerment and oppression of women in particular. Thus, *The Exorcist* allegorically depicts female agency and sexuality[18] as an abjection that opposes the governing rules and laws of the "paternal symbolic,"[19] and thereby troubles dominant sociocultural notions of identity, system, and order.

Creed further applies psychoanalytic and feminist theories to observe that *The Exorcist*'s core struggle involves the conflict between fathers and mothers, and thus between the maternal and the paternal. Moreover, she argues that in the absence of any sort of father figure, Chris and Regan's domestic relationship takes on lesbian overtones, and she points to their "unusual physical intimacy" and tendency to plan the details of their life together as evidence for this assertion.[20] Indeed, though their relationship initially appears caring, happy, and intimate, it quickly becomes perverse and crudely sexual. Creed isolates the sequence in which Regan violently and graphically masturbates with a crucifix to illustrate how the film positions the girl's behavior as abject and thus as a threat to prevailing cultural norms, particularly those regarding familial and/or sexual relationships.[21] Regan expresses sexual desire for her mother during this sequence and even shoves Chris's face in her crotch in a startling parody of cunnilingus. In the process, Regan violates the incest taboo even as she violates the sanctity of religion by defiling the cross.

Indulging in these cultural taboos seemingly increases Regan's possession, which in turn causes her behavior to worsen, yet the film exonerates her for breaking these taboos by placing the blame squarely on the entity inhabiting her. The possessed child motif grants the makers of satanic films more leeway to depict culturally taboo subjects like incest or blasphemy, because it allows them to portray such material in a "less threatening or objectionable way."[22] Indeed, Regan cannot control her actions while demonically possessed, and therefore cannot be held responsible for challenging the symbolic order. In essence, Regan epitomizes the "invasion metamorphosis"[23] subtype of horror films because she succumbs to the whims of an invasive power that alters her behavior and causes her to question the patriarchal order. This scenario mirrors real-world anxieties, particularly those arising from the perception that second-wave feminism represented an invasive ideology that inspired women to question their roles in society and challenge the authority of patriarchal order or paternal law.

For Andrew Scahill, the possessed Regan exemplifies the "revolting child" figure, a recurring horror trope that reflects contemporary sociocultural concerns regarding children, but also relates to a critique of patriarchy. According to Scahill, revolting or monstrous children typify the abject because their bodies openly challenge the laws of order and normality by transgressing several different boundaries (i.e., between children and adults, humans and animals, natural and supernatural).[24] At the same time, revolting children represent the "rebel" because they disrupt the sense of "harmonious community" that traditionally signifies order and normality.[25] Regan challenges "the avatars of a patriarchal culture (the family, the church, the military, educational system)" as well as "the very developmental narrative that upends that hierarchy."[26] Scahill argues that revolting children threaten order because they "represent the horror of incomplete narratives by their refusal to enter the social contract that marks them as 'adult.'"[27] He contends that this revolting child trope resembles queerness because it transgresses the boundaries between children and adults and thereby suggests a stunted development. In other words, the revolting child becomes a transgressive figure that completely upsets the natural order inhabited by adults, and Regan exemplifies this phenomenon.

Similarly, dominant cultural narratives routinely position young women in the space between childhood and adulthood, as they conceptualize female adolescence as a precarious time when innocent girls become helpless victims of their own burgeoning sexuality and only patriarchal guidance can align them with dominant notions of "normative development."[28] The adolescent Regan inhabits such a revolting body because she exists in the liminal space between girl and woman. As such, only Karras and Merrin's intervention can discipline her unruly body and her emergent sexuality and subsequently return her to the path of so-called normal adult development.[29] Metaphorically, then, the film portrays Regan as an adolescent girl who either cannot or will not accept her subservient role in the symbolic order, and this denotes another way the film positions her as abject; she threatens both tradition and the prescribed order.[30]

The Exorcist positions Regan's rebellion as both abnormal and monstrous, particularly with regard to her increasingly brazen attitude toward her own sexuality. Peter Biskind observes that the film represents a "male nightmare of female puberty," and it equates emergent female sexuality with demonic possession in an effort to reflect widespread societal disgust regarding female bodily functions like menstruation.[31] Likewise, Creed notes that Regan's possession occurs around the same time she enters puberty, a time when "adolescent sexual desires find shape and expression," and this explains why her behavior becomes increasingly "unladylike" and "aggressively sexual."[32] Simon Hewitt contends that the events unfolding onscreen reflect sociocultural anxieties regarding teenage sexuality, as Regan's possession grants her access to knowledge normally forbidden to children because it could potentially corrupt them.[33] According to Hewitt, sexuality represents adulthood's defining feature, and its influence must therefore remain separate from children's lives. Thus, Pazuzu causes Regan to cross "the boundary between two distinct modes of existence, a pre-sexual childhood and a sexual adulthood,"[34] rendering her both corrupt and abject. Creed's reading supports this analysis as she argues that Regan's name and possession each associate her with Christian snake symbolism,[35] which characterizes women as disobedient, treacherous, and wanton.[36] By inhabiting the body of a prepubescent girl, Pazuzu upsets the boundary between childhood and sexuality, but Father Karras intervenes and restores order through an act of male violence, which in turn absolves Regan of committing the "sin of adolescent sexuality" and allows her to re-enter the patriarchal order.[37]

In addition to transgressing the boundaries between childhood and sexual maturity, Regan's possession also transgresses patriarchal notions regarding gender identity and sexual orientation. Most critics argue that the demon sounds male, and therefore serves to masculinize Regan's own voice.[38] According to Clover, coding the possessed Regan's voice as masculine reflects a tradition in possession stories wherein "the invading devil or dybbuk has been construed as a male being."[39] Furthermore, Pazuzu's role as consort to the Assyrian snake goddess, Lamia,[40] also renders the male demon as a sexual entity.[41] Thus, the possession's aural nature suggests a transgression of gender boundaries, as a male entity appears to inhabit and operate within a female body, compelling it to engage in sexual behaviors.[42] Thus, during her possession, Regan exists as neither fully male nor fully female.

Yet, this reading becomes complicated when considering that actress Mercedes McCambridge, who initially did not receive credit for her work on the film, provided Pazuzu's voice. McCambridge frequently played butch characters that reflected her own "deviant female persona"[43] and her chronic bronchitis reportedly added to the otherworldly noises made by the possessed Regan.[44] Thus, it makes sense to metatextually code Pazuzu's voice as that of a perverse "female devil" that resides within the body of a preteen girl and induces her to act in a sexual—even homosexual—way toward those around her. Thus, the film also positions lesbianism as deviant.[45] Whether read as masculine or lesbian, the demon's voice inhabits the liminal space between male and female, and therefore leads to confusion regarding the possessed Regan's sexual orientation and the intent behind the sexual acts she performs. As Creed notes, gender boundaries become violated when an individual succumbs to possession or invasion by a differently-gendered personality, and this in turn increases the resulting sense of abjection.[46] Regardless of the transgression's ultimate nature, it nevertheless threatens patriarchal stability and therefore requires suppression.

Additionally, the film links Regan's dangerous sexuality and abjection to Chris's failure or refusal to inhabit the traditional maternal role. Critics note that *The Exorcist* uses Regan's ordeal to punish Chris because she does not fulfill the stereotypical role of wife and mother.[47] According to Thomas Kapacinskas, Chris's success drove away her husband, since he "could not tolerate becoming 'Mr. Chris MacNeil.'"[48] In many ways, Regan's possession serves to rebuke Chris's status as a career-minded single mother who actively enjoys her sexual freedom, and therefore condemns the sort of female empowerment encouraged by second-wave feminism. This disapproval manifests most clearly during the scene in which Regan overhears Chris cursing out her ex-husband for failing to call and wish his daughter a happy birthday. Regan's "visible signs of possession begin in the very next scene," implying that "a single mother is not powerful enough to protect her family from such pressures."[49] Thus, the film reflects the backlash to feminism's perceived impact on the breakdown of the family unit; while *The Exorcist* may appear to subvert stereotypes, it nevertheless ends with the affirmation of traditional gender roles.[50]

As a divorced career woman, Chris assumes a masculine breadwinner role to care and provide for her daughter. Furthermore, her short haircut and tendency to wear pants rather than skirts or dresses render her either androgynous or overtly masculine. Yet, as Regan's rebellious behavior escalates along with her possession, Chris increasingly turns to men for assistance, and her masculine characteristics recede as she grows more fearful of her daughter and submissive to the men around her. The film portrays this disempowerment through Chris's voice, which becomes strangled by sobs and outbursts over the course of the film. Indeed, Chris becomes noticeably meeker as she relinquishes her control to patriarchal institutions (i.e., medicine and religion) in an effort to deal with her daughter's rapidly intensifying possession. Whereas Regan becomes more aggressive and dominant due to her possession, Chris's agency decreases as a result of the demonic invasion. Thus, the film depicts dual female rebellions but ultimately chastises both, as the denouement serves to reassure audiences that punishment and repression await any woman who dares to transgress the boundaries and social norms regarding gender and sexuality.

Moreover, Hewitt's analysis of *The Exorcist* suggests that the stability secured by the film's ending results from the use of masculine violence.[51] He contends that the possessed Regan represents the oncoming onslaught of "explosive social change" that not only threatened to upset the patriarchal social order, but actively sought its destruction. Violence exemplifies the only way to stop such change and restore order, thus calming the fears of those who seek to maintain the patriarchal status quo. In *The Exorcist*, this violence manifests in the treatment of Regan's physical body during her possession. Kermode notes that Regan repeatedly appears restrained throughout the film;[52] she spends much of the runtime bound to her own bed, confined inside an assortment of intimidating medical devices, and, perhaps most significantly, restricted by adult men roughly twice her size. Kermode maintains that this theme of restraint establishes a claustrophobic or oppressive atmosphere, but we believe Regan's continued restriction represents another way the film metaphorically depicts female oppression or repression.

Ultimately, the heroes quell Regan's rebellion through the use of violence, and thus the film's narrative mirrors the violent sociocultural struggles of the late 1960s and early 1970s.[53] This theme of violent suppression culminates with Regan returning to the confines of normality and decency only after Father Karras, a former amateur boxer, pummels the twelve-year-old girl in a final desperate attempt to drive the insolent evil from her body. Karras—who assumes the role of the symbolic father due to his status as a priest—beats Regan and forces the demon from her body, thereby restoring her innocence and allowing her to resume her prescribed subservient role in the patriarchal social order. Meanwhile, the now-possessed Karras maintains control long enough to throw himself out the bedroom window and down a long flight of stairs in a final act of self-sacrifice that absolves him of his failure to assume the role of dutiful son while simultaneously proving his righteousness as a defender of the paternal order.[54] According to William Paul, this attack, which makes no sense narratively, indicates that Pazuzu becomes undone "when finally confronted with a muscular male who seeks not a feminized compassionate cure, but rather the emotional satisfaction of a good battering."[55] Thus, the film suggests that patriarchy must reassert itself through violence to end Pazuzu's threat.

Yet, Karras and Merrin die while Regan lives to ride off into an uncertain future with her mother. Thus, at the film's heart lies the abject woman, whose victims include two men "destroyed by the uncontainable power that is feminine sexuality."[56] Moreover, while Regan's burgeoning sexuality and rebellious nature become repressed once more, the film's ambiguous ending suggests they could re-emerge at any time. Thus, the film implies that the threat of second-wave feminism always lurks in the shadows.

THE TRADITIONAL EXORCISM NARRATIVE

The Exorcist was not the first feature film to feature a possession that required the intervention of an exorcism ritual. As mentioned in the previous chapter, *Der Dibuk* appears to be the first film—or, at least the first surviving film—to feature such a storyline. Other films were released before *The Exorcist*, but they did not have the same impact on global pop culture. For instance, the Polish film *Matka Joanna od aniołów* (aka *Mother Joan of the Angels*, aka *The Devil and the Nun*) was released in 1961. Directed by Jerzy Kawalerowicz, the film portrays a Catholic exorcism, but it does so by sexualizing Catholic nuns, rendering it a "nunsploitation" film that more closely aligns with the movies discussed in chapter 3. Other exorcism films include Italy's *Il demonio* (aka *The Demon*; 1963, Brunello Rondi); Britain's *Naked Evil* (aka *Exorcism at Midnight*; 1966, Stanley Goulder); Spain's *Las melancólicas* (aka *Exorcism's Daughter*; 1971, Rafael Moreno Alba); and *The Devils* (1971, Ken Russell) and *The Possession of Joel Delaney* (1972, Waris Hussein), both from the United States. Of these films, all but *Naked Evil* and *Joel Delaney* feature women becoming possessed and requiring the assistance of a spiritual man to perform an exorcism and expel the invasive entity. With the success of *The Exorcist*, this common narrative structure—which we term the traditional exorcism narrative—became the foundation for the emergent exorcism subgenre.

The five films that feature women becoming possessed in the manner described above conform to Clover's designation of "occult films," which in many ways provides the basis for the traditional exorcism narrative. Clover defines the occult film as "a dual focus narrative concerning a female character as portal to possession (a penetrability coded as feminine)."[57] In such narratives, "a male character (representing Western science/rationality) in crisis [. . .] must 'open up' (i.e., become feminized) to the possibility of supernatural acts" in his effort to vanquish the invading evil and subsequently restore order.[58] Clover's definition applies to *The Exorcist*, because Regan's possession leads Father Karras to challenge his reliance on Western science and reaffirm his Catholic faith. As demonstrated above, Regan's possession causes a variety of transgressions, abjections, and threats that Karras must confront and vanquish. Examined through the lens of Clover's definition of occult films, *The Exorcist* initially appears hopeful in terms of feminism, because it positions the resolution to Karras' crisis as feminine and potentially transgressive in itself. Yet, our reading of exorcism cinema's narrative tropes and metaphorical meanings reveals the opposite. Such films repeatedly depict a girl or young woman transgressing the boundaries of female sexuality and/or propriety only to become punished and oppressed, and thus these films appear to reaffirm paternal law and patriarchal authority. Furthermore, the same depictions, tropes, and metaphors recur throughout the exorcism cinema subgenre, and thereby perpetuate the traditional exorcism narrative.

From the start, horror films have tended to situate women in two primary roles, both of which position them as an "Other": either they lack agency and must therefore rely entirely upon the hero's efforts, or they become positioned as a threat the hero must overcome. Aside from the recurring "Final Girl" or "Survivor Girl" trope common to slasher films, which we discuss further in chapter 5, women in horror films tend to occupy the position of Other: the damsel in distress or the monster. Horror films frequently reduce women to the role of the Other because they lack the phallus, and thus lack power and control.[59] The cinematic apparatus situates the castrated woman as a passive, non-threatening entity unable to nullify the threat she either experiences or poses. In other words, horror films routinely deny women any sort of subjectivity or agency, and define them almost entirely in relation to men, who become active agents within the narrative. The imagery and discourses that recur throughout horror cinema normalize this depiction, creating an ideology in which women only occupy the roles of victims or damsels in distress.

At the same time, horror films often situate women as the Other by depicting them as monstrous. According to Creed, the "monstrous-feminine" situates the woman as a threat to patriarchal society, establishing and reinforcing this positioning by symbolically portraying her as a deviant, non-human creature.[60] Creed contends that horror films primarily concern the "purification of the abject," an act that involves the hero defeating the monster and subsequently restoring the symbolic order.[61] As discussed in chapter 1, horror films reestablish order and stability by demarcating distinct boundaries between human and non-human, and they often accomplish this through direct confrontations with the abject and the monstrous-feminine. The woman-as-monster figure represents an abjection that exists outside the boundaries of good, symbolic, patriarchal order. Thus, women become Othered because horror films routinely position them as monstrous representations of that which should not exist and therefore must be undone, silenced, and ultimately erased from existence.

While nearly all the various subgenres of horror cinema portray Other women by depicting them as manifestations of the monstrous-feminine, exorcism cinema foregrounds the idea that the monstrous-feminine actively threatens patriarchal order. Indeed, throughout exorcism cinema, women (mainly young women) and girls become positioned as monsters due to the abnormality of their possession; they exist simultaneously as human and demon, representing two diametrically opposed identities in one body. This monstrousness reflects the tension between innocence and temptation, which itself relates to Western religious and sociocultural conceptualizations of the virgin/whore dichotomy that positions women along an axis with the virgin on one end and the whore on the other. In Christianity, for instance, the figures of the Virgin Mary and Mary Magdalene exemplify this dichotomy. According to Creed, sin and abjection emerge from within, and this might account for why patriarchal discourse often perpetuates stereotypes of feminine evil in which a woman's beauty and virtue harbor wickedness and treachery.[62] From this perspective, women embody both the role of the innocent lover and the dangerous temptress, seemingly able to switch from one to the other without warning.

While this binary depiction of women recurs throughout the horror genre, it often represents exorcism cinema's dominant theme, as established by *The Exorcist*. For instance, Regan initially appears innocent and virginal, but her possession twists this chastity as she performs depraved sexual acts and challenges sociocultural conventions regarding feminine decency. Regan moves from virgin to whore due to her demonic possession, and then from whore to virgin due to exorcism. The virgin/whore dichotomy reflects systemic and institutionalized notions of feminine behavior; when Regan acts as the whore, she endangers both herself and others. Yet, when she inhabits the role of the virgin, both before the possession and after the exorcism, she appears beatific in the eyes of those around her. The influence of patriarchal institutions like the Catholic Church often account for such notions regarding the parameters of feminine sexuality and female conduct.

This influence has been exerted for centuries. Clover asserts that possession has been historically gendered as feminine.[63] As such, films that depict possession and exorcism align with a storytelling tradition that extends all the way back to the Bible. Indeed, from the story of Eve and the snake, to ideas regarding the sibyls and prophetesses of the Middle Ages, to the psychics and wiccans of today, Western narratives routinely portray women as portals that allow the devil to enter this world.[64] Furthermore, Western civilization has historically characterized women as the "weaker sex," due in large part to medieval conceptions of the female body as mutable and impressionable, and the female spirit as less faithful and less well-defined than the male body and spirit.[65]

Similarly, medieval philosophers argued that woman was not made in the image of God, and therefore the devil had little to fear when entering her body. Thus, women were considered more open to demonic manipulation and attack.[66] Indeed, the patriarchal order of the time regularly attributed women's emotional and social disturbances to the influence of "a malevolent spiritual force."[67] According to these characterizations and arguments, by the very nature of her femininity, even a virtuous woman could succumb to possession. Thus, it becomes easy to see why patriarchal institutions such as the Church advanced arguments regarding the likelihood that women could experience possession and thereby threaten themselves and others. From this perspective, all women hold the potential to experience possession, which in turn renders them interstitial and abject. As such, women in general become avatars for the monstrous-feminine that threatens society.

Following from this tradition, the exorcism cinema subgenre regularly positions women as monsters that jeopardize patriarchal order or paternal law, primarily because they embody both female innocence and sexual temptation. In exorcism cinema, possessed girls and young women exemplify this dichotomy, and thus become categorically interstitial.[68] Exorcism films position these girls and young women as terrifying figures that alternately threaten and entice the male protagonists, thereby positioning female sexuality and agency as twin sites of male anxiety. Indeed, exorcism films frequently portray girls and young women discovering a newfound power—that is, the ability to harness and express their burgeoning sexuality—and this power aligns them with the devil, the ultimate incarnation of evil and chaos.

At the same time, exorcism films situate the possessed girl or young woman as a victim in need of saving, as the "demon" inside her causes her to act in such abject, whorish ways.[69] Exorcism narratives further reify masculinity's dominance by depicting the male priests as saviors of virtue and defenders of patriarchal tradition because they restore the possessed girl or woman to a previous state of virginal innocence and respectful obedience.[70] In essence, exorcism films depict female sexuality as a threat, which in turn positions masculinity as the normal, dominant, and proper source of identification.[71] This positioning applies to a film like *The Exorcist*, which represents a battle between the symbolic order of the patriarchy and paternal law (as embodied by Fathers Merrin and Karras) and pre-symbolic anarchy (portrayed in the film as a young girl on the verge of discovering her own sexuality and agency).

The onscreen struggle between possession and exorcism allows for the examination of sociocultural anxieties regarding female sexuality and agency, because this struggle often mirrors tensions experienced in patriarchal Western societies, in which so-called aberrant displays of female sexuality inspire feelings of both disgust and desire.[72] Through their depiction of demonic possession, exorcism films examine the consequences that occur when a woman learns to take charge of her own sexual desires, which patriarchal institutions have repressed. This repression in turn causes any outburst of female independence or agency to become labeled as monstrous and threatening; in other words, patriarchal notions of normalcy have contributed to the creation of the very monster that threatens to undo patriarchal authority.[73] Viewers are meant to fear the possession, just as they are meant to cheer the male hero's attempts to exorcise the invasive force. Creed, however, argues that the possessed woman's sexuality appeals in its abject, graphic depiction.[74] As King has said, horror films allow viewers to experience sensations often deemed socially unacceptable.[75] Outside of the cinematic apparatus, uninhibited feminine sexuality threatens society's stability. Exorcism cinema reassures audiences that this larger threat can be contained and suppressed should repression prove inadequate. Thus, viewers of exorcism films can revel in the idea of untamed female sexuality, while remaining confident that the male hero will ultimately restore order.

This struggle characterizes the tension between feminine innocence and the sort of overt female sexuality that patriarchal institutions often fear and seek to control. In exorcism films, a woman who develops and controls her sexual desires and appetites becomes a dangerous aberration, and therefore the patriarchy must prevent her from gaining agency over this aspect of her life and identity. Indeed, for women, horror films often perpetuate the idea that sex leads to death, particularly if they enjoy it.[76] Cinematic possessions tend to afflict women primarily during the period when they transition from innocent girl to sexually active young woman, thus positioning sexual activity as a corrupting force that renders the girl impure and/or deviant.

Conversely, the possession could reflect traditional conceptualizations of women as the weaker sex, and the idea that men have more stable identities than women. This perception regarding women's malleability and lack of a strong inner spirit reveals why men sometimes consider women incapable of making responsible choices regarding their own bodies, particularly when it comes to a potentially life-altering experience like sex.[77] Possession, then, reflects the assumption that only deviant women would attempt to take charge of their sexuality.[78] Possession indicates that a masculine entity has usurped control of the girl or woman and seeks to unduly influence her to make the transition from the virgin to the whore, as no "good" woman would choose to engage in such inappropriate behavior. Exorcism, meanwhile, serves to return the girl or young woman to a state of pre-sexual innocence, wherein she no longer threatens herself or those around her.

This subtext exists in nearly every exorcism film produced after *The Exorcist*. Such films regularly utilize possession as a metaphor for the emergence of an empowered woman. Throughout the exorcism cinema subgenre, possession most often affects girls and young women who have not yet become sexually active or aware; thus, these possessions appear to metaphorically situate a girl or woman's burgeoning sexual agency as a threat that requires containment or outright elimination. Thus, the possessed-woman-as-threat figure represents a primary component of the traditional exorcism narrative. Male figures acting on behalf of patriarchal institutions, such as priests and other religious leaders, often become tasked with the job of suppressing this threat, therefore restoring the natural (i.e., patriarchal) order.[79] Indeed, many exorcism films barely concern the possessed girl or woman, and instead focus on the struggles of the male priests tasked with saving her. Traditional exorcism narratives position the priests as the heroes of the story, and subsequently emphasize their subjective experience of confronting and saving the possessed individual. Thus, the male savior figure, often taking the form of the doubting priest trope, represents the other primary component of the traditional exorcism narrative.

Clover underscores this point when she observes that while the possessed Regan's actions generate much of the film's horror, the true dread results from Karras's tortured relations with his mother, his fellow priests, and even God.[80] According to Clover, "for all its spectacle value, Regan's story is finally significant only insofar as it affects the lives of others, above all the tormented spiritual life of Karras."[81] In other words, the narrative uses Regan's predicament as a means to restore Karras's faith in God. The film portrays Karras as a tragic figure with a tormented psyche whose death saves Regan from her harrowing experience and allows her to lead a supposedly "normal" life.[82] The priest's struggle with the possessed girl and her metaphorical sexual awakening appears to reflect the patriarchy's fears regarding unleashed female sexuality. The holy man alleviates viewers' fears because his actions serve to repress the woman's uninhibited sexuality and end the threat it poses, at least temporarily. As a result, exorcism films frequently downplay the possessed girl or woman's subjective experience, and her predicament functions primarily as motivation for the male hero to rediscover his faith and allegiance to patriarchal institutions and paternal authority.

Of course, the tensions that recur throughout the exorcism cinema subgenre do not simply reflect those surrounding a woman's discovery, embracing, and expression of her emerging sexuality. These tensions also reflect the idea that women can enact and take control of their power and agency through such expression; possession allows these women to find their voice within the confines of a patriarchal order that would otherwise silence them.[83] As the symbolic manifestation of voice, language has been created largely by patriarchal structures as a way to "limit what can be said and how it can be said."[84] Furthermore, because dominant groups (i.e., men) tend to develop language, the masculine perspective becomes normalized as the default in language, privileging men over women.[85]

This struggle involving women's voice serves a dual function in these films. First, the demonic possession relates to gender transgression, as it empowers women to enter a masculine (i.e., patriarchal) realm through aggression, violence, and sexual dominance. In exorcism films, women frequently use masculine language (e.g., swearing, taunting, etc.) to assert themselves and make their voices heard within the confines of this patriarchal language. This transgression, however, indicates that masculinization results in empowerment, indicating the further oppression of feminine power (i.e., feminine ways of speaking) as a form of liberation. Indeed, since the invading spirits are often coded as masculine, the possessed woman's power hinges on this "masculinization from the inside out."[86] Thus, exorcism films suggest the women's power arises from her willingness to embrace a masculine nature rather than a feminine one.

In addition, this transgression threatens order because it reflects the masculine concern regarding women speaking in such masculinized ways and thus invading male spaces and encroaching on men's dominance. Because men have been able to construct their dominance through language, women's appropriation of that same language to gain equal footing sometimes appears as a threat that must be expelled; as Chris Boeskool explains, for those in positions of power, the idea of equality often implies a reduction in power and thus a threat to said power.[87] As such, exorcism films frequently position women's voices as a threat because they use them to speak out against those repressive societal structures that favor men and thus transgress gender boundaries. Such movies visually represent this threat by associating that voice with the physical ugliness of the possessed; the films establish these women as innocent and beautiful, and therefore the corruption of their physical body renders anything that comes out of it (i.e., anything they say) equally corrupt. Possession provides women with an empowering voice, and exorcism subsequently disempowers women because it silences their voices and thus removes the threat they pose to patriarchal order and authority.

APPLYING THE TRADITIONAL EXORCISM NARRATIVE

By exerting control over their sexuality, voices, and thus agency, women gain power over their own lives, and also potentially over the lives of men. Exorcism films convey this empowerment through the experience of possession, which grants girls and young women the ability to speak their minds without fear of repercussion, since the demon actually speaks in their place.[88] Furthermore, coding the demonic voice as masculine adds to this metaphorical reading; the possessed girl or woman gains strength because she draws on the power of the masculine, which in turn grants her the ability to speak against the patriarchy and finally make her voice heard.

As with melodramatic stories and real-life incidents of hysteria, it becomes possible to read possession as an act of breaking through patriarchal repression of female voices and experiences.[89] The possessed girl or woman not only speaks freely about her emerging sexual desires, but she also gains the power and agency to express unguarded, insightful, disruptive, and potentially insensitive comments about the people around her. Thus, exorcism cinema's use of demonic possession does not simply reveal the tensions that exist within modern societies and cultures regarding female sexuality; it also demonstrates that sociocultural tensions occur when women discover their voices and the power to take control of their own lives.

Furthermore, the traditional exorcism narrative functions as a dual narrative, similar to the occult film as described by Clover.[90] On the one hand, demonic possession metaphorically creates an empowered woman, because it allows her to express her burgeoning sexuality. More than that, it allows her to discover her voice and her sense of agency, and grants her the ability to speak and act out against patriarchal forces of suppression, oppression, and repression. This narrative creates a possessed-woman-as-threat archetypal figure that becomes a central trope of the subgenre.[91] At the same time, a male figure struggles to find his faith and save the possessed person's soul, which represents an attempt to restore patriarchal tradition and reestablish parameters regarding female propriety. In doing so, the doubting priest figure comes to realize the validity of his faith in the patriarchy and becomes the male savior figure, acts that represent two other key central tropes of this subgenre.

Andrew Britton argues that *The Exorcist* "allows the repressed to find expression, and gratification, in an absolutely objectified form (possession by the devil)" and it therefore "moves inexorably towards the punishment (renewed repression) of that gratification."[92] Possession grants power, but because a woman exerts that power, it threatens patriarchal order and therefore requires suppression lest it upset the stability of the surrounding society and culture. The possessed individual's abject nature provides viewers with the pleasure of seeing the subversion of patriarchal and heteronormative ideology, while reassuring them that the hero will ultimately uphold such ideology and end the threat posed by this monstrous subversion.[93]

Thus, the exorcism ritual metaphorically represents the idea that the protagonist (usually the male priest) must actively repress the possessed girl or woman (often positioned as the victim and the monster), and thereby prevent her from dismantling the patriarchal order (i.e., the forces of normality, decency, and propriety).[94] As such, exorcism films function as morality tales,[95] meant to alert viewers to the dangers posed by empowered women, who experience punishment for harboring aberrant notions of female sexuality and agency. These "monsters" reflect actions, ideologies, and identities that deviate from so-called normal, respectable society; their grotesqueness resides less in their form (although special effects often visually depict the possessed as physically deformed to allude to their inner ugliness) than in their ability to threaten society.[96] As Clover argues, these stories routinely depict men acting to return unruly women to a state of normalcy, often through violence and repression, and thus they serve as stark reminders of "what happens to the woman who drifts out of the orbit of male control."[97] The narratives of such films potentially reflect traditional religious ideologies that dictate proper feminine behavior, and while these ideologies may not always echo the prevailing wisdom of the time, they nevertheless remain part of the fabric of Western civilization.

The remainder of this book utilizes this understanding of the traditional exorcism narrative to examine other exorcism films that hail from a variety of nations, cultures, and time periods. Nevertheless, they all tend to reflect the narrative tropes and metaphors discussed above, which contribute to the construction of the traditional exorcism narrative. Indeed, few exorcism films challenge this narrative, and these challenges seem relatively small compared to how often those same films exemplify the metaphorical oppression expressed in this narrative. Moreover, as our analyses of the films indicate, the traditional exorcism narrative contributes to our understanding of how dominant patriarchal forces operating in the world habitually oppress and marginalize non-dominant groups, from women to people of color to non-heteronormative individuals.

NOTES

1. Mark Kermode, *The Exorcist: Revised 2nd Edition* (London: British Film Institute, 2003), 8–9.
2. For more, see Kermode, *The Exorcist*, 8 and Alexandra Heller-Nicholas, "'The Power of Christ Compels You': Moral Spectacle and The Exorcist Universe," in *Roman Catholicism in Fantastic Film: Essays on Belief, Spectacle, Ritual and Imagery*, ed. Regina Hansen (Jefferson: McFarland & Company, Inc., 2011), 65–80.
3. Kevin J. Wetmore, *Post-9/11 Horror in American Cinema* (New York: Continuum, 2012), 139–40.
4. Juan B. Cortés and Florence M. Gatti, "Demonology and Witchcraft," in *The Case Against Possessions and Exorcisms: A Historical, Biblical, and Psychological Analysis of Demons, Devils, and Demoniacs* (New York: Vantage Press, 1975), 44.
5. Kermode (2003) notes that director William Friedkin claims he did not intend for *The Exorcist* to reflect the prevailing social mood of the time. In fact, he finds the idea that the film functions as an allegory for anxieties surrounding feminism and the generational crisis amusing, stating, "I'm not aware of any far-reaching social problems that *The Exorcist* dealt with. That usually comes later—when people have run out of things to say about the film, they start describing the social implications of it" (35).
6. According to Andrew Scahill (2010), the film's "hyperbolic structure" supports a variety of readings, and critics have considered it "a misogynist indictment of working mothers, an anxious response to student political protests, a historical artifact verifying the presence of capital 'e' Evil, a Nixon-era loss of innocence allegory for the nation, the disillusionment of the American public with Positivism, the projection of anti-Islamic anxieties, or a Catholic call to arms against liberal humanism" (40).
7. Stephen King, *Danse Macabre* (New York: Pocket Books, 1982/2010), 177.
8. Vivian Sobchack, "Bringing it All Back Home: Family Economy and Generic Exchange," in *The Dread of Difference: Gender and the Horror Film*, ed. Barry Keith Grant (Austin: University of Texas Press, 1996), 150.
9. Robert F. Willson Jr., "*The Exorcist* and Multicinema Aesthetics," *The Journal of Popular Film* 3, no. 2 (1974): 183–87.
10. Barbara Creed, *The Monstrous-Feminine: Film, Feminism, and Psychoanalysis* (New York: Routledge, 1993), 34.
11. Carol J. Clover, *Men, Women and Chainsaws: Gender in the Modern Horror Film* (Princeton: Princeton University Press, 1992), 65.
12. Peter Hutchings, "Masculinity and the Horror Film," in *You Tarzan: Masculinity, Movies and Men*, eds. Pat Kirkham and Janet Thumim (New York: St. Martin's Press, 1993), 84.
13. Harry M. Benshoff, *Monsters in the Closet: Homosexuality and the Horror Film* (Manchester: Manchester University Press, 1997), 182.
14. Conversely, Kermode (2003) contends that the theatrical cut's abrupt ending leaves the audience feeling "startled and disorientated, unable to recover their composure, with no time to reflect on the horrors they have seen or draw any reassurance that everything is indeed 'going to be all right'" (84).
15. We should note that the demon actually remains unnamed throughout *The Exorcist*. Scholars and critics often refer to it as Pazuzu, likely because Father Philip Lamont (Richard Burton) names it as such in *Exorcist II: The Heretic*. One of the first occurrences of naming the demon Pazuzu appears in Andrew Britton's 1979 review of the film, in which he refers to the invasive entity as Pazuzu, "a minor Mesopotamian deity with none of the connotations of the Christian Satan" (50).

16. Creed, *Monstrous-Feminine*, 9.

17. Barbara Creed, "Kristeva, Femininity, Abjection," in *The Horror Reader*, ed. Ken Gelder (New York: Routledge, 2000), 64–65.

18. According to Jacquelyn W. White, Barrie Bondurant, and Cheryl Brown Travis (2000), "sexuality" refers "to a variety of phenomena, including sexual identity, sexual preference, and sexual behavior" (11). Similarly, Chris Dumas (2014) draws upon the work of Sigmund Freud to argue that sexuality "pervades every aspect of human life and behavior" and involves "nearly any behavior that works toward achieving some kind of pleasure (or even displeasure)" (24). Thus, when we use the term "sexuality," we refer to a range of identities and proclivities that are and have been routinely oppressed in the context of patriarchal societies and cultures.

19. Creed, *Monstrous-Feminine*, 37.

20. Ibid., 40.

21. Ibid., 35.

22. Carrol L. Fry, "Sign, Symbol and Primal Fears in the Satanic Film," in *Cinema of the Occult: New Age, Satanism, Wicca, and Spiritualism in Film* (Bethlehem: Lehigh University Press, 2008), 129.

23. For more on this horror subtype, see Bruce Ballon and Molyn Leszcz, "Horror Films: Tales to Master Terror or Shapers of Trauma?," *American Journal of Psychotherapy* 61, no. 2 (2007), 216.

24. Andrew Scahill, "Demons Are a Girl's Best Friend: Queering the Revolting Child in *The Exorcist*," *Red Feather Journal* 1, no. 1 (2010): 39–55.

25. Ibid., 41.

26. Ibid.

27. Ibid., 42.

28. Ibid., 43.

29. Ibid.

30. Scahill (2010) argues that "the putridity, the decay, and the flow of bodily fluids from the young girls all represent what the symbolic order (here represented by the medical and religious professions as well as the family) seeks to reject and repress in order to maintain its stability and coherency" (47).

31. Peter Biskind, *Easy Riders, Raging Bulls: How the Sex-Drugs-and-Rock 'N' Roll Generation Saved Hollywood* (New York: Simon & Schuster, 1998), 223.

32. Creed, *Monstrous-Feminine*, 35.

33. Simon Hewitt, "I'm Not Sure I Like the Sound of That: Palliative Effects of the 'Synchronous Monster' in Cinema" (presentation, Fear, Horror, & Terror at the Interface, 7th Global Conference, Oxford, United Kingdom, September 5–7, 2013).

34. Ibid.

35. In reference to one of King Lear's monstrous daughters, whom Shakespeare characterized as "sharper than a serpent's tooth." For more, see Creed, *Monstrous-Feminine*, 33.

36. Ibid.

37. Hewitt, "Palliative Effects."

38. Creed, *Monstrous-Feminine*, 39.

39. Clover, *Chain Saws*, 103.

40. We discuss a postcolonial reading of Pazuzu's nature in chapter 4, but we should note that *The Exorcist* films establish the demon as Middle Eastern/African. Pazuzu's invasion therefore serves to disrupt Regan's Whiteness in this film, but the demon ultimately becomes oppressed and defeated by Western ideology via the Catholic exorcism ritual.

41. Creed, *Monstrous-Feminine*, 33.

42. Andrew Britton, "The Exorcist," in *American Nightmare: Essays on the Horror Film*, eds. Andrew Britton, Richard Lippe, Tony Williams, and Robin Wood (Toronto: Festival of Festivals, 1979), 51.

43. Patricia White, *Uninvited: Classical Hollywood Cinema and Lesbian Representability* (Indianapolis: Indiana University Press, 1999), 180.

44. David Konow, *Reel Terror: The Scary, Bloody, Gory, Hundred-Year History of Classic Horror Films* (New York: Thomas Dunne Books, 2012), 148.

45. White, *Uninvited*, 180.

46. Creed, *Monstrous-Feminine*, 32.

47. For more on this idea, see Bianca Marcus, "A Single Woman: Rebellion Against and Reinforcement of Traditional Gender Roles in *The Exorcist*," *Kino: The Western Undergraduate Journal of Film Studies* 2, no. 1 (2011): 1–3.

48. Thomas J. Kapacinskas, "'The Exorcist' and the Spiritual Problem of Modern Woman," *Psychological Perspectives: A Quarterly Journal of Jungian Thought* 6, no. 2 (1975): 179.

49. Chris Dumas, "Horror and Psychoanalysis: An Introductory Primer," in *A Companion to the Horror Film*, ed. Harry M. Benshoff (Malden: Wiley Blackwell, 2014), 33.

50. Adrian Schober, *Possessed Child Narratives in Literature and Film: Contrary States* (New York: Palgrave, 2004), 74–75.

51. Hewitt, "Palliative Effects."

52. Kermode, *The Exorcist*, 32–33.

53. As Kermode (2003) notes, the early 1970s were a time defined by great cultural and social strife, when army soldiers gunned down college protestors, hippies became associated with serial killers, and President Richard Nixon's involvement in the Watergate scandal caused many to question the government's credibility and legitimacy.

54. Moreover, Karras's sacrifice seems to suggest a Christ-like characterization, as he becomes a martyr to the cause of defending patriarchy from the threat of female sexuality/agency.

55. William Paul, *Laughing Screaming: Modern Hollywood Horror and Comedy* (New York: Columbia University Press, 1994), 308.

56. Dumas, "Horror and Psychoanalysis," 32.

57. David Church, "Review: *The Exorcism of Emily Rose*," *Disability Studies Quarterly* 26, No. 2 (2006): 1.

58. Ibid.

59. Jill Dolan, "Ideology in Performance: Looking Through the Male Gaze," in *The Feminist Spectator as Critic* (Ann Arbor: UMI Research Press, 1988), 49.

60. Creed, *Monstrous-Feminine*, 251.

61. Ibid., 257.

62. Ibid., 42.

63. Clover, *Chain Saws*, 70.

64. Ibid., 71–72.

65. Nancy Caciola, *Discerning Spirits: Divine and Demonic Possession in the Middle Ages* (Ithaca: Cornell University Press, 2003), 130.

66. In our interview with Daniel Stamm, the director echoes this idea, saying "Why to me it makes sense to have it be a girl is that in our society . . . it seems the most vulnerable and worthy of protection entity you could expose to the demon force." Daniel Stamm (film director) in discussion with the authors, June 7, 2015.

67. Nathaniel Deutsch, *The Maiden of Ludmir: A Jewish Holy Woman and Her World* (Los Angeles: University of California Press, 2003), 132.

68. Noël Carroll, *The Philosophy of Horror, Or, Paradoxes of the Heart* (New York: Routledge, 1990), 32.

69. This duality reflects Peter Hutchings's (1993) assertion that an individual sometimes embodies both the victim and the victimizer, as in the case of classic monsters such as King Kong and Dracula (86).

70. William Paul (1994) argues this repression manifests symbolically in *The Exorcist* during the sequence in which Regan masturbates with the crucifix. He contends that in this sequence, the devil grants Regan an awareness of her own sexuality, and that the Church seeks to curtail her newfound sexual awakening. Paul points out that by violently masturbating with the crucifix, one of the most recognizable symbols associated with the Catholic Church, the possessed Regan essentially represses her own burgeoning sexuality. For more, see Paul, *Laughing Screaming*, 306.

71. Mark Jancovich (ed.), *Horror, The Film Reader* (New York: Routledge, 2002), 15.

72. Creed, *Monstrous-Feminine*, 31.

73. Dumas, "Horror and Psychoanalysis," 31.

74. Creed, *Monstrous-Feminine*, 31.

75. King, *Danse*, 297.

76. Ibid., 70.

77. Caciola, *Discerning Spirits*, 146.

78. White, Bondurant, and Travis (2000) note that twentieth century literature frequently conceptualized men as "naturally dominant" and women as "naturally submissive." They argue that such notions of sexuality imply that "achieving femininity lies in surrendering the body (and the self) to men; that women are a sexual problem and need men to teach them mature sexual responsiveness. Finally, it conveys the message that women who reject these roles will be psychologically flawed" (18). Thus, a woman who seeks to control her sexuality becomes aberrant within the context of a traditional patriarchal gender order.

79. We should explicate our use of the term "natural" here. In his rhetorical analysis of *The Exorcist*, Martin J. Medhurst (1978) contends that the film is less about good versus evil, and more about "a natural man confronting a supernatural evil" (82). Even if the film does not depict the battle between good and evil, it still portrays a struggle between natural/normal (aka masculine, patriarchal) and unnatural/abnormal (aka feminine).

80. Clover, *Chain Saws*, 85.

81. Ibid., 87.

82. Kim Nicolini, "Chasing Hell: The Films of William Friedkin," *CounterPunch* 20, no. 5 (2013): 25–26.

83. Sobchack, "Family Economy," 162.

84. Jacquelyn W. White, Barrie Bondurant and Cheryl Brown Travis, "Social Constructions of Sexuality: Unpacking Hidden Meanings," in *Sexuality, Society, and Feminism*, eds. Cheryl Brown Travis and Jacquelyn W. White (Washington, DC: American Psychological Association, 2000), 17.

85. Ibid.

86. Clover, *Chain Saws*, 103.

87. Chris Boeskool, "'When You're Accustomed to Privilege, Equality Feels Like Oppression,'" *Huffpost Politics*, last modified March 14, 2016, http://www.huffingtonpost.com/chris-boeskool/when-youre-accustomed-to-privilege_b_9460662.html.

88. Caciola, *Discerning Spirits*, 129.

89. Jan Campbell, *Film and Cinema Spectatorship: Melodrama and Mimesis* (Malden: Polity Press, 2005), 45.

90. Clover, *Chain Saws*, 66.

91. While concretized in *The Exorcist*, this trope reached perhaps its utmost expression in *The Vatican Tapes* (2015, Mark Neveldine). In this film, the possessed woman becomes the Antichrist, the very harbinger of Armageddon in Christian faith.

92. Britton, "The Exorcist," 51.

93. Ibid., 52–53.

94. According to Creed (1993), "*The Exorcist* is not unlike a 'ritual' of purification in that it permits the spectator to wallow vicariously in normally taboo forms of behavior before restoring order" (37). Furthermore, she argues that rituals such as exorcism allow societies to return to a state of normality because they allow for a confrontation with the abject, which ultimately results in that element's expulsion. Thus, society redraws the lines between dichotomous states of being such as human and non-human, living and dead, and natural and supernatural, becoming stronger in the process.

95. Rick Pieto, "'The Devil Made Me Do It: Catholicism, Verisimilitude and the Reception of Horror Films," in *Roman Catholicism in Fantastic Film: Essays on Belief, Spectacle, Ritual and Imagery*, ed. Regina Hansen (Jefferson: McFarland & Company, Inc., 2011), 57.

96. Lester D. Friedman, "'Canyons of Nightmare': The Jewish Horror Film," in *Planks of Reason: Essays on the Horror Film*, eds. Barry Keith Grant and Christopher Sharrett (Lanham: Scarecrow Press, Inc., 2004), 83–84.

97. Clover, *Chain Saws*, 103.

THREE

Rip-offs and Homages of the 1970s

Spotlighting Exploitation with Abby *and* Şeytan

As discussed in the previous chapter, *The Exorcist* premiered during a time of great sociocultural upheaval, as people around the world reexamined traditional ideas about gender, sexuality, religion, race, youth, and more. The film implicitly (and sometimes explicitly) targeted the anxieties that accompanied this sociocultural turmoil, and this might explain why it caused hysterical reactions in some viewers. Reports from the time indicate that audience members routinely fainted, vomited, and even suffered heart attacks.[1] In one notable incident, a woman reportedly miscarried while watching the film. In another, four women were allegedly confined to psychiatric care after a screening in Toronto.[2] Mark Kermode describes an incident in Berkeley, California, in which "a man threw himself at the screen in a misguided attempt to 'get the demon.'"[3] Doctors issued warnings about the film, while theater owners complained about having to clean up vomit. European officials blamed *The Exorcist* for an increase in suicidal and criminal behavior after a teenager claiming he became possessed while watching the film murdered a nine-year-old girl.[4] Surprised by these hysterical reactions, director William Friedkin argued that his film also inspired an increase in public service and church attendance, but such positive acts did not elicit the same attention from a news media oriented toward sensationalism.[5]

Along with the hysteria, the film also inspired a great deal of controversy upon release. Citing a lack of excessive sex or violence, the Motion Picture Association of America's ratings board initially awarded *The Exorcist* a mild R rating, meaning children could see it with their parent's permission.[6] However, public outcry over this decision prompted district attorneys in Washington, DC, and Boston to overturn the ruling, prohibiting children under seventeen from seeing the film even if accompanied by a parent.[7] Meanwhile, the film received an X certificate in Britain, where it met with protests and picketing from the Christian "Festival of Light" lobby.[8] Town councils throughout the UK subsequently banned *The Exorcist* outright, though enterprising travel companies offered bus trips to towns screening the film.[9] Tunisia also banned the movie outright, labeling it Christian propaganda.[10]

The controversy extended beyond the film's rating and exhibition; as noted in the previous chapter, actress Mercedes McCambridge voiced the demon Pazuzu in an uncredited performance, but to enhance the shock value of the possession scenes, the film's marketing stressed that Linda Blair performed this dialogue herself.[11] McCambridge eventually sued Warner Bros. to obtain her screen credit.[12] News of the lawsuit emerged just as actress Linda Blair received a Best Supporting Actress Oscar nomination for her performance as Regan, though she did not win the award (likely because of the legal battle).[13] More disturbingly, following the film's theatrical debut, Blair received death threats from individuals who accused her of glorifying Satan. To ensure the young actress's safety, the studio assigned bodyguards to watch over her for six months.[14]

Despite all this, or perhaps because of it, *The Exorcist* became a hugely successful international hit, remaining in theaters for two full years. During its initial theatrical release in 1973, the film netted $193 million domestically, while two subsequent rereleases in 2000 and 2010 generated another $232 million in domestic ticket sales and $208 million worldwide.[15] Adjusted for inflation, *The Exorcist* currently stands as the ninth highest grossing movie of all time. Such phenomenal success could explain why so many imitators arose in the film's wake. According to Andrew Tudor, genres and their subgenres develop and become crystalized "through a kind of survival of the commercially fittest."[16] Financially successful like *The Exorcist* sometimes spawn new genres or subgenres because producers seeking comparable success will utilize similar aesthetics and/or narrative aspects (i.e., its tropes and conventions) in their own films. Tudor notes that *The Exorcist*'s success kicked off a horror boom in the early 1970s, and that many of those films in some way featured possession.[17] For this reason, *The Exorcist* essentially established the exorcism cinema subgenre.

Indeed, many producers and distributors have tried to replicate the film's remarkably effective formula by either producing films that copied its narrative outright, or by altering the content or advertising campaigns of pre-existing films. At the time of publication, 117 exorcism films have been produced and released worldwide since 1973, and nearly all of them follow the same narrative structure and contain the same thematic conventions as *The Exorcist*. In this chapter, we discuss various foreign and domestic attempts to capitalize on *The Exorcist*'s success throughout the 1970s. The movies discussed in this chapter originate from a variety of national cinemas, including Germany, Brazil, Italy, France, Spain, and the United Kingdom, and we argue that a political economic consideration of their production, circulation, and reception highlights the transcultural and globalized nature of the cinematic medium.

In this chapter, we also consider two specific exorcism films that thus far have received limited scholarly and critical attention: *Abby* (1974, William Girdler) and *Şeytan* (1974, Metin Erksan). We draw on the critical frameworks of feminist and postcolonial theories to examine how each film's narrative and characters relate to the traditional exorcism narrative as established by *The Exorcist*. Postcolonial theory allows us to historically situate both films within their respective cultural and historical contexts, while feminist theory forms the basis for our argument that these two films perpetuate and reaffirm the traditional exorcism narrative. Throughout this chapter, we argue that exploring culturally situated exorcism cinema allows us to understand how such films appropriate, reflect, challenge, and ultimately respond to the traditional exorcism narrative. This consideration in turn allows us to understand how individuals from these cultures either adopt or resist the ideologies embedded in exorcism films.

RIP-OFFS, HOMAGES, AND EXPLOITATION

Horror frequently taps into widespread fears that resonate with audiences around the world, and therefore the genre often transcends national or cultural borders.[18] This could explain why producers of the 1960s and 1970s frequently thought of horror films as cult items able to play in markets beyond their national boundaries.[19] National cinemas of this period often embraced the genre because it allowed them to highlight their own national identities, while still producing films that could relate to or fit within the confines of Hollywood's industrial cinema system.[20] Thus, non-Western nations and cultures frequently use horror to explore or highlight local traditions and lore that differ from European or North American traditions, and render them more or less recognizable to Western audiences. Furthermore, and perhaps more importantly, by depicting horrors that originate outside of the Western psychoanalytic perspective, such films displace the universal Western subject frequently situated as the central figure in horror films,[21] which in turn destabilizes the primacy of the Western ideological perspective. Thus, international horror can offer glimpses into what other cultures consider fearsome.

This ability to traverse national boundaries—either by exceeding those boundaries or reflecting conditions within them—and thereby succeed globally often aligns international horror films with exploitation cinema.[22] According to David Church, the term "exploitation" functions as "an overarching generic label loosely applied to various genre products" and emerges out of aesthetic considerations concerning a film's budget, style, and sensibilities.[23] Exploitation films often rely on sensationalized subject matter to compensate for low budgets and a lack of recognizable stars. Furthermore, these "spectacles in bad taste" often feature depictions of drug use, gratuitous violence, extreme gore, explicit nudity, and sexual deviance.[24] Throughout the 1960s and 1970s, exploitation films routinely screened in "cheap, sleazy places like grind houses, drawing audiences through spectacularly lurid advertising," and thus the films themselves became thought of as cheap, tawdry, and altogether disreputable.[25] Of course, the goal with exploitation was not to make art, but to quickly produce cheap movies that satisfied the audience's "desire for transgressive spectacle."[26]

In an attempt to cash in on the demand for international art films that featured explicitly erotic content but maintained a much more prestigious reputation, producers and distributors often marketed exploitation films as artistic experiences that similarly offered a universal sensual appeal. They accomplished this by foregrounding the sensationalistic content, such as the "sexuality at play in the mythologies of horror," while de-emphasizing anything that appeared too culturally specific.[27] Additionally, exploitation films catered to a global youth market that rebelled against the traditions of various nations and cultures; thus, young people in the United States gathered in grindhouses and drive-ins to watch movies that contained perspectives and experiences often vastly different from their own. While exploitation films existed in relation to films produced within the hegemonic structures of the Hollywood system, they still catered to this youth market by challenging traditional movies and institutional systems.[28] An example of this occurs in the Spanish horror films produced during this period; such films frequently employed generic codes that challenged or subverted "the socially accepted norms of sex and sexuality, religion, class and the family."[29] Other exploitation subgenres, such as blaxploitation, offer comparable challenges to prevailing ideologies regarding race, masculinity, and sexuality.

While some horror films appear to critique national and cultural norms and thus support progressive readings, the majority tend to align more closely with tradition and prevailing ideologies, such as those produced within the Hollywood system. This latter tendency arises primarily from horror's conservative and reactionary nature, and may explain why many foreign and domestic films advance conservative ideologies similar to those found in *The Exorcist*; in their bid to generate similar box office revenue, producers of domestic and foreign rip-offs would have likely included similar ideological stances in their own films. As Danny Shipka observes, European horror films reflect the patriarchal perspective on women's liberation and the sexual revolution, because they tend to focus on how men react to women's sexual liberation rather than on how women become empowered by embracing their own sexuality.[30]

Furthermore, with its transgressive sexuality and graphic and blasphe-mous content, *The Exorcist* already aligns with exploitation cinema in many ways,[31] and this reason, along with the film's financial success and ideological nature, might indicate why numerous nations and cultures produced their own exploitation rip-offs and homages in the decade fol-lowing its release.

Between 1973 and 1980, producers and distributors around the world sought to capitalize on *The Exorcist's* impressive worldwide success in four distinct ways. First, the marketing for many films promised or sug-gested scenes of possession and exorcism, even if the film itself included neither. Second, producers or distributors rewrote or re-edited existing films to include new scenes or sequences clearly meant to evoke *The Exorcist*. Third, some producers developed outright rip-offs of *The Exor-cist*, while others produced culturally or nationally specific homages to the film. Finally, producers developed sexploitation films that focused on and extended the sexual aspects of possession as depicted in *The Exorcist*. These efforts resulted in at least two dozen European, horror, and exploi-tation films that emulated that landmark film in one way or another.[32] Some of these films do not include a depiction of exorcism, and thus were not considered in our filmography, which lists only twenty-one as true exorcism films. Moreover, these rip-offs reflect *The Exorcist's* conserva-tive, reactionary response to feminism, even though the majority of them originated from outside of the United States and thus reflect different cultural perspectives and experiences. Thus, the traditional exorcism nar-rative established by *The Exorcist* became replicated, perpetuated, and appropriated on a global scale.[33]

As noted above, producers of this period often marketed their low-budget horror or exploitation movies as exorcism films even if they did not explicitly deal with the topic. For instance, the French film *Les possé-dées du diable* (1974, Jesús "Jess" Franco) depicts a spiritual rather than demonic possession, but does not feature a subsequent exorcism ritual. Yet, North American distributors retitled the film *Lorna the Exorcist* for its U.S. release in 1976.[34] The Spanish film *Las melancólicas* (1971, Rafael Mo-reno Alba) tells the story of a woman who descends into madness after witnessing her mother's exorcism, which likely inspired producers to rerelease the film internationally as *Exorcism's Daughter* in 1974. The fol-lowing year, director Jess Franco helmed *L'éventreur de Notre-Dame*, which played in the United States under the titles *Exorcisms*, *Demoniac*, and *Exorcism and Black Masses* (a heavily re-edited version that empha-sized the film's hardcore pornographic elements). In the film, a deranged priest accuses sexually active women of succumbing to demonic posses-sion, but in reality their behavior is part of a theatrical performance of Black Mass rituals. Also from Spain, *El juego del diablo* (1975, Jorge Dar-nell) more closely resembles a traditional gothic horror story than a pos-session and exorcism story, though producers still released it under the

English title *The Devil's Exorcist*. While these films hail from Europe, Western distributors also imported Hong Kong martial arts films during the 1970s, and employed similar marketing tactics. For instance, *Shao Lin Zu Shi* (1976, Fu Di Lin) was retitled *Kung Fu Exorcist* for its 1978 release in the United States.

Throughout the 1970s, producers also attempted to cash in on *The Exorcist* by either rewriting or re-editing existing films to include new material dealing with exorcism. For instance, producers of the British film *Naked Evil* (1966, Stanley Goulder) added new footage meant to evoke the scientific and medical investigation featured in *The Exorcist* and then rereleased the film as *Exorcism at Midnight* in 1974. Similarly, Italian producer Alfredo Leone rewrote and re-edited *Lisa e il diavolo* (aka *Lisa and the Devil*; 1974, Mario Bava) to include a lurid exorcism subplot, and rereleased it in 1975 as *The House of Exorcism*.[35] A similar fate befell the Spanish film *Exorcismo* (1975, Juan Bosch), in which a young woman becomes possessed after inadvertently participating in a satanic ritual. Screenwriter and star Paul Naschy claims he wrote the film three years before the release of *The Exorcist*, and that he intended the themes of possession and exorcism to remain peripheral to the narrative.[36] The producers, meanwhile, wanted Naschy's story to align with *The Exorcist*'s more successful depiction of possession and exorcism. Thus, *Exorcismo* was rewritten to emphasize the main character's struggle with doubt as he works to save a young woman from demonic possession, which in this film functions as a cautionary tale for the rebellious youth of the time (indeed, the girl and her friends engage in all sorts of deviant behavior, from smoking pot to performing pagan or satanic rituals).[37]

This period also saw the release of several rip-offs and homages that examined possession and exorcism from different national or cultural perspectives even as they imitated *The Exorcist*'s specific narrative tropes and conventions. Co-directors Ovidio G. Assonitis and Robert Barrett produced one of the most notable rip-offs;[38] released in the United States as *Beyond the Door*, the Italian-American co-production *Chi sei?* (1974) more closely resembles *Rosemary's Baby* than *The Exorcist*, but it nevertheless portrays a woman becoming demonically possessed and then apparently impregnated with the Antichrist. She cannot save herself, however, and she requires "the help of a wizened white man"[39] who essentially beats the demon out of her. Warner Bros. filed a copyright infringement lawsuit against the movie, which featured scenes of the possessed woman projectile vomiting and spinning her head completely around.[40] Warner Bros. lost the suit, however, because courts ruled that the production company held no copyright claim on the horror subgenre.[41]

Other examples include the Italian film *L'esorciccio*, released internationally as *The Exorcist: Italian Style* (1975, Ciccio Ingrassia). Intended as a parody, the film utilizes Italian comedic sensibilities to satirize *The Exorcist*'s characters and legacy. The Brazilian film *O Exorcismo Negro* (1974,

José Mojica Marins) features a highly metatextual narrative, in which the director exorcises a family possessed by Coffin Joe, a character from his films. The Spanish film *La endemoniada* (1975, Amando de Ossorio)—also known as *Demon Witch Child* and released in the United States as *The Possessed* in 1976—depicts a girl becoming possessed by a Gypsy witch and requiring an exorcism from a local priest.[42] *The Manitou* (1978, William Girdler), meanwhile, draws on Native American lore to explain and explore possession, while the American TV movie *Good Against Evil* (1977, Paul Wendkos) was intended as a pilot for an unproduced TV series.

Finally, several sexploitation films released during this period evoked the violent and sexual transgressions featured in *The Exorcist*. For instance, in the German film *Magdalena, vom Teufel besessen* (1974, Walter Boos) a virginal teenage girl terrorizes her boarding school and engages in a variety of sexual acts after she becomes possessed. In the United States, the film played under the English titles *Magdalena, Possessed by the Devil, Beyond the Darkness*, and *Devil's Female*. Italy also produced its fair share of sexploitation films during this period, including *L'anticristo* (aka *The Antichrist*; 1974, Alberto De Martino),[43] in which a young disabled woman becomes possessed after recalling her past life as a witch during the Inquisition.[44] Italy also produced the sexually charged *L'ossessa* (1974, Mario Gariazzo), which included an act of bondage sex play and went by numerous titles during its North American release in 1977, including *Enter the Devil, The Devil Obsession, The Eerie Midnight Horror Show, The Sexorcist*, and *The Tormented*. Another Italian production, *Un urlo dalla tenebre* (1975, Franco Lo Cascio and Angelo Pannaccio), depicts a young man becoming possessed by the spirit of a mysterious woman and engaging in numerous sexual and satanic acts. The film played as both *The Possessor* and *The Return of the Exorcist* in the United States. Finally, the Mexican film *Alucarda, la hija de las tinieblas* (1977, Juan López Moctezuma) portrays lesbianism, orgies, nunsploitation, and exorcism.

The movies described above attest to *The Exorcist*'s lasting global impact, because they either covertly or overtly emulate its narrative in their attempts to replicate the film's massive success. At the same time, and perhaps more importantly, these rip-offs and homages also serve to perpetuate the traditional exorcism narrative on a global scale, because they tend to reproduce or even amplify *The Exorcist*'s conservative ideologies. Such films metaphorically portray patriarchy's attempts to disempower women by preventing them from fully embracing their own sexuality and agency, and, as Shipka notes, instead reduce them to "what the male-dominated society demands: a good little girl"[45] by the end. The rest of this chapter consists of our examination of two films that not only reaffirm the traditional exorcism narrative, but expand it to portray the oppression of other marginalized groups, namely African American and Islamic women. The blaxploitation horror film *Abby* and the Turkish production *Şeytan* both demonstrate that oppression can occur at the inter-section of different marginalized identities.

THE BLAXORCIST

Brooks E. Hefner notes that by August 1972, films like *Sweet Sweetback's Baadasssss Song* (1971, Melvin Van Peebles) and *Shaft* (1971, Gordon Parks) had established the blaxploitation genre as a serious cultural and financial force. Blaxploitation films offered a new, socially relevant image of black masculinity, which proved quite popular with both white and African American audiences.[46] In addition, such films regularly featured "socially and politically conscious" men and women who inhabited a range of occupations and positions in their lives and communities.[47] Though often considered a genre unto itself, blaxploitation actually en-compasses several other genres, including crime, action, martial arts, westerns, comedy, nostalgia, drama, musical, and horror. Significantly, the blaxploitation horror films of the early 1970s frequently contained "*some* degree of African American input, not necessarily through the di-rector but perhaps through a screenwriter, producer and/or even an ac-tor,"[48] which in turn allowed them to challenge or subvert the white, European ideological perspective frequently situated at the center of hor-ror texts.

While horror films traditionally position racial, sexual, or other differ-ences as a monstrous threat to the natural (i.e., white, European) order, the often romanticized monsters lurking in Blaxploitation horror films foreground blackness as a way of reversing such marginalization.[49] In-deed, as Lester Friedman notes, horror films that highlight a monster's ethnicity or race explicitly or implicitly deal with matters of racism and xenophobia.[50] Blaxploitation horror films routinely appropriated main-stream cinema's most recognizable monsters and reinterpreted them from an Afrocentric perspective. Such films reinforce normality and stability through depictions of "black heterosexual couples and black (and white) authority figures," but they often position the monster as a "specifically black *avenger* who justifiably fights against the dominant order—which is often explicitly coded as racist."[51] Thus, Dracula, Fran-kenstein's monster, the werewolf, and others became reimagined as rep-resentatives of black pride and black power.

Blaxploitation horror films routinely challenge the genre's "Other-phobic assumptions" even as they reify prevailing cultural ideas regard-ing gender and female sexuality, both of which remain coded as threaten-ing or monstrous.[52] In any event, African American audiences no longer had to struggle to uncover the racial subtext in horror films, because blaxploitation horror films offered them "a more complicated version of monstrous difference, heavily influenced by the critiques of white power structures common in Blaxploitation films."[53] While this notion applies to a film like *Blacula* (1972, William Crain), which portrays the titular monster as a tragic and noble figure, it does not necessarily apply to *Abby* (sometimes referred to as *The Blaxorcist*), which depicts the possessed woman as deviant due to her non-traditional sexual attitudes and desire to undo the symbolic patriarchal order. The film does not portray Abby as a black avenger but rather as a danger to black masculinity and white morality.

Abby opens with Catholic bishop Dr. Garnet Williams (played by William Marshall, star of *Blacula*) supervising an archaeological dig in Nigeria. In a sequence that recalls *The Exorcist*'s opening scenes, Dr. Williams discovers a puzzle box carved with images of a whirlwind, a cock's comb, and an erect penis. Williams identifies these as the symbols of Eshu, the powerful Yoruba trickster god of chaos and sexuality.[54] Upon closer inspection, Williams discovers that the penis carving opens the box. He unlocks it, and unleashes a terrifying supernatural entity that attacks him and his men before fleeing to Louisville, Kentucky, where it possesses Abby (Carol Speed), the devoted young wife of Williams' son, Emmet (Terry Carter), a reverend at the local church.

The possession causes Abby's behavior to turn increasingly bizarre and self-destructive, such as when she slashes her own arm with a knife. At the same time, she becomes far more sexually aggressive; she masturbates in the shower and makes bold advances toward the male members of Emmet's congregation. Confused and distraught by his wife's sudden uncontrollable behavior, Emmet nevertheless tries to care for her, but receives only contempt and abuse in return. Not knowing where else to turn after white doctors determine that Abby does not suffer from any known medical conditions, Emmet contacts his father in Nigeria. Realizing the truth behind Abby's condition, Dr. Williams returns to Louisville to exorcise the young woman and free her from the demon's hold. Emmet and his father follow the possessed woman to a seedy bar, where they confront Eshu (or at least, an entity claiming to be Eshu) and cast out the unclean spirit. Afterward, Emmet and Abby—who has no memory of her possession—board a plane for a vacation to an unnamed location.

Abby generated few positive responses upon release, but it did play well in the blaxploitation market. The film accumulated $2.6 million in rentals,[55] and would have done more business had it remained in theaters. As with *Beyond the Door*, however, Warner Bros. argued that *Abby* infringed on their copyrighted work and threatened to sue. The allegation had more traction with *Abby*, however, because the film included "entire sequences of dialogue" from *The Exorcist*.[56] Unfazed by these allegations of cinematic plagiarism, director William Girdler lauded *Abby* for replicating many of *The Exorcist*'s most terrifying scenes on a much smaller budget.

Harry M. Benshoff notes that white filmmakers produced the majority of American horror films, and therefore it should come as no surprise that many of these films use racial or gender difference to connote monstrousness.[57] This practice becomes significant when considering that white men wrote and directed *Abby*; Girdler conceived the story with screenwriter Gordon Cornell Layne, who wrote the script. Desperate to avoid the criticisms that greeted their earlier blaxploitation films, however, distributor American International Pictures ordered a series of rewrites based on input from African American advisors, including star William Marshall.[58] These revisions likely led to the film's overwhelmingly positive depiction of black Christianity, but also gave rise to its decidedly sex-negative attitudes regarding women and the Yoruba religion.[59] Indeed, while blaxploitation films such as *Abby* regularly position whiteness as dangerous, they also subtly reinforce white heteronormative patriarchal attitudes by exposing the commercial considerations that drive the exoticization of blackness.[60] Nevertheless, our analysis reveals that the film contains a positive and potentially postcolonial reading of the Yoruba religion, because it ultimately works alongside Christianity to redeem Abby by the film's end and thereby resolves the tensions between Eastern and Western ideologies.[61]

Various other tensions become metaphorically encoded in the struggles between the possessed Abby and the men in her life; Abby, Emmet, and Emmet's father represent the tensions between Christian morality and Yoruba spirituality, and between female liberation and traditional patriarchal attitudes regarding sexuality. While Emmet embodies ideas of Christianity and black religiosity, he primarily stands in for black masculinity, which becomes threatened and abused following Abby's possession and subsequent sexual awakening. Emmet harbors a great deal of skepticism, and frequently questions whether his father truly performs the Lord's work as a good minister should. Thus, the character also reifies traditional Christian and patriarchal ideologies. Furthermore, the name Emmet takes on profound significance when considering that in Hebrew "emet" means "truth." Thus, by aligning Emmet with the twin forces of tradition and patriarchy—which Abby threatens when she dares to take control of her sexuality and agency—the film situates his traditional Christian and heteronormative perspective as the "true" ideological position for both individuals and society.

Abby portrays the conflict between these ideologies in a variety of ways. For example, early in the film, following Eshu's release, Emmet raises a glass in toast to the Lord, and it shatters in his hand, thus signaling the clash between Christianity and the African-based Yoruba religion. Additionally, the film positions the Yoruba deity Eshu as a threat to Christianity and thus to the symbolic order, and *Abby* thereby reflects a colonialist rhetoric by suggesting that ceding "improper" pagan spirituality to "proper" Christian ideology represents the only way to maintain order. This theme recalls *The Exorcist*, which implied a similar clash between Christianity and an "invasive" pagan religion as embodied by Pazuzu. Interestingly, a similar incident occurs in *Exorcism at Midnight*, which features a conflict between the Anglican religion and Jamaican Obeah spirituality.

Abby also tackles the tensions between science and religion, with science yielding to religion. The film initially portrays Williams as a rational scientist, and at first he dismisses Emmet's concerns. While in Nigeria, Williams inhabits the role of the doubting priest figure because the film initially portrays him as a detached archaeologist who rejects ancient beliefs as nothing more than superstition. When he returns to Kentucky, however, he increasingly relies upon his Christian faith to battle Eshu. The film reinforces this spiritual awakening through costuming, as Williams dons his clerical collar and shirt when he embraces his faith. Further, Williams prays for God to grant him the strength to combat the sinister forces unleashed by his doubt, as well as for the guidance and insight that will allow him to free Abby from the malevolent spirit. Thus, Williams comes to represent black Christianity, which the film positions as dominant over the African religion.

A prominent example of this positioning occurs after Abby escapes from the hospital; Williams and Emmet return home to find Abby waiting for them. She acts demurely at first, but becomes increasingly sexual throughout this sequence and even attempts to seduce Williams. Her voice assumes a deep, masculine quality, indicating that Eshu has taken control once again. Williams demands the demon relinquish control of Abby's spirit, but Eshu simply laughs and threatens him in return. Williams' failure to defeat Eshu at this point suggests that his skepticism and rationality has weakened his faith. During the film's climactic exorcism sequence, however, Williams calls on God's power to successfully drive the demon out. Thus, *Abby* situates Christian morality as the answer to the world's ills, particularly those caused by uninhibited feminine sexuality. Furthermore, these events appear to support a colonialist reading of the film, as Christianity suppresses and supplants a pagan religion.

While establishing the Church's power, *Abby* also depicts this institution as under threat from feminine sexuality and agency. The film equates sexuality—particularly female sexuality—with destruction and disorder,[62] aligning it with many blaxploitation horror films that sought to uphold male-dominated heteronormativity.[63] The film establishes Abby as a pious young woman who wants nothing more than to love and honor her man as they build a traditional home together. Abby sings in the church choir, performs community service, and studies to become a marriage counselor, but she avoids taking pride in her accomplishments, because she believes pride is one of the devil's favorite sins. After succumbing to possession, however, Abby exhibits a deviant and aggressive

sexuality that threatens those around her. The film establishes her possession and subsequent sexual deviance during the sequence in which she
masturbates in the shower. Abby writhes as she touches herself and
moans ecstatically, completely oblivious to the massive, inhuman shad-
ow that creeps up behind her and appears to merge with her. The following day, Abby stabs herself in the arm with a kitchen knife, as if to atone
for her sinful indulgence.[64]

From there, Abby's situation rapidly deteriorates, as her newfound
sexuality becomes less about her own pleasure and more about causing
her husband pain and embarrassment. After she succumbs to possession,
Abby physically and psychologically abuses Emmet, actions that position
assertive female sexuality as a transgressive and emasculating force intent on toppling the traditional masculine order. For example, Emmet
tries to seduce Abby by paraphrasing the Song of Solomon,[65] but she
rebuffs his declaration of love and dismisses sex as nothing more than
animalistic lust. She then mocks Emmet's sexual prowess before kicking
him in the groin and laughing at him as he lies on the floor writhing in
pain. This sequence situates Emmet in a feminine role as he attempts to
establish an emotional connection with Abby, who occupies the masculine role by speaking out against love and emotion. Furthermore, Abby
asserts dominance over Emmet because she refuses his efforts to initiate
sex and questions his manhood. Significantly, her voice deepens during
this sequence, until it finally inhabits a liminal space between the feminine and the masculine. The nature of Abby's newfound voice—which
allows her to express her thoughts and desires regarding sex—suggests
that sexual dominance represents a masculine or male quality, and wom-
en who attempt to access this power transgress the boundaries between
masculinity and femininity.[66]

This struggle for dominance soon moves out of their private bedroom
as Abby psychologically torments Emmett in public settings. Shortly after
she becomes possessed, Abby counsels a nervous young couple on the
verge of marriage. Emmet enters, and Abby's voice once again deepens
as she tells the woman about the importance of sexually satisfying her
betrothed. Abby then rips her blouse open and throws herself at the
woman's fiancée, declaring that she plans to "fuck the shit out of him."
Emmet stops her and pulls her away as she laughs manically. He drags
her up to the bedroom and attempts to discipline her, but Eshu's visage
flashes across the screen during this sequence, indicating that the demon
has taken control of Abby once more. She manages to momentarily regain control and begs Emmet to help restore her innocence. He tries to
reassure her, but Eshu reasserts control and pledges to show Emmet
what a real marriage ceremony looks like. The possessed Abby then
tosses Emmet onto the bed and attacks him. Throughout this sequence,
Abby becomes the sexual aggressor, and the film positions this activity as
both ludicrous and physically dangerous for Emmet.

The film further establishes feminine sexuality as potentially harmful during an adulterous encounter that occurs late in the film, in which Abby seduces the local funeral director. Abby accompanies the man to his car and attempts to initiate sex, but he worries that Emmet might learn of their affair and thus cannot perform. Abby uses her masculine demonic voice to mock the man, rejecting his puritanism and denying her marriage. Abby then attacks the man, at which point the film cuts to a shot of the car rocking wildly as smoke pours out of the windows. Suddenly, Eshu's face flashes across the screen yet again, but this time it is intercut with images of Abby shrieking, implying that the entity's influence over her continues to grow. Horrified screams ring out as Eshu laughs and growls with delight, and finally announces that Abby belongs to him now.

Afterward, the now fully possessed Abby enters a nightclub, where she flirts and dances with two men at the same time, while a song about a dangerous woman plays on the jukebox.[67] Emmet arrives and asks her to come home, but she undermines his patriarchal authority once more by mocking him and denying their marriage. She then tries to undress Emmet while the other men watch and goad her on, and Emmet's discomfort and ineffectiveness in this sequence suggests a symbolic impotence; removed from a traditional, patriarchal context, Emmet can no longer control Abby. Her sexuality threatens his authority,[68] and by extension patriarchal authority.

In addition to portraying the repression of female sexuality, *Abby* also marginalizes African sexuality in a more general sense. For instance, Dr. Williams opens the puzzle box and unleashes Eshu using a carving of an erect penis, an act that implicates the black phallus as a threat, which in turn positions African males as a dangerous Other.[69] Furthermore, Williams explains that Eshu uses sex to destroy his enemies. The film explicitly positions Eshu as a malevolent force, and as such reinforces a conservative ideology regarding African sex and sexuality, both of which become coded as threats to the symbolic order. Additionally, like Pazuzu in *The Exorcist*, Eshu does not actually want to harm Abby directly, but rather uses her to attack Williams, a representative of Christian dogma. Thus, Eshu threatens Christian morality and the order it represents. As previously mentioned, this clash between religions reflects a colonialist struggle between Eastern and Western ideologies, or between an untamed carnal savagery and the twin forces of modernity and civilization.

Despite this conflict between belief systems, the power of the African religion ultimately saves Abby. During the exorcism, Williams wears traditional African ceremonial garb, donning a dashiki over his Christian vestments. Williams then sprinkles dust on Abby and beseeches the Yoruba god Olorun to remove the wicked spirit from her body. The room bursts into flames as images of the demon flash rapidly across the screen. Williams uses the puzzle box from earlier in the film to collect the dust he sprinkled on Abby, and he quickly seals it, thus ending Eshu's threat. Williams announces that Olorun saved Abby's body and will soon restore her emotionally as well. Hence, *Abby* does not simply depict a struggle between Christianity and paganism, but rather a potential merging of the Yoruba and Christian beliefs, because Williams draws on both to repel Eshu. Therefore, the film also supports a postcolonial reading, because it suggests that Christian beliefs must reside alongside and in accordance with other forms of spirituality to sufficiently uphold patriarchal values. This tension between the Christian and Yoruba beliefs reflects a larger sociocultural tension, wherein white society simultaneously fears and fetishizes primitive religious traditions.[70] Having the religions somewhat coexist onscreen demonstrates a postcolonial resolution to this tension.

Nonetheless, *Abby* still maintains the necessity of suppressing feminine and African sexuality and agency to uphold white, patriarchal values. By depicting the possessed as an African American woman—who, in the West, occupies "the outermost reaches of 'otherness'" and thus becomes rendered "highly invisible"[71]—the oppression exists at its fullest, since the exorcism simply returns Abby to the "normal" state for an African American woman in the United States in the 1970s. This repression actually contrasts with many blaxploitation films, which depict both black men and women as sexually liberated and empowered;[72] by seeking to replicate *The Exorcist* and thus align with the traditional exorcism narrative, *Abby* portrays the repression of black female sexuality.

THE TURKISH *EXORCIST*

Like *Abby*, director Metin Erksan's film *Şeytan* supports a postcolonial reading because it attempts to reconcile *The Exorcist*'s Christian elements by reinterpreting them within a non-Western, non-white cultural context.[73] Iain Robert Smith asserts that Turkey functions as both a geographical and cultural bridge between Europe and Asia.[74] Indeed, from a cultural perspective, Turkey exists at the intersection of Muslim and secular ideologies, as well as Eastern and Western sensibilities.[75] Such cultural overlap might explain why Turkish cinema of the 1970s frequently appropriated elements from Western popular culture and rendered them more acceptable to Turkish sensibilities. This practice of transcultural appropriation—which Savas Arslan terms "Turkification"[76]—emerged due to the nation's strict censorship guidelines; throughout the 1970s, Turkish censors heavily edited Hollywood films, or banned them outright. For instance, *The Exorcist* was not officially released in Turkey until 1982. Thanks to widespread media coverage, however, Turkish audiences expressed great interest in such films, thus prompting the local film industry to produce their own cheap rip-off versions. Suggesting a postcolonial approach to adaptation and appropriation, this phenomenon led directly to the production of *Şeytan*, which replicated *The Exorcist*'s narrative and tone almost wholesale even as it de-emphasized elements Turkish censors might consider blasphemous or offensive.[77]

Like *The Exorcist* and *Abby* before it, *Şeytan* begins with an unnamed elderly scholar (Agah Hün) discovering demonic artifacts at an archaeological site. The film then transitions to the spacious, upper-class home of Ayten (Meral Taygun) and her twelve-year-old daughter Gul (Canan Perver). The events that follow closely resemble those portrayed in *The Exorcist*, as Gul becomes possessed and exhibits increasingly deviant and threatening behavior, and modern medical science fails to account for her malady. Unlike Chris MacNeil, however, Ayten does not turn to religion for answers but instead consults secular journalist Tugrul Bilge (Cihan Ünal) after finding a copy of his book, in which he applies a modern understanding of mental health to the phenomenon of demonic possession. Bilge investigates the case, and his arc mirrors that of Father Karras; initially skeptical, Bilge soon accepts the reality of the situation after he listens to a recording of Gul's demonically altered voice and bears witness as the words "HELP ME" (or "BANA YARDIM EDİN" in Turkish) appear in the flesh across her stomach.

After consulting with a *hoja*,[78] Bilge seeks the aid of the elderly scholar from the film's prologue. Familiar with the ancient rite of exorcism, the scholar agrees to exorcise Gul. The climax plays out almost exactly like that of *The Exorcist*, as Bilge and the scholar confront the unnamed demon in a desperate bid to cast it out. The entity mocks Bilge for failing to prevent his mother's death, much like Pazuzu mocked Father Karras. The scholar escorts Bilge from the room and reassures the exhausted journalist that the demon speaks falsely. The scholar then returns to complete the ritual alone, despite a sudden burst of pain in his chest. Bilge re-enters shortly thereafter to discover the scholar lying dead on the floor, while Gul stands over his body laughing. Filled with righteous anger, Bilge physically attacks the girl and pummels her until the demon flees her body and enters his, at which point Bilge throws himself out the window to his death. The next day, Ayten and Gul—who, like Regan and Abby, does not recall her possession—visit a mosque, and Gul embraces the hoja from earlier in the film.

Like *The Exorcist*, *Şeytan* foregrounds the dangers of female sexuality, while at the same time de-emphasizing the possession's overtly religious connotations, likely to conform to cultural restrictions.[79] The film downplays the religious aspects in two key ways: first, it establishes Tugrul Bilge as a non-believer. While he agonizes over his mother's ultimate fate, he does not struggle with the same spiritual angst that afflicted Father Karras.[80] Smith argues that placing a secular journalist in the Father Karras role allows the film to avoid "the problem of having a central character who is questioning his faith in Allah."[81] Yet, like Karras, Bilge does

not believe in the reality of demonic possession or exorcisms, and that
doubt indicates a similar crisis of faith or religious skepticism. At first, the
film's characters turn to science to resolve the problem, but when modern
medicine fails to cure Gul's increasingly erratic behavior, Ayten and Bilge
must turn to religion and traditional patriarchy.

Second, *Şeytan*'s climactic exorcism sequence is a fairly generic affair
that features few concrete references to Islam, and thus it serves to mini-
mize the possession story's religious connotations. Though he does not
wear religious garments, the unnamed scholar apparently understands
and accepts that Gul has become possessed by a demon.[82] During the
exorcism, the scholar reads from the Quran, and splashes the possessed
Gul with sacred Zamzam water,[83] which causes her to writhe in pain. In
one of the film's few overtly religious acts, the scholar beseeches Allah to
save Gul from evil. Rather than Father Merrin's lament of "The Power of
Christ compels you," Bilge and the scholar chant "Allah's grace be upon
you." Yet, the incidents described here do not reflect any orthodox Islamic beliefs or practices. As Kaya Özkaracalar explains, Islam has not institutionalized exorcism to the same degree as the Catholic Church, but the
Quran nevertheless supports the folk belief in malign, invasive entities
known as djinns, and Islamic practitioners employed rituals to drive
these spirits out.[84] Thus, unlike *The Exorcist*, the film depicts a spiritual or
folkloric belief rather than an explicitly religious one.

The film also deviates from *The Exorcist* because the possession causes
both Gul and Ayten to undergo an overt conversion, and this represents
perhaps the film's most explicit reference to religion. Prior to the possession, neither Gul nor her mother appear to believe in or practice any form
of religion. After the possession, however, Gul makes repeated reference
to religious beliefs and actions. For instance, in a sequence that directly
recalls *The Exorcist*, Gul wets herself during one of her mother's parties,
and afterward asks why Allah allows people to become confused. Later,
Ayten brings her daughter to the hospital, and nurses restrain the increasingly unruly Gul, who screams at them and declares that God will
curse them all. Following this incident, a doctor visits Gul at home just as
she experiences a violent, uncontrollable convulsion that causes her body
to thrash about in a perverse parody of Islamic prayer. These sequences
all indicate that the entity inhabiting Gul threatens the symbolic order,
represented here in the form of the Islamic faith.

Şeytan reinforces the idea that Gul's possession stands in for an invasive permissiveness that threatens to topple Islam's stability. Following
the exorcism, Gul and her mother visit a mosque, and they both wear
head scarves that resemble traditional Islamic garb. Gul spots the hoja
who helped them contact the scholar, and she runs to him and kisses his
hand. He smiles at her and strokes her hair, and she smiles at him in
return. She then embraces her mother, who looks up as traditional Islamic music plays on the soundtrack. This final sequence suggests that after

Bilge and the scholar gave their lives to free Gul's soul from the devil's embrace, both Gul and Ayten rediscovered their faith in Islam.[85] Indeed, as Özkaracalar observes, the film's central theme reaffirms Islamic power and legitimacy, which Şeytan positions as the resolution to "the conflict between modernization and tradition in general and between materialism and religion in particular."[86] The film reinforces this position when Gul — finally freed from the devil's control thanks to the power of Islam — impulsively yet piously kisses the hand of the hoja who helped deliver her from evil.

While the film excises all references to Catholicism and does not replace such references with similar ones from Islam, and similarly removes any foul language, Şeytan nevertheless condemns second-wave feminism. Significantly, the film appears to blame Gul's predicament on Ayten, whose independence and assertiveness seemingly encourage the girl's disobedient behavior. Like Chris in *The Exorcist*, Ayten exemplifies the liberated woman of second-wave feminism due to her status as a single mother. Moreover, Ayten's dress and mannerisms reflect the Western affluence and decadence seen in earlier Turkish Yeşilçam melodramas that often aligned with Western social and cultural values.[87] However, while *The Exorcist* establishes Chris as a driven actress, Şeytan leaves Ayten's career goals ambiguous while still clearly establishing her wealthy lifestyle. Furthermore, her independence calls into question her moral character. The film conveys this characterization during a scene in which mother and daughter lie in bed together, and Ayten declares that she could never love another man as much as she loved Gul's father. Yet, in the very next scene, Ayten berates Gul's absent father over the phone. Gul's tutor, Suzan, warns against speaking to a man like that, but Ayten ignores her. Gul overhears this exchange, and shortly after exhibits signs of possession. The film thereby implicates Ayten's defiant attitude as the cause of Gul's own rebelliousness, thus aligning the film with Yeşilçam melodramas that routinely punished the wealthy. In Şeytan, Ayten's punishment further results from her lack of Islamic faith and her adherence to the tenets of second-wave feminism.

Thus, Şeytan represents an explicit act of cultural appropriation. As Smith notes, the film lifts elements from *The Exorcist* and reinterprets them into a Turkish cultural context in an attempt to "comment on, and reflect upon, issues that had significant resonance in the Turkish culture of the time."[88] In effect, Şeytan becomes more than just "an incoherent attempt to simply plagiarise a Western style horror film."[89] Rather, the film merges elements of Western culture into a Middle Eastern context, and thus renders them more or less understandable to audiences from both cultural perspectives. Thus, Şeytan does not challenge the traditional exorcism narrative, but rather reinterprets that narrative into a new context that reinforces some of the thematic tropes that recur across this narrative.

This tendency to appropriate and recontextualize elements from Western horror films supports our reading of Şeytan as a postcolonialist text that nevertheless perpetuates the traditional exorcism narrative. While Turkey does not represent a colonized people to the extent that African Americans do in *Abby*, it still reflects a non-dominant culture on a global level in comparison to countries like the United States. Şeytan represents an act of transcultural appropriation, in which a text produced by a dominant culture becomes altered by a non-dominant culture to include symbols recognizable to those hailing from that non-dominant culture. Furthermore, such appropriation allows the non-dominant culture to speak back against the dominant culture. Şeytan changed aspects of *The Exorcist* to better align the story with Turkish culture, thereby highlighting the ability of non-Western cultures to push back against colonizing forces from the West.[90] Even in asserting the position of Islamic faith in the modern world, the film nevertheless reinforces patriarchal attitudes regarding appropriate feminine behavior. Like *Abby* before it, Şeytan recontextualizes *The Exorcist*'s embedded ideological messages to reflect a new cultural setting, but ultimately resolves the feminist tensions by once again restoring the patriarchal order.

EXPANDING THE TRADITIONAL EXORCISM NARRATIVE

Shipka notes that the sort of exploitation films discussed in this chapter reflect the "modern mass-communication and mass-cultural environment that relied on increasing globalization to facilitate its success."[91] Yet, such films do not simply result from cultural imperialism, in which Hollywood cinema imposes Western culture and ideologies onto other nations. Instead, these films reflect the identities of the nations and cultures that produced them.[92] Culturally specific representations of exorcism films made outside the borders of the United States demonstrate the extent to which the traditional exorcism narrative circulates and reflects sociocultural tensions that occur on a global scale. Each national cinema seemingly appropriated aspects of this narrative in their efforts to replicate *The Exorcist*'s success. Films such as *Exorcismos*, *Şeytan*, *Abby*, and *The Exorcist* all feature similar resolutions, in which a male protagonist reaffirms his faith after struggling with doubt throughout the film, and this in turn grants him the power to repress a threatening Other.[93] The repetition of this characterization appears to reflect the global tensions that result from the clash between modern liberal religious ideologies and more traditional or conservative conceptualizations of belief.

The cycle of exploitation films produced during the 1970s demonstrates that exorcism films from around the world tended to replicate the traditional exorcism narrative established by and rooted in *The Exorcist*'s conservative approach to female sexuality and religion. Therefore, these films offer profound insight into the repression experienced by women and other non-dominant groups during that time. Horror films produced in the United States deal with the fear of the Other, which often represents a prevailing anxiety in any given historical period.[94] Similarly, exorcism films produced during this period, even those made outside of Hollywood or mainstream Western culture, often depict the Other along gendered racial and religious lines. In these films, possession empowers the Other, who then becomes silenced via exorcism, which effectively prevents these non-dominant (i.e., non-white, non-Western, non-Christian, non-male, non-heteronormative) identities from challenging or proposing an alternative to the dominant ideological perspective.

Thus, the possessed-woman-as-threat figure expands to include other marginalized identities, suggesting a related possessed-Other-as-threat trope. This extension of the traditional exorcism narrative then links women to other non-dominant groups that become oppressed by the dominant, symbolic order.[95] This link in turn reflects the idea that women's struggles often equate to the struggles of other non-dominant groups. Arguing from a materialist feminist perspective, Jill Dolan notes that "[l]ess powerful people are subjected to social structures that benefit the interests of the more powerful."[96] When applied to the traditional exorcism narrative, the materialist feminist critique demonstrates exorcism cinema's tendency to reflect and shape the ideological suppression of a variety of marginalized or non-dominant identities.

This idea particularly applies to exorcism films produced outside of the Hollywood system, especially when they fail to challenge the traditional exorcism narrative. Kyle Bishop argues that such films perpetuate a form of colonial imperialism, because they reflect a Western cultural sensibility that romanticizes the Other to allow for easier consumption by Western audiences.[97] According to Bishop, the dominant culture silences and enslaves the Other, and effectively prevents them from participating in the culture.[98] It becomes possible to expand this argument to possessed individuals, as the victims gain the power to speak out and make their voices heard, only to become silenced again by the film's end.

Viewed from a Western perspective, *Abby* and *Şeytan* exploit and romanticize the mysterious and exotic nature of Othered individuals. In each film, the possessed individuals stand in for non-dominant groups and ideologies, thus situating them as an Other in relation to the dominant group and traditional ideologies. Thus, these films position the individual as peripheral to the symbolic order, even before they succumb to possession. Possession furthers this Othering, and situates the individual as an active threat to the symbolic order. Only a representative of traditional ideologies can return the possessed individual to a non-dominant or marginalized and thus non-threatening position. While these films may allow for postcolonial readings, they also contain overarching colonial narratives in how they portray Other non-dominant groups. As Benshoff writes, "the horror film functions hegemonically, in effect enabling socially oppressed people to contribute to their own oppression by consenting to the manufacture of their own identities as monstrous Others."[99] The films discussed in this chapter accomplish just that by expanding the traditional exorcism narrative to other marginalized groups without challenging its ideological positions.

Abby and *Şeytan* demonstrate how these tensions can result in the oppression of identities that exist at a demographic intersection. In *Abby*, an African American woman whose voice and sexuality threatens those around her is saved (i.e., disempowered) by a mixture of African and Christian religions. In *Şeytan*, Turkish beliefs restore a disobedient Middle Eastern girl to a state of innocence, and thereby align her with the Islamic faith. As we discuss in subsequent chapters, other films utilize the traditional exorcism narrative to explore the silencing of various non-dominant groups, which in turn reveals this narrative as a metaphor for the act of repressing alternative modes of thought to maintain white, heterosexual, masculine, and/or Christian ideological structures.

The two films analyzed in this chapter align with the traditional exorcism narrative primarily because they position other religions—that is, other manifestations of patriarchal authority—as the oppressor. In *Abby*, a colonized people (i.e., African American people) ultimately help their colonizers (i.e., the white, Christian patriarchy) reify and reaffirm an oppressive hegemonic or dominant ideology.[100] Similarly, *Şeytan* utilizes this narrative structure to perpetuate an ideology that aligns with Turkey's dominant Islamic identity. Thus, while both films allow for progressive postcolonial readings, they ultimately depict the restoration of a culturally-specific dominant order, and this return to tradition advances a conservative ideology.

Ultimately, the rip-offs and homages produced around the world served to perpetuate the traditional exorcism narrative and solidify the conventions of this emerging horror subgenre throughout the 1970s. At the same time, Hollywood sought to capitalize on this phenomenon by expanding *The Exorcist* into a franchise that would span decades, despite suffering from narrative inconsistencies and poor critical and commercial reception. Nevertheless, *The Exorcist*'s sequels and prequels continued to expand the traditional exorcism narrative's oppressive ideologies, particularly with regards to non-heteronormative identities—although one film in the franchise did challenge this narrative by deviating somewhat from the conventions established in the original film.

NOTES

1. William Peter Blatty himself denied any direct knowledge or experience of people vomiting in the theaters, and said the cases of fainting had more to do with the scenes of Regan undergoing medical procedures, such as the arteriography scene that

involved blood spurting from her neck. For more, see Matt Slovick, "The Exorcist," *The Washington Post*, 1996, at http://www.washingtonpost.com/wp-srv/style/longterm/movies/features/dcmovies/exorcist.htm, accessed February 13, 2016.

2. Bob McCabe, *The Exorcist: Out of the Shadows* (New York: Omnibus Press, 1999), 136–37.

3. Mark Kermode, *The Exorcist: Revised 2nd Edition* (London: British Film Institute, 2003), 84.

4. McCabe, *Shadows*, 140.

5. Kermode, *The Exorcist*, 84.

6. McCabe, *Shadows*, 132.

7. Kermode, *The Exorcist*, 86.

8. Ibid.

9. Listverse staff, "25 Fascinating Facts About *The Exorcist*," *Listverse*, last modified October 30, 2009, http://listverse.com/2009/10/30/25-fascinating-facts-about-the-exorcist/.

10. Ibid.

11. Andrew Scahill, "Demons Are a Girl's Best Friend: Queering the Revolting Child in *The Exorcist*," *Red Feather Journal* 1, no. 1 (2010): 42.

12. McCabe, *Shadows*, 143.

13. Listverse staff, "25 Fascinating Facts."

14. Ibid.

15. "The Exorcist," *Box Office Mojo*, accessed July 27, 2015, http://www.boxofficemojo.com/movies/?id=exorcist.htm.

16. Andrew Tudor, *Monsters and Mad Scientists: A Cultural History of the Horror Movie* (Cambridge: Basil Blackwell, Ltd., 1989), 23.

17. Ibid., 56, 62.

18. Kirsten Strayer "Art, Horror, and International Identity in 1970s Exploitation Films," in *Transnational Horror Across Visual Media: Fragmented Bodies*, eds. Dana Och and Kristen Strayer, (New York: Routledge, 2013), 111.

19. Ibid., 109.

20. Ibid., 110.

21. Ibid., 112.

22. Ibid.

23. David Church, "From Exhibition to Genre: The Case of Grind-House Films," *Cinema Journal* 50, no. 4 (2011): 20.

24. Ibid.

25. Ibid.

26. I. Q. Hunter, "Trash Horror and the Cult of the Bad Film," in *A Companion to the Horror Film*, ed. Harry M. Benshoff (Malden: John Wily & Sons, Inc., 2014), 483.

27. Strayer, "International Identity," 112.

28. Ibid., 112–13.

29. Andy Willis, "Paul Naschy, *Exorcismo* and the Reactionary Horrors of Spanish Popular Cinema in the Early 1970s," in *European Nightmares: Horror Cinema in Europe Since 1945*, eds. Patricia Allmer, Emily Brick, and David Huxley, (New York: Columbia University Press, 2012), 122.

30. Danny Shipka, *Perverse Titillation: The Exploitation Cinema of Italy, Spain and France, 1960–1980* (Jefferson: McFarland & Company, Inc., 2011), 148.

31. Shipka, *Perverse Titillation*, 144.

32. Ibid., 123.

33. Ian Olney argues that many occult films destabilize patriarchy because they celebrate transgressive femininity and queerness. Yet, his primary example, *Lorna the Exorcist*, does not actually depict an exorcism, the central element that perpetuates the sort of repression seen in the traditional exorcism narrative. Furthermore, while the films Olney discusses do portray transgressive sexuality, it was often included for the purposes of exploitation, meant to titillate male viewers and thereby reaffirm their dominant position in the social order. For more, see Ian Olney, "Unmanning *The*

Exorcist: Sex, Gender and Excess in the 1970s Euro-Horror Possession Film," *Quarterly Review of Film and Video* 31, no. 6 (2014): 561–71.

34. Olney notes that this movie repurposes horror movie tropes "to challenge the norms governing female identity and sexuality." For more, see Ian Olney, "Spanish Horror Cinema," in *A Companion to the Horror Film*, ed. Harry M. Benshoff (Malden: John Wiley & Sons, Inc., 2014), 382.

35. According to Danny Shipka (2011), Bava had his name removed from this altered version of the film because it offended him. For more on *Lisa e il diavolo*'s production and distribution, see also Kevin Heffernan, "Art House or House of Exorcism? The Changing Distribution and Reception Contexts of Mario Bava's *Lisa and the Devil*," in *Sleaze Artists: Cinema at the Margins of Taste, Style, and Politics*, ed. Jeffrey Sconce (Durham, NC: Duke University Press, 2007), 145, and Brian Collins, "*Lisa and the Devil* and (Later) Some Pea Soup," *Birth. Movies. Death.*, last modified July 10, 2015, http://birthmoviesdeath.com/2015/07/10/lisa-and-the-devil-and-later-some-pea-soup.

36. Willis, "Paul Naschy," 124.

37. Ibid., 126–28.

38. Assonitis, who also produced the film, would go on to become known as the "Rip-Off King" for overseeing several other obvious attempts to cash-in on Hollywood success through Italian-American co-productions, including a *Jaws* rip-off called *Tentacles* (1977, Ovidio G. Assonitis) and a knockoff of *The Omen* called *The Visitor* (1979, Giulio Paradisi). For more, see Jonathan Smith, "'The Visitor' is All of 70s Horror Shoved into One Film," *Vice*, last modified October 31, 2013, http://www.vice.com/read/the-visitor-is-the-entirety-of-70s-horror-shoved-into-one-film.

39. Shipka, *Perverse Titillation*, 146.

40. Father Richard Woods provided a deposition in this case in 1978. Father Richard Woods (theology professor) in discussion with the authors, October 14, 2015.

41. Ibid.

42. Peter Hutchings argues that this film suggests a troubled patriarchy, because it depicts a weak father unable to protect his daughter from the possession. Thus, the film appears to challenge the traditional exorcism narrative. For more, see Peter Hutchings, "International Horror in the 1970s," in *A Companion to the Horror Film*, ed. Harry M. Benshoff (Malden, MA: John Wiley & Sons, Inc., 2014), 292–309.

43. For a more detailed discussion of this film, see ibid, 306–37.

44. Shipka (2011) notes that the film appears to perpetuate conservative gender roles, because the narrative serves to return women to their traditional positions. The woman, while handicapped and repressed, remains chaste prior to her possession, and thus conforms to appropriate notions regarding female behavior and feminine propriety. Shipka notes, however, that "Once she is possessed and able to leave her wheelchair she exhibits all the signs of a sinner and her freedom must be curtailed, leaving it up to a dominant male priest to put her back in her place" (146). Thus, *L'anticristo* clearly aligns with the traditional exorcism narrative.

45. Ibid., 150.

46. Brooks E. Hefner, "Rethinking *Blacula*: Ideological Critique at the Intersection of Genres," *Journal of Popular Film and Television* 40, no. 2 (2012): 64.

47. Novotny Lawrence, *Blaxploitation Films of the 1970s: Blackness and Genre* (New York: Routledge, 2008), 18.

48. Harry M. Benshoff, "Blaxploitation Horror Films: Generic Reappropriation or Reinscription?," *Cinema Journal* 39, no. 2 (2000): 31. Italics in the original.

49. Hefner, "Rethinking *Blacula*," 63.

50. Lester D. Friedman, "'Canyons of Nightmare': The Jewish Horror Film," in *Planks of Reason: Essays on the Horror Film*, eds. Barry Keith Grant and Christopher Sharrett (Lanham: Scarecrow press, Inc., 2004), 83–84.

51. Benshoff, "Blaxploitation Horror," 37. Italics in original.

52. Ibid., 31.

53. Hefner, "Rethinking *Blacula*," 65.

54. The Yoruba trickster figure Esu-Elegbara likely served as the inspiration for Eshu. In popular culture, the trickster figure often highlights the struggles faced by racial or sexual minorities. Furthermore, Herry M. Benshoff identifies "the mythic figure of Esu-Elegbara" as a "primordial queer figure, 'at once both male and female . . . his [sic] enormous sexuality ambiguous, contrary, and genderless'" (206). Benshoff contends that "the trickster figure might be well suited for expressing a queer revenge fantasy as well as a black one" (206). For more, see Harry M. Benshoff, *Monsters in the Closet: Homosexuality and the Horror Film* (New York: Manchester University Press, 1997), 173–229.

55. Lawrence, *Blaxploitation Films*, 60.

56. Ibid., 61.

57. Benshoff, "Blaxploitation Horror," 31.

58. As Benshoff (2000) notes, "Blaxploitation film in its white-controlled studio-backed form (as compared to the more independent black auteur production), was a money-making endeavor first and foremost" (202).

59. Benshoff, "Blaxploitation Horror," 40.

60. Ibid., 37.

61. According to Ania Loomba (1998), the colonized can exist in the West as they do in the "third world" and can "share a history of colonial exploitation, may share cultural roots, and may also share an opposition to the legacy of colonial domination" (14). Yet, there exists a need to recognize that African American and African "histories and present concerns cannot simply be merged" (14). Both Africans and African Americans may resist the colonizing force, but in different ways. Both of these locations of resistance manifest in *Abby*, yet they ultimately become undone by white Christian patriarchy.

62. Benshoff, "Blaxploitation Horror," 40.

63. Ibid.

64. Dean Brandum, "Abby Ho'ed," *Filmbunnies*, accessed July 27, 2015, https://film-bunnies.wordpress.com/2008/08/13/abby-hoed-william-girdlers-abby-1974/.

65. Emmet recites, "I am black, and comely, like the curtains of Solomon. O ye daughters of Jerusalem, let me kiss thee with the kisses of my mouth. Thy love is better than wine."

66. After becoming possessed, Abby loses the ability to sing in the church choir, for which she had earlier been celebrated. Singing in praise of the Lord represents the traditional, acceptable way for Abby to use her voice. Possession grants her the ability to speak her mind about sex, and the film positions this as grounds for punishment.

67. "Gone Woman," written by Robert O. Ragland (music) and William Girdler (lyrics), and performed by George Gentre Griffin.

68. Brandum, "Abby Ho'ed."

69. By portraying Williams touching the penis carving, this sequence also appears to implicate homosexuality, or at least non-heteronormativity, as a threat to the symbolic order.

70. Bryan Stone, "The Sanctification of Fear: Images of the Religious in Horror Films," *The Journal of Religion and Film* 5, no. 2 (2001): Online.

71. Lorraine O'Grady, "Olympia's Maid: Reclaiming Black Female Subjectivity," in *The Feminism and Visual Culture Reader* (2nd Ed.), ed. Amelia Jones (New York: Routledge, 2010), 208.

72. Lawrence, *Blaxploitation Films*, 19.

73. Aside from contributing to the somewhat lamentable Turkish exploitation genre, Erksan also directed such notable films as *Revenge of the Snakes* (1962) and *Dry Summer* (1963), widely regarded as two of the best Turkish films of the 1960s.

74. Iain Robert Smith, "The Exorcist in Istanbul: Processes of Transcultural Appropriation Within Turkish Popular Cinema," *PORTAL Journal of Multidisciplinary International Studies* 5, no. 1 (2008): 1–12.

75. Though, as Burcu Sari Karademir notes, from the time of the Ottoman Empire the country has sought to align itself more with Western standards of civilization. For

more, see Burcu Sari Karademir, "Turkey as a 'Willing Receiver' of American Soft Power: Hollywood Movies in Turkey during the Cold War," *Turkish Studies* 13, no. 4 (2012): 634.

76. As quoted in ibid., 7.

77. Kaya Özkaracalar, "Horror Films in Turkish Cinema: To Use or Not to Use Local Cultural Motifs, That is the Question," in *European Nightmares: Horror Cinema in Europe Since 1945*, eds. Patricia Allmer, Emily Brick, and David Huxley (New York: Columbia University Press, 2012), 252.

78. A Turkish honorific used when addressing well-known Islamic scholars.

79. "Şeytan (1974)," *And You Call Yourself a Scientist!* accessed July 30, 2015, http://www.aycyas.com/turkishexorcist.htm.

80. Özkaracalar, "Turkish Cinema," 252.

81. Smith, "Transcultural Appropriation," 8.

82. *The Exorcist* establishes Pazuzu as an Assyrian wind demon, and thus foreign to Catholicism. In that sense, Pazuzu becomes further Othered and repressed by Christianity during the exorcism, which signifies a colonialist act. In *Şeytan*, it becomes possible to read the unnamed demon as a "local" devil or djinn displaced by the local religion—that is, Islam, and this could signify a form of colonialism.

83. Water retrieved from a well in Mecca and considered sacred by Muslims. For more, see Karademir, "Hollywood Movies in Turkey," 639.

84. Özkaracalar, "Turkish Cinema," 259.

85. Ibid., 252.

86. Ibid.

87. Karademir, "Hollywood Movies in Turkey," 638.

88. Smith, "Transcultural Appropriation," 10.

89. Ibid.

90. A more recent Turkish horror movie, *Semum* (2008, Kasan Karacadag), similarly appropriates tropes found in the *The Exorcist* in particular and Western horror tropes in general, and recontextualizes them so they more closely align with Turkish culture and the Islamic faith.

91. Shipka, *Perverse Titillation*, 9.

92. Ibid., 8.

93. Willis, "Paul Naschy," 126–27.

94. Benshoff, "Blaxploitation Horror," 31.

95. Kyle Bishop, "The Sub-Subaltern Monster: Imperialist Hegemony and the Cinematic Voodoo Zombie," *The Journal of American Culture* 31, no. 2 (2008): 146.

96. Jill Dolan, "Ideology in Performance: Looking Through the Male Gaze," in *The Feminist Spectator as Critic* (Ann Arbor: UMI Research Press, 1988), 15

97. Bishop, "Sub-Subaltern Monster," 141.

98. Ibid.

99. Benshoff, "Blaxploitation Horror," 32.

100. Loomba, *Colonialism*, 43.

FOUR

Revisiting *The Exorcist*

Challenging and Extending the Traditional Exorcism Narrative

Aside from inspiring the rip-offs and homages discussed in the previous chapter, *The Exorcist* also spawned a series of official sequels and prequels. After the film became an enormous financial success in 1973, producers almost immediately turned their attention to developing a follow-up. Yet, *Exorcist II: The Heretic* would not arrive in theaters until June 17, 1977, nearly four years after the original. Neither screenwriter William Peter Blatty nor director William Friedkin opted to return for the sequel, so the studio turned to John Boorman,[1] director of *Point Blank* (1967) and *Deliverance* (1972). Following a famously troubled production, the sequel opened to scathing reviews and quickly bombed at the box office. According to film critic Mark Kermode, American audiences routinely jeered *Exorcist II*, prompting the studio to withdraw the film from theaters and recut it.[2] Despite all this effort, it still attained a reputation as one of the worst films ever made. Friedkin dismissed the sequel as "the product of a demented mind,"[3] and Blatty recalled laughing at it while watching it in the theater. Indeed, audiences considered *Exorcist II* an unintentional comedy,[4] and no amount of reshoots or re-editing could salvage the film.[5]

A few years later, Blatty would make his directorial debut with an adaptation of his novel *The Ninth Configuration* (1980), a post-Vietnam War drama set in a mental institution and featuring the astronaut character who briefly appeared in *The Exorcist*. While both films differ wildly in terms of tone and story, Blatty nevertheless considers *The Ninth Configuration* the true sequel to *The Exorcist*.[6] Despite critical acclaim, the film

67

failed at the box office, and Blatty would not direct another film until 1990, when he oversaw production of *The Exorcist III*. Based on his novel, *Legion*, the story no longer focused on Regan MacNeil, who had since become the subject of parody in other films.[7] Instead, *Exorcist III* concentrates on Lieutenant William Kinderman (a peripheral character from *The Exorcist*) as he investigates a series of murders that somehow link to the deaths of both Father Karras and the Gemini Killer, a serial murderer executed fifteen years earlier. The film received mixed reviews,[8] and performed poorly at the box office (despite opening at number one during its first weekend of release).[9] Overall, the apparent dissolution of the *Exorcist* franchise seems to correspond to the lull period of the 1980s and 1990s, which produced only thirteen true exorcism films.

Exorcism cinema experienced a renaissance in the twenty-first century. We explore this resurgence in more detail in chapter 7, but for now we should note that *The Exorcist*'s highly successful rerelease in 2000—complete with additional footage—also spurred attempts to relaunch the franchise that started it all,[10] as Morgan Creek Productions developed a prequel almost immediately afterward. However, this attempt resulted in a schism that seemingly ended the franchise altogether. As detailed in this chapter, a series of well-documented mishaps (a common occurrence with this franchise) led to the production and release of two separate prequel films: *Exorcist: The Beginning* (2004, Renny Harlin) and *Dominion: Prequel to the Exorcist* (2005, Paul Schrader). Both films failed critically and commercially, and this failure likely accounts for the absence of any further cinematic sequels, prequels, or "sidequels" that expand *The Exorcist* cinematic universe to this day.[11]

In addition to this diminishing critical reputation and commercial success, *The Exorcist* franchise also suffers from issues with internal continuity. Three of the sequels and prequels document Father Merrin's experiences with the demon Pazuzu while in Africa; yet, none of them portray the story in the same way, and each entry contradicts the last. As Kermode notes,[12] *Exorcist II* depicts the young Father Merrin (Max von Sydow) exorcising an Ethiopian boy possessed by the demon Pazuzu in the 1930s. *The Beginning*, meanwhile, relocates this confrontation to 1947 Kenya, where Merrin discovers a statue of Pazuzu in the buried ruins of a pagan church. *Dominion* tells essentially the same story as *The Beginning*, but the circumstances surrounding the exorcism differ in a number of significant ways. This lack of oversight and cohesiveness might explain why none of the other films in *The Exorcist* franchise had the same sort of cultural impact as the original.

Despite their rather poor reputations, the sequels and prequels all represent interesting extensions and even possible subversions of the traditional exorcism narrative. *Exorcist II* explores possession and exorcism in a non-Western context by positioning Regan as a possible modern-day saint. Both prequels depict Merrin's initial conflict with Pazuzu during his time in Africa, but each film features different (though still marginalized) people succumbing to possession. *Exorcist III*, meanwhile, portrays a white man becoming possessed, which sets it apart from the vast majority of exorcism films, which tend to position women, people of color, or other marginalized individuals as the victim of possession. While *Exorcist III* appears to challenge the traditional exorcism narrative established by the original film, overall the franchise advances this narrative and helps to cement the subgenre's boundaries.

THE SEQUELS

Given *The Exorcist*'s enormous financial success, it should come as no surprise that producers scrambled to produce a sequel. Richard Lederer, co-producer of *Exorcist II*, recalled how the initial intent was to produce a low-budget rehash of the original film.[13] The sequel would explore the first film's story from the angle of a priest investigating the events surrounding Regan's possession and subsequent exorcism, allowing producers to use previously unseen footage from the first film. While this basic idea formed the backbone of *Exorcist II* when it finally reached the production phase, producers included a new explanation for Regan's possession that ultimately complicated the original film's story, apparently to the dismay of both critics and audiences.

Set roughly three years after the events of the first film, *Exorcist II* opens with Regan MacNeil (Linda Blair) now living in New York with her guardian, Sharon Spencer (Kitty Wynn). Regan does not remember being possessed by the demon Pazuzu, and her psychiatrist, Dr. Gene Tuskin (Louise Fletcher), worries that the young woman has simply repressed the traumatic memories. Meanwhile, the Vatican dispatches Father Philip Lamont (Richard Burton), a priest questioning his faith because he sees only darkness in the world, to investigate Father Merrin's death. Lamont meets with Dr. Tuskin, but she refuses to allow him to question Regan because she believes he might damage the girl's psyche. Instead, she proposes they use a machine called a "synchronizer" that will allow Lamont to enter Regan's mind and uncover her memories of the exorcism. Pazuzu intervenes, however, and sends Lamont's consciousness to the past. While there, he observes Father Merrin exorcising a young Ethiopian boy named Kokumo, a powerful psychic who uses his abilities to battle Pazuzu, who manifests as a swarm of locusts.

Lamont eventually journeys to Africa to seek out the adult Kokumo (James Earl Jones), now a scientist studying grasshoppers to understand why they swarm. While there, Lamont learns that Pazuzu primarily targets individuals with psychic abilities. *Exorcist II* then reveals that Regan can communicate telepathically with others, and that Father Merrin belonged to a group of theologians who believed psychic power would someday connect all of humanity in a global consciousness and thus initiate a new phase of human existence. Lamont returns to New York, and from there he accompanies Regan to her old house in Georgetown, where Pazuzu assumes the girl's form and offers Lamont unlimited power. Lamont initially succumbs to this temptation, but Regan uses her power to free him from the demon's influence. Lamont then rips the demon's heart out with his bare hands just as a locust swarm crashes through the window. Regan banishes Pazuzu by performing the same ritual Kokumo used to expel the locusts in Africa. Afterward, Dr. Tuskin implores Lamont to watch over Regan. He consents and departs with the girl, while Tuskin stays behind to answer the police's questions.

Regan's developing relationship to and importance within the Catholic Church is perhaps the most interesting aspect of *Exorcist II*. The film aligns with *The Exorcist* because it positions independent women as a threat to traditional order, and only a patriarchal institution like the Church can neutralize that threat. With her mother out of the picture, Regan assumes the role of the independent woman, only now her agency manifests in the form of her newfound psychic healing abilities rather than her possession. Of course, Regan's powers still threaten patriarchal order because they render her more open to the devil's corruption. To that end, much like the first film, a doubting priest battling his own inner demons (perhaps he, too, has become possessed) ushers this young woman back into the Church's embrace and thus restores her to her proper (i.e., submissive) place within the natural, masculine social order.[14] In other words, Father Lamont must reaffirm his faith and suppress Regan's powers before they can undo the symbolic order.

Yet, *Exorcist II* deviates from the traditional exorcism narrative because neither Regan (the monstrous-feminine) nor Lamont (the patriarchal defender) become directly involved with the possession and exorcism. Instead, the film uses Merrin and Kokumo to depict the struggle between chaos and order, a story later revisited and revamped in the *Exorcist* prequels. Unlike the exorcism films analyzed thus far, all of which focus on the possession of a girl or young woman, *Exorcist II* depicts a young boy becoming possessed. The young Kokumo initially appears as a force for good, drawing on his great spiritual power to combat the locust swarms. Thus, rather than a member of the "weaker" sex and therefore vulnerable to possession, *Exorcist II* features a powerful male figure who can suppress evil at the center of the exorcism narrative.

Initially, this portrayal appears to challenge the traditional exorcism narrative. Yet, closer inspection reveals that, like *Abby*, *Exorcist II* actually extends the narrative because it portrays a member of a non-dominant group becoming possessed, and thus emerging as a threat to the traditional order established by dominant Western, Christian values. Kokumo's African heritage and pagan roots render him a non-dominant outsider, thereby setting him apart from the dominant symbolic order exemplified by Fathers Merrin and Lamont. These differences become further accentuated when Kokumo succumbs to possession by a demon previously identified as Assyrian but now positioned as African; as such, both the possessed individual and the possessing entity actively threaten the symbolic order. To end the threat and save Kokumo, Father Merrin — the exemplar of white, Christian morality — takes the boy to a Christian holy site and performs a Catholic exorcism ritual. Thus, the film advances a colonialist rhetoric, because it implies Kokumo's salvation lies with the Christian faith, rather than his own pagan magic. *Exorcist II* thereby portrays a clash between Eastern and Western cultures, much like the one seen in *Abby* and discussed in chapter 3. Unlike *Abby*, however, *Exorcist II* does not support a postcolonialist reading because it explicitly portrays Catholicism as superior to Kokumo's pagan magic, and therefore positions Western ideology as superior to non-Western modes of belief.

Additionally, the film extends the traditional exorcism narrative to include queer individuals, because Kokumo's possession causes him to transgress gender norms. *Exorcist II* initially Others Kokumo by portraying him as a member of a non-dominant cultural group, but he also becomes Othered after he succumbs to possession because he violates gender boundaries. As discussed in chapter 2, Pazuzu's voice inhabits a liminal space between male and female throughout *The Exorcist*, and this in turn Others Regan because she transgresses gender norms during her possession. This type of transgression also occurs in *Exorcist II*, because the film codes the invading entity as female.[15] For instance, during the flashback sequence, when Kokumo becomes possessed, he growls "My name is Pazuzu" in a distinctly feminine voice. Later, Kokumo wails during the exorcism ritual, and once again his voice takes on feminine qualities.[16] Observing the scene, Lamont speaks directly to Pazuzu, who responds in an unmistakably female voice. We should note, however, that the film's dialogue positions the demon as male; for example, characters often use male pronouns when discussing Pazuzu, and Lamont refers to the demon as "king of the evil spirits of the air." Nonetheless, the demon's voice consistently situates it as feminine, and as such the film portrays the feminine as a threat to the natural order.

According to Harry M. Benshoff, "the male homosexual or queer is monstrous precisely because he embodies characteristics of the feminine" such as in outward displays like voice and behavior.[17] When men become possessed by a feminine demon, this transgression indicates the removal of the man's voice and power; indeed, such removal appears to have been the demon's goal all along, given that Satan targets gifted individuals. Furthermore, *Exorcist II* transfers the uncertainty surrounding Pazuzu's gender identity onto Kokumo, resulting in an uncertainty regarding his own gender identity while possessed. In other exorcism films, a masculine entity possesses a female body, thereby lending masculine power to the woman and granting her the voice and agency to speak out against those seeking to oppress her. In this instance, however, a feminine entity possesses a male body, which results in a gender identity more aligned with a non-heteronormative (and thus marginalized) conception of masculinity. This non-heteronormative masculinity becomes associated with the feminine Pazuzu, rendering Kokumo even more of a threat to patriarchal ideologies than if he had become possessed by a masculine entity.

Kokumo's possession, then, highlights the film's main thematic message: women and minorities threaten the white, masculine order unless they establish a connection to patriarchal institutions like the Church. For example, the adult Kokumo explains to Lamont that locusts swarm because their wings brush against one another and they become agitated, which essentially transforms them into an angry mob. He then shows Lamont a female locust bred to resist such agitation. Kokumo refers to her as the "Good Locust" and explains that her children will someday negate the swarm by calming the other locusts. Thus, the film metaphorically reinforces the need to create a "good" woman—and, by extension, a well-behaved representative of a non-dominant group—who can model appropriate feminine qualities such as serenity and obedience. Furthermore, the film implies that women and minorities can only embody such qualities if they align with the values advocated by patriarchal organizations like the Catholic Church. Pazuzu represents the monstrous-feminine, because the demon does not align with either the Church or the patriarchy; the possessed Kokumo thus embodies this monstrous-feminine and must therefore be repressed through the act of Christian exorcism. Once saved, Kokumo benefits his community through the patriarchal institution of science. Thus, *Exorcist II* appears to tolerate the feminine, the queer, and non-dominant minorities only if they align with heteronormative and patriarchal values.

According to Ken Gelder, two primary thematic concerns dominated horror throughout the 1970s, and they both exemplify a postcolonial rhetoric.[18] First, horror films of the 1970s regularly depict the transgression of boundaries, and they increasingly explored issues of "circulation: one thing passing into another, mutating, even melting identities along the way."[19] Second, horror often portrayed the conflict between the modern and the traditional, which manifested in clashes between science and religion, or in tensions between Eastern and Western ideologies. Gelder's ideas apply to possession narratives in particular, because the possessed individual experiences a melding of identities, and also exists at the intersection of the tensions between tradition and modernity. Kokumo's possession exemplifies Gelder's argument because it involves a melding of identities that threaten to undo traditional order. Such a melding appears to support a postcolonial reading, but only if Kokumo's possession was resolved in a way similar to the one depicted in *Abby*. Because *Exorcist II* positions this melding as a threat that only Christianity can negate, Kokumo's exorcism therefore represents the triumph of tradition over modernity, and thus the film advances a colonialist rhetoric.

While we will return to a discussion of colonialism with the analysis of the prequels, the second sequel leaves Africa and Regan behind. In many ways, *Exorcist III* feels more like a crime thriller than a true exorcism narrative, and thus aligns more closely with the slasher movies that emerged in the 1970s and dominated horror throughout 1980s and 1990s. At the same time, however, the narrative recalls *The Exorcist* because the serial murders committed throughout the film connect to Regan's possession. Additionally, the film's original title, *Legion*, refers to a biblical passage that recounts an episode in which Jesus meets a man possessed by hundreds of demons, a story recalled by various other exorcism films. With *Exorcist III*, the series further moves away from the idea of the possessed woman, but it still portrays the feminine as monstrous. Indeed, *Exorcist III* depicts similar struggles of power that become highlighted via feminist critique, namely because a man gains the ability to possess other people—mainly women—and compel them to do his bidding.

Blatty originally intended the film as a subdued psychological thriller that would generate scares through mood and tone rather than gruesome special effects.[20] More importantly, perhaps, he originally envisioned the film as having nothing to do with exorcism. Morgan Creek Productions had other ideas, however, and they demanded a series of reshoots to bring the film more in line with *The Exorcist*.[21] Most notably, they changed the title from *Legion* to *Exorcist III*. Next, they brought in Jason Miller to reprise his role as Father Karras, while simultaneously trimming Brad Dourif's performance as the Gemini Killer.[22] Finally, studio executives instructed Blatty to shoot an expensive exorcism sequence (at a reported cost of $4 million) that would feature "fire, lightning, explosions, levitation, a sea of snakes, and even face-ripping dismemberment."[23] A resigned Blatty made the changes, and the compromised film opened to mixed reviews and an overall poor reception at the box office.

Ignoring the events of *Exorcist II*—likely due to Blatty's lack of participation in that film's production—*Exorcist III* begins with Lieutenant William Kinderman (George C. Scott) investigating the murder and crucifixion of a twelve-year-old African American boy. Later that day, Kinderman relates the gruesome details of the murder to his friend, Father Joseph Dyer (Ed Flanders). Soon afterward, police discover a decapitated priest in a church confessional. Around the same time, Dyer admits himself to the hospital for some routine testing, only to fall victim to the murderer. Kinderman learns that the fingerprints found at the various crime scenes do not match, indicating that different people committed each murder. Furthermore, the homicides all bear an uncanny resemblance to those committed by the infamous Gemini Killer (Brad Dourif), a serial murderer executed fifteen years earlier.

During the investigation, Kinderman learns that an unidentified psychiatric patient recently woke from a fifteen-year-long catatonic stupor and identified himself as the Gemini Killer. Kinderman visits Patient X, who bears an uncanny resemblance to the deceased Father Damien Karras (Jason Miller). Patient X claims that demons visited the Gemini Killer during his execution and offered to insert his soul into Karras's dying body. He also declares that his soul leaves Karras's body each night and compels the hospital's elderly female dementia patients to commit murders. A few nights later, an old woman attacks Kinderman's daughter, but the assassination attempt fails when Father Paul Morning (Nicol Williamson) arrives to exorcise Father Karras. However, demonic forces violently prevent the priest from casting out the invasive spirit. Kinderman arrives shortly thereafter and discovers Morning's mutilated body slumped in the corner of Patient X's cell. Kinderman tries to shoot Karras, but the demons stop him. Father Morning momentarily regains consciousness and urges Karras to fight the demonic influence. Karras manages to reassert his personality long enough to beg for death. Kinderman shoots Karras, thus saving the priest's soul and ending the Gemini Killer's threat once more.

Of all the sequels and prequels, *Exorcist III* offers perhaps the most overt challenges to the traditional exorcism narrative, largely because it situates a white man as the primary victim of possession. While confusion remains regarding Patient X's identity, our reading assumes that demonic intervention allows the Gemini Killer to possess Father Karras. Furthermore, Karras appears to have become possessed by more than one invasive entity. When Kinderman questions him, Patient X recites the biblical passage that refers to Legion: "I am no one; I am many." Significantly, Patient X manifests different personalities throughout the film, and each one speaks with a different voice; sometimes the voice sounds higher pitched (though still clearly male), while at other times it sounds disembodied, demonic, and deeply masculine. All of this suggests multiple possessions (hence, Legion), although only the Gemini Killer physically manifests in the room to speak with Kinderman. Thus, *Exorcist III* depicts a heteronormative, white male who represents the patriarchy succumbing to possession, and the film thereby portrays a different kind of possession story. Karras becomes possessed by the Gemini Killer (a fellow man) rather than Pazuzu, and this portrays the patriarchy as susceptible to corruption.

Yet, the possessed man's Othered nature also situates non-traditional masculinity as a form of corruption. During the times when the Gemini Killer physically manifests, *Exorcist III* portrays him as somewhat feminized due to his bearing (e.g., the way he moves, his hairstyle, etc.) and his lisping way of speaking. He becomes particularly feminized when contrasted with the more visibly masculine Father Karras. Thus, the possessing entity indicates an effeminate, non-heteronormative masculinity, and thus threatens due to its queer nature.

Furthermore, the Gemini Killer only compels women to commit crimes, which indicates another form of gender transgression; he imbues these women with his masculine power and allows them to become violent, but his tendency to remotely possess only women indicates an affinity for the feminine. When looked at on a continuum, Karras exists on the masculine side, and the women inhabit the feminine side, with the Gemini Killer occupying the liminal space between these opposing poles. As discussed above, when women become possessed by male demons, they gain access to masculine power that allows them to struggle against patriarchal oppression, but it also renders them as abject because they transgress gender boundaries. When men become possessed by male demons, however, they often gain more power, and can infect others with that power. Male demons thereby function as a reaffirmation of masculine power and dominance over others, as in *Exorcist III*, in which old women succumb to the Gemini Killer's will. Thus, the possessed individual becomes positioned as a threat to order in two ways: first, he is Othered, and second, he reveals the dark side of dominant masculinity.

At the same time, however, *Exorcist III* reflects the traditional exorcism narrative because it positions the feminine as a threat to order. The Gemini Killer possesses the hospital's elderly female dementia patients and compels them to commit murder, and thus the film reinforces one of the traditional exorcism narrative's central ideas: the feminine threatens patriarchal order and stability because women are more susceptible to temptation and thus desirable targets for demonic possession. *Exorcist III* establishes this idea early on, during a scene in which one of the dementia patients confesses her sins to an unwitting and increasingly worried priest. Throughout the sequence, the woman's voice grows deeper and more masculine as she confesses to murdering seventeen people. She then kills the priest, and returns to the hospital with no memory of her actions. Later, after Father Dyer's murder, Kinderman learns that the fingerprints found at the scene of the crime belong to another patient, Mrs. Clelia (Mary Jackson), who has no memory of what happened. Later, however, Mrs. Clelia crawls on the ceiling, clearly empowered by her possession. Near the end of the film, another female dementia patient kills a nurse and steals her uniform, and then tries to kill Kinderman's daughter. During the attack, the old woman emits a demonic howl as she performs feats of superhuman strength. The Gemini Killer imbues these women with strength and agency they would not otherwise have.

Thus, while the Gemini Killer inspires the murders, women actually commit them, and the film thereby situates the feminine as deadly. Furthermore, these possessed and murderous old women align with the archetypal figure known as the hag,[24] which links possession to witchcraft, one of the primary threats to man and patriarchy. Moreover, these possessed women indicate both gender-bending and abjection, because their bodies become possessed by an apparently male entity or personality during these incidents. Therefore, while the film does not situate a possessed woman as the primary victim/antagonist, it nevertheless portrays women as lethal agents of demonic forces, and therefore as a form of chaos that threatens masculine stability. Like other exorcism films, *Exorcist III* depicts this stability in the form of a man regaining his faith and using his renewed masculine resolve to end the demonic infestation and thereby restore order.

Exorcist III most closely reflects the traditional exorcism narrative during the tacked on exorcism sequence, primarily because of who performs the ritual and how the possession ultimately ends. As discussed in previous chapters, the doubting priest figure recurs throughout exorcism cinema, and both Kinderman and Father Morning embody elements of this figure. Years earlier, Morning performed an exorcism that frightened him so badly his hair turned completely white. While he still believes in God, his fear indicates that he lacks faith (if he truly believed, he would not feel fear), and this might explain why he fails to successfully exorcise Karras. Similarly, Kinderman sees only evil in the world, and he doubts the existence of God. When viewed together, Kinderman and Morning appear to fulfill the same role as Lamont in *Exorcist II*; Kinderman sees only darkness, and the film situates him as the "classic existentialist figure struggling with what little faith he has left."[25] These two men must work together to exorcise Karras. Significantly, they do not succeed through spiritual strength, but rather through masculine violence; Kinderman shoots Karras upon the possessed man's request and thereby ends the Gemini Killer's threat. This decidedly bleak conclusion suggests that patriarchy will always find a way to turn back the darkness, either through religious belief or masculine violence.

By concluding with such violence, *Exorcist III* reveals traditional exorcism as weak, inferior, and altogether incapable of saving a possessed man, and the film reinforces this idea through how quickly the demon dispatches the feeble Father Morning. Only masculine violence can free the possessed man's soul. Significantly, a man representing a different patriarchal institution (e.g., law enforcement) still vanquishes the demon, but only with assistance from the representative of another patriarchal institution (e.g., religion); indeed, Morning's near-death intervention prevents Kinderman from succumbing to the demon's tricks. In other words, *Exorcist III* reinforces the idea that patriarchy will ultimately prevail, whether through the language of Roman Rites, or through the retort of a snub-nosed revolver.

THE PREQUELS

As mentioned earlier, controversy plagued the *Exorcist* series, yet no other movie in the franchise experienced quite as much misfortune as the planned prequel that would explore Father Merrin's conflict with the demon Pazuzu during his time in Africa. Kermode notes that the prequel suffered a death, a walk-off, a firing, Internet slander, and disavowal by the series' creator.[26] The official prequel that was eventually shot and released does not even align with the canon established in the previous films. *Exorcist II* reveals some of Merrin's back story, hinted at in *The Exorcist*, but the official prequel contradicts this information because it features different locations, different time periods, and different people becoming possessed and exorcised.

The prequel's troubled production likely led to this jumbled continuity; the studio only greenlit the prequel after the financially successful twenty-fifth anniversary rerelease of *The Exorcist*, but the revolving door of names attached to the film signaled doom from the start.[27] Morgan Creek contracted William Wisher, screenwriter of *Terminator 2: Judgment Day* (1991, James Cameron), to write a film for Tom McLoughlin, director of *One Dark Night* (1982).[28] However, rewrites by bestselling author Caleb Carr attracted the attention of John Frankenheimer, director of *The Manchurian Candidate* (1962), prompting McLoughlin to leave the project, which had bloomed in both scope and budget.[29] Liam Neeson signed on to play Father Merrin, with shooting scheduled to begin in 2002.[30] Unfortunately, Frankenheimer's death in July of 2002 caused the studio to put the film on hold, at which point Neeson left to fulfill other commitments.[31] Morgan Creek then hired maverick director and screenwriter Paul Schrader to helm the picture, though they soon came to regret that decision.[32]

Schrader made it through principal photography with Stellan Skarsgård stepping in as Merrin, and at first the writer/director seemed a great fit for the project. As Kermode writes:

> Raised as a strict Calvinist, Schrader had once famously described *The Exorcist* as "the greatest metaphor in cinema. . . . God and the Devil in the same room arguing over the body of a little girl." [. . .] For Schrader, *Exorcist: The Beginning* offered the chance to command a $40m movie while simultaneously exploring his own tortured vision of religious faith.[33]

Yet, the first cut left studio executives crying foul because the film did not include nearly enough blood, gore, and shocks to befit the series.[34] Rather than letting Schrader conduct reshoots, or perhaps because Schrader did not think such scare tactics were necessary, Morgan Creek turned the film over to director Renny Harlin, whose previous films included *A Nightmare on Elm Street 4: The Dream Master* (1988), *Die Hard 2: Die Harder*

(1990), and *The Long Kiss Goodnight* (1996). In January 2004, rumors surfaced that none of Schrader's footage would survive in Harlin's film, and its release in August 2004 seemed to confirm such rumors.[35] *The Beginning* failed both critically and commercially, and so the studio, perhaps humbly, once again offered Schrader the resources to complete his version, released nearly a year later as *Dominion*.[36]

While both films ostensibly cover the same material, they differ wildly in the details. The key separation occurs in how each film approaches the traditional exorcism narrative. Both films concern Father Merrin questioning God's existence (or lack thereof) and ability to intervene in the world.[37] Thus, both films feature a holy man questioning his faith, one of the central tropes in the traditional exorcism narrative. Yet, *The Beginning* foregrounds this theme much more explicitly than *Dominion*. More significantly, *The Beginning* ultimately reveals a possessed woman as the source of the film's troubles, while *Dominion* features a possessed African boy. Thus, *The Beginning* appears to align most closely with the traditional exorcism narrative, and therefore with the tropes and themes portrayed in *The Exorcist*. Meanwhile, *Dominion* demonstrates the same type of extension seen in *Exorcist II* because it hews more closely to the franchise's established canon.

In *The Beginning*, Father Merrin (Stellan Skarsgård) has been left traumatized by the horrific events he witnessed during World War II, and so he takes a sabbatical from the Church. He travels to East Africa, where he devotes himself to archaeology and works to restore his shaken faith. One day, an antiquities collector approaches Merrin and invites him to participate in the excavation of a Christian Byzantine church discovered by the British in Kenya's Turkana region. The collector divulges that the church dates back to around 500 AD, centuries before Christianity arrived in that region of Africa, and that he wants Merrin to recover an ancient demonic artifact before the British soldiers overseeing the dig learn of its existence. Intrigued, Merrin agrees. He travels to the site along with Father Francis (James D'Arcy), a scholar dispatched by the Vatican to ensure that no one desecrates the church. Upon arrival, Merrin meets Major Granville (Julian Wadham), the British officer leading the dig, and Sarah (Izabella Scorupco), a doctor haunted by her experiences in a Nazi concentration camp.

Merrin and Father Francis visit the dig site with their translator, Chuma (Andrew French), and they enter the church—which remains in pristine condition, as though buried immediately upon completion—where they discover statues of angels holding spears pointed downward, as if to subdue something buried beneath the church. More disturbingly, someone (or something) tore the enormous crucifix from the altar and hung it upside-down in an act of blatant desecration. Determined to learn more about the operation, Merrin travels to an asylum in Nairobi to visit Monsieur Bession (Patrick O'Kane), the lead archaeologist who suffered a mental breakdown three weeks earlier. Merrin arrives to find that Bession has carved a swastika into his own chest, and he speaks with the voice of the Nazi commandant who tormented Merrin during the war. Before Merrin can question him, however, Bession slashes his own throat. The asylum's warden, Father Gionetti (David Bradley), declares that a demon drove Bession to insanity and suicide. Gionetti then provides the skeptical Merrin with a book of Roman exorcism rituals and sends him on his way.

Back at the village, a boy named Joseph (Remy Sweeney) falls into a catatonic state after a pack of hyenas kills his older brother. The villagers believe that an evil spirit has possessed the boy, and they unsuccessfully attempt to exorcise him. Around this time, Merrin learns that the church was built atop the ruins of an even older temple, one that predates Christianity, and the excavation has unleashed an ancient evil. Meanwhile, Sarah and Father Francis usher Joseph into the church to perform an exorcism, but Sarah kills the priest before he can complete the ritual. Eventually, Merrin discerns that the demon actually possessed Sarah rather than Joseph. Mustering his faith, Merrin descends into the church once more and attempts to exorcise Sarah, but she dies in the process. Defeated, Merrin and Joseph flee the ruins, only to find that the British soldiers and the local tribesmen have annihilated one another. Despite the horrors he encountered, Merrin's battle with the demon has renewed his faith in God. Clad in his priestly garments once more, Merrin returns to Rome and informs the collector that he could not retrieve the artifact.

Of all the sequels and prequels, *The Beginning* most closely aligns with the traditional exorcism narrative. This time around, Merrin assumes the role of the doubting priest who has lost faith, and the film establishes him as sort of rugged, hard-drinking archaeologist on a quest to find an ancient religious icon (not unlike Indiana Jones). At the same time, the film firmly establishes his lack of faith; for instance, Father Francis mentions Merrin's knowledge of exorcisms, but the older priest quickly changes the subject, explaining that he became an archaeologist to work with something real, something he could touch. Merrin goes on to explain that he sees no point to religion. Most tellingly, perhaps, Merrin cannot successfully perform the exorcism ritual until he reaffirms his relationship with God. He attempts to exorcise Joseph, but because he no longer believes in God, Merrin fails to drive the demon out. Nor can he see that the demon has actually possessed Sarah; his lack of faith blinds him to the true threat. Merrin only becomes empowered once more when he rekindles his faith in God, which also allows him to resume his role within the patriarchal order. Thus, *The Beginning* marks another appearance of the doubting priest figure, as Merrin assumes the role of the man who lost his faith, but regains it after a confrontation with the supernatural, thereby re-establishing his allegiance to the Church's patriarchal values.

In addition to the doubting priest figure, *The Beginning* also portrays a possessed woman whose uninhibited sexuality threatens patriarchal order. The young doctor, Sarah, ultimately emerges as the true danger in the film. Interestingly, *The Beginning* does not chronicle her possession the way many other exorcism films do; instead, the film only reveals Sarah's possession during the climax, perhaps to capitalize on the "twist ending" phenomenon popularized by *The Sixth Sense* (1999, M. Night Shyamalan). In this way, *The Beginning* does not allow viewers to sympathize with Sarah's plight, because it does not depict her personal struggle against the possession. Rather, the film situates her as an object of lust, both before and after the possession. Indeed, Sarah tempts Merrin throughout the film; she flirts with him, and later kisses him. During the exorcism, she asks Merrin why he no longer desires her. She exists primarily to illustrate how far Merrin has fallen from faith. Sarah exists at both ends of the virgin/whore dichotomy throughout the film; prior to possession, she represents innocence, but she becomes a threatening temptress once she succumbs to demonic influence. While the film establishes Sarah as a competent doctor who plays an important role in the archaeological dig, she also acts as an agent of the evil that blights the area and causes the death of many British and Turkana during their bloody war. Thus, *The Beginning* simultaneously portrays Sarah as an object of lust and an object of fear, and therefore she exemplifies the abject role of women in exorcism films.

As mentioned above, *Dominion* tells essentially the same story as *The Beginning*, but many of the details differ. For instance, in *The Beginning*, an antiquities collector prompts Merrin (once again played by Stellan Skarsgård) to investigate the excavation of the church. In *Dominion*, however, Merrin chooses to join the archaeological dig on his own. More importantly, the character of Sarah does not appear in *Dominion*; instead, Merrin meets a young female doctor named Rachel (Clara Bellar) in the village near the dig site, but Rachel shares no characterizations with Sarah other than her profession. While many of the events and characters overlap, different actors inhabit some of the roles (for instance, Gabriel Mann plays Father Francis in this version). The biggest difference between Schrader's version and Harlin's occurs in the third act, when Pazuzu possesses a deformed African boy named Cheche (Billy Crawford) and Father Merrin must exorcise him.

Like *Exorcist II*, *Dominion* reflects and extends the traditional exorcism narrative, largely because it focuses on the same type of exorcism even as it offers a contradicting account of Merrin's past. As in *The Beginning*, *Dominion* uses Merrin's traumatic encounter with the Nazis to introduce the character and establish why he lost his faith. In this version of the story, however, the Nazi commander forces Merrin to sacrifice members of his "flock" to save others. Thus, the film provides a different motivation for Merrin's shaken belief. Furthermore, *Dominion* does not portray

Merrin as a frightened man who drinks as a way to cope with his uncertainty, but rather as a resolute scholar questioning the true nature of the universe. Similarly, whereas Sarah tempts Merrin, Rachel does not. Thus, while *The Beginning* explicitly establishes Merrin as a flawed man who lost his faith and succumbs to temptation, he does not seem to have fallen quite as far in *Dominion*.

As with *Exorcist II*, *Dominion* uses possession and exorcism to extend the traditional exorcism narrative. Like Kokumo, Cheche becomes Othered thanks to his African heritage, but also because the Turkana people consider him an outsider due to his mental and physical disabilities. At the same time, the film positions Merrin—and by extension, the Christian faith—as Cheche's savior. By situating an African boy in the role of the possessed individual, *Dominion* supports a colonialist reading because it once again portrays Christianity's domination over other religions and modes of belief. The film reinforces this view of Christianity through its depiction of the church; as in *The Beginning*, the church contains four statues of angels standing guard over the entrance to Hell, and demonic petroglyphs once again cover the walls. Further investigation reveals another temple beneath the church, one dedicated to a "pagan god" or "mountain demon." By situating the Christian church on top of the pagan temple, *Dominion* implies that the old gods threaten the world and therefore must succumb to the One True God, the Symbolic Father who maintains patriarchal order.

Also, like *Abby*, *Dominion* depicts non-white, non-heteronormative individuals as a threat to the dominant white, heterosexual order. Unlike *Abby*, however, the film implies that only a white male can dispel that threat. This power discrepancy also manifests in the parallel story of the British military entering the region to subdue the Turkana people. *Dominion* thereby portrays white patriarchy as the only force capable of neutralizing the threat posed by the possessed individual, whose subjugation effects the restoration of patriarchal order and values. Thus, while the demon may empower Cheche and grant him the means to heal his disabilities, such empowerment threatens the natural order and therefore requires suppression. Removed from the Sarah character, Cheche represents an intersection of marginalized identities that requires oppression.

The possessed Cheche also endangers the natural order because he transgresses gender boundaries, and this supports a queer reading of the possession. Prior to the exorcism, the demon gains full control of Cheche and transforms him into a hairless, androgynous being. In the temple beneath the church, he proclaims "I am perfection" in a feminine voice, which recalls Kokumo's possession in *Exorcist II*. While Pazuzu's gender identity remains unclear in this film, Cheche's behavior while possessed suggests gender and sexual transgressions. Furthermore, the possessed Cheche lounges in a sexually suggestive position as he offers Father Merrin the thing he desires most: a chance to absolve his guilt. Merrin rejects this temptation and casts the demon out, but the film sends a clear message: the feminine represents a monstrous threat to masculine order, and only the patriarchal institution of the holy Church can repel this menace and protect mankind from temptation. As with Kokumo, possession heightens this threat because the possessed individual transgresses the boundaries of gender and sexual orientation, and thus aligns with dominant, heteronormative anxieties regarding homosexual identity.

ADVANCING THE TRADITIONAL EXORCISM NARRATIVE

While the later films in the *Exorcist* franchise offer some challenges to the traditional exorcism narrative, they nevertheless maintain the tropes and metaphors established by the original film. In each, a man struggles with his faith, and this essential feature has reinforced the traditional exorcism narrative for over three decades. This same type of spiritual angst even afflicts secular men, such as Kinderman. Furthermore, these men can only settle this spiritual crisis when they confront and exorcise a supernatural evil. Metaphorically, then, these men experience crises of masculine power and control that they can only resolve by suppressing members of non-dominant groups—sometimes violently—who they blame for causing this crisis in the first place. The challenges to this narrative emerge via the possessed individuals' natures, but only in one film is that individual a woman. In *Exorcist III*, a man assumes the role of the possessed individual in need of exorcism. Even then, the demon possesses various women throughout the film, all of whom become deadly while possessed, and the possessed man appears to experience a queering. In *Exorcist II* and *Dominion*, a young boy becomes possessed, but the boy's African identity and queer representation indicate that the film ultimately supports the traditional exorcism narrative.

Overall, the analysis of these possessions reveals that non-dominant groups function as the primary targets of these possessions; the demons empower these Othered individuals, who then become oppressed and marginalized once more via exorcism. Specifically, the franchise expanded which non-dominant groups could become Othered. In *Exorcist II* and *Dominion*, possession empowers African boys and renders them dangerous, necessitating their subsequent oppression through exorcism, and this indicates a need to apply a colonial analysis to the films. Only the Western religious ideology can save the boys, supplanting both the possession and their own pagan belief systems.

In his discussion of films featuring Haitian zombies, Kyle Bishop notes that perceptions of superiority such as those discussed above reinforce a Hegelian master/slave dialectic, and result in a tendency to dehumanize members of the subjugated culture.[38] The *Exorcist* franchise extends this dialectic into the traditional exorcism narrative. *Dominion* and

Exorcist II offer similar conceptualizations of the imperialist hegemonic model, because they depict an African boy becoming more or less enslaved by a demon, while a white priest fights to save him. Unlike the African locals, Merrin genuinely cares for and wants to help the possessed Cheche; the film nevertheless reinforces the idea that the boy threatens order, and situates Merrin as the only person who can neutralize that threat. From a metaphorical standpoint, then, Cheche's possession grants him access to unlimited power and agency, but because this power subsequently renders him a threat to the symbolic order, Merrin must intervene and actively suppress that power. Thus, unlike *Abby*, the *Exorcist* franchise appears to maintain a colonialist rhetoric via how the films portray possession and exorcism.

Additionally, the portrayals of possession in *Exorcist II* and *Dominion* suggest the need for a queer analysis of possession. Indeed, exorcism films routinely depict transgressions against gender and sexuality boundaries, and such transgressions have thereby emerged as one of the traditional exorcism narrative's central concerns. A prominent example occurs in *The Exorcist*, wherein Regan's possession and her actions towards her mother represent blatant transgressions against gender boundaries and cultural taboos regarding sexuality. Similarly, Kokumo's and Cheche's (and to an extent Karras's) possessions situate them in the liminal space between male and female, which means they have transgressed gender and sexual identity and become societal outsiders.

Jill Dolan argues that Western society in particular has naturalized heterosexuality as the dominant ideology, and that such ideologies result in oppositional gender classes such as masculine and feminine.[39] It then becomes possible to destabilize the hegemony of gender and sexual binaries by "[r]ecasting sexuality as a choice" and thus subvert the idea that heterosexuality represents a compulsory state of being.[40] When applying Dolan's argument to the traditional exorcism narrative, the queer identity becomes abject because it demonstrates that notions of sexuality and gender are not inherent to biology, and such ideas can upset tradition and order. This reliance on the queer identity as a form of abjection recurs throughout *The Exorcist* franchise, from the use of Mercedes McCambridge's voice in *The Exorcist* to Cheche's androgyny in *Dominion*.[41] The continued reliance on this type of queer abjection suggest that from the beginning, in addition to portraying the oppression of female sexuality, the traditional exorcism narrative also concerns the oppression of non-heteronormative, or queer, identities.

Thus, while *The Exorcist* franchise offers some challenges to the traditional exorcism narrative, the sequels and prequels ultimately serve to expand the ways in which filmmakers can use it (either implicitly or explicitly) to comment on and maintain sociocultural norms. As such, the repeated use of this narrative establishes the boundaries and expectations of this subgenre. Moreover, the traditional exorcism narrative frequently adapts to reflect on the nature of various non-dominant groups in different historical periods, and thereby reinforces the idea that these groups must be treated with caution and fear due to their ability to upset tradition. While women apparently received the focus of oppression in the 1970s, this oppression extended to racial, gendered, and sexual orientation minorities over time, particularly as these non-dominant groups increased their activism to make their voices heard and establish themselves as equals. After the 1970s, however, exorcism cinema entered a lull period and a new horror subgenre arose to dominate the silver screen throughout the 1980s and 1990s; as that subgenre rose, exorcism cinema descended into parody.

NOTES

1. Interestingly, studio executives originally approached Boorman to direct *The Exorcist*, but the director turned it down because he considered the story "repulsive." For more, see Bob McCabe, *The Exorcist: Out of the Shadows* (New York: Omnibus Press, 1999), 158.

2. Mark Kermode "Better the Devil You Know," *The Guardian*, last modified January 24, 2004, http://www.theguardian.com/film/2004/jan/25/features.review.

3. Ibid.

4. Ibid.

5. McCabe, *Shadows*, 164.

6. Alex Fitch, "Light in the Darkness: William Peter Blatty's Faith Trilogy," *Electric Sheep Magazine*, last modified February 25, 2011, http://www.electricsheepmagazine.co.uk/features/2011/02/25/light-in-the-darkness-william-peter-blattys-faith-trilogy/comment-page-1/.

7. See chapter 5 for a more in-depth discussion of these parodies.

8. "The Exorcist III (1990)," *Rotten Tomatoes*, accessed August 7, 2015, http://www.rottentomatoes.com/m/exorcist_3/.

9. "The Exorcist III," *Box Office Mojo*, accessed August 7, 2015, http://www.boxofficemojo.com/movies/?page=main&id=exorcist3.htm.

10. According to Mark Kermode (2004), the rerelease featured eleven minutes of additional footage that helped the film "earn more than $100 million worldwide" (Online).

11. *The Exorcist* TV series debuted on the Fox Network in September 2016. For more on this project, see chapter 9 in this book.

12. Kermode, "Devil You Know."

13. Richard Lederer, quoted in McCabe, *Shadows*, 156.

14. A similar storyline occurs in *The Exorcism of Anna Ecklund* (2016, Andrew Jones) in which a young woman's exorcism ultimately reveals that she has the power to help exorcize others.

15. We should also note that while *The Exorcist* implies that the demon (which remains unnamed throughout the film) hails from the Middle East, *Exorcist II* seems to establish Pazuzu as an African deity.

16. Kokumo means "immortal" in the African and Yoruba languages. The name also suggests a liminal identity, since it is primarily bestowed upon children thought to reside in the space between the spirit realm and the world of the living. For more, see Kayode Omoniyi Ogunfolabi, "History, Horror, Reality: The Idea of the Marvelous in Postcolonial Fiction" (PhD diss., Michigan State University, 2008), 185–86.

17. Harry M. Benshoff, *Monsters in the Closet: Homosexuality and the Horror Film* (Manchester: Manchester University Press, 1997), 6.

18. Ken Gelder, "Global/Postcolonial Horror: Introduction," *Postcolonial Studies* 3, no. 1 (2000): 35–38. Italics in original.

19. Ibid., 35.

20. Kermode "Devil You Know."

21. Ibid.

22. Ibid.

23. Ibid.

24. Katharine M. Briggs describes the hag as an aged crone, or a magical creature (such as a fairy or goddess) that assumes the appearance of such a woman. The hag figure recurs throughout folklore and children's tales such as *Snow White* and *Hansel and Gretel*. Significantly, these tales frequently depict hags as malevolent, supernatural beings capable of causing great harm. For more, see Katharine M. Briggs, "Hags," in *An Encyclopedia of Fairies, Hobgoblins, Brownies, Bogies, and Other Supernatural Creatures*, (New York: Pantheon Books, 1976), 216 and Katharine M. Briggs, *The Fairies in English Tradition and Literature*, (New York: Routledge, 1967), 66–67.

25. Martyn Conterio, "Films That Time Forgot: *The Exorcist III* (1990)," *New Empress Magazine*, last modified January 22, 2013, http://newempressmagazine.com/2013/01/films-that-time-forgot-the-exorcist-iii-1990/.

26. Kermode, "Devil You Know."

27. Ibid.

28. Ibid.

29. Ibid.

30. Ibid.

31. Ibid.

32. Ibid.

33. Ibid.

34. Ibid.

35. Ibid.

36. Ibid.

37. Douglas E. Cowan, "Religion and Cinema Horror," in *Understanding Religion and Popular Culture: Theories, Themes, Products and Practices*, eds. Terry Ray Clark and Dan W. Clanton, Jr. (New York: Routledge, 2012), 66.

38. Kyle Bishop, "The Sub-Subaltern Monster: Imperialist Hegemony and the Cinematic Voodoo Zombie," *The Journal of American Culture* 31, no. 2 (2008):141–52.

39. Jill Dolan, "Ideology in Performance: Looking Through the Male Gaze," in *The Feminist Spectator as Critic* (Ann Arbor: UMI Research Press, 1988), 63.

40. Ibid., 63.

41. Daniel Humphrey, "Gender and Sexuality Haunts the Horror Film," in *A Companion to the Horror Film*, ed. Harry M. Benshoff (Malden: John Wiley & Sons, Inc., 2014), 43.

FIVE

Keeping the Devil at Bay

Slashers, Parodies, and Satirizing Religion

As discussed in the previous chapters, *The Exorcist*'s lasting cultural legacy allowed audiences around the world to become so familiar with its
narrative conventions and aesthetics that they could deconstruct these
elements and thereby uncover what made the film so terrifying. Such
insight into the film's construction likely granted viewers a greater ability
to poke fun at the artificiality of its terror-inducing moments. When a
film or an entire genre or subgenre reaches a saturation point within a
culture, audiences can more easily recognize its artifice, thus revealing its
inherent humor. Marrying humor and horror effectively removes the
threat of terror and the sensation of fear that accompanies it;[1] parodies
allow for the deconstruction and removal of horror by encouraging viewers to laugh at that which frightens them. In other words, the exorcism
parodies produced in the 1980s and 1990s highlighted *The Exorcist*'s artifice, which in turn exposed its intrinsic silliness. These parodies coincided with a relative lull period for exorcism cinema, when it seemed as
though the subgenre's time had passed.

Sotiris Petridis observes that film genres and subgenres experience
cycles of growth and decline, in part because they are "influenced by the
social, political and economic aspects of the period that they were/are
produced in."[2] Petridis's observation applies to the exorcism cinema subgenre; exorcism films primarily function as allegories for widespread sociocultural concerns regarding female sexuality and non-dominant
groups, and therefore the subgenre's effectiveness waxes and wanes in
relation to such fears. Indeed, after a brief uptick in the 1970s, the exorcism film cycle declined in the 1980s and 1990s. Only thirteen true exorcism films were produced during this period. Perhaps the sociocultural

conditions that allowed for the exorcism subgenre's rise only existed during the tumultuous 1970s. Perhaps the sense of optimism that accompanied the Reagan and Clinton administrations altered the global sociocultural landscape enough that audiences around the world became less concerned with tales of demonic influence and religious conviction, and therefore less interested in movies about possession and exorcism. In fact, for a time it appeared as though cinematic depictions of possession and exorcism might fade into obscurity altogether as Western society shifted toward neoconservative values, which in turn allowed for the emergence of a host of new social, political, and economic concerns.

A historical analysis suggests that the exorcism cinema subgenre's "lean years" coincide with an increasingly prosperous period marked by improved job growth, greater individual and corporate wealth, and an overall sense of economic stability for the mainstream middle class. Of course, the 1980s and 1990s also experienced a great deal of social and economic upheaval; indeed, the media of this period suggests widespread anxieties regarding teen sexuality and increased drug use. Yet, unlike the 1970s—a decade when the prevailing sociocultural concerns largely involved widespread economic stresses—the mainstream media and political rhetoric of the 1980s and 1990s was primarily defined by a perception of stability and prosperity, and thus any similar concerns became positioned as outliers or aberrations.

The attempt to reconcile this sense of increased affluence with persistent sociocultural anxieties regarding sex and drug use likely contributed to the exorcism cinema subgenre's decline and the slasher film's subsequent rise throughout the 1980s and into the early 1990s. While the people of the 1970s also fretted over issues of sexuality, the emergence of the neoconservative movement in the 1980s resulted in an altogether different approach to dealing with these anxieties.[3] Following his election in 1980, U.S. President Ronald Reagan urged a return to the traditional "family values" and conservative religious beliefs of the 1950s.[4] Moreover, his policies often seemed specifically designed to counteract the advances of the various civil rights movements of the 1960s and 1970s (particularly those involving women, people of color, and the non-heteronormative).[5] These radical new ideologies and sociocultural values became inextricably linked to the economic uncertainty of the 1970s, and conservatives often blamed such liberal principles for the nation's financial woes.[6] At the same time, the Christian Right ascended during the late 1970s and the United States subsequently experienced a religious revival.[7]

Additionally, the AIDS epidemic first gained widespread attention during the late 1980s and early 1990s, and for many Americans this deadly disease only reinforced the need to reinstate traditional (i.e., patriarchal and heteronormative) values regarding sex and sexuality.[8] In a sense, the AIDS epidemic reaffirmed the notion that social order depended on the suppression of non-dominant, "deviant" groups such as the non-heteronormative, and particularly the male homosexual. While exorcism cinema may seem like the perfect vehicle to explore such fears, the slasher subgenre offers a more explicit portrayal of the link between sex and death as exemplified by the AIDS epidemic,[9] which effectively ended the "free love" movement of the 1960s and 1970s. Throughout the 1980s and 1990s, stories emerged of individuals suffering slow and painful deaths caused by a poorly understood disease contracted primarily via sexual intercourse, and as a result people came to equate sex with death. Moreover, many people believed that only those who engaged in "abnormal"—that is, homosexual—behavior would succumb to this disease, initially labelled GRID (Gay Related Immune Deficiency) to reflect this perception.[10] For many people, AIDS became "an opportunity to pass moral judgement" on those who did not conform to mainstream values.[11] All of this resulted in widespread cultural anxieties regarding non-monogamous and non-heterosexual sex, which in turn contributed to the rise of neoconservatism.

Slasher films reflect such anxieties because they depict relentless killers stalking and slaying sexually uninhibited individuals who also frequently use drugs, the very activities that allowed AIDS to spread. Slashers target and kill those who indulge in behavior deemed unacceptable by society at large,[12] and thus they function as stand-ins for the disease. Carol J. Clover has argued that the slasher figure often transgresses "normal" sexual and gender boundaries,[13] which in turn links the killer to fears surrounding homosexuality and the AIDS epidemic.[14] Furthermore, the killer appears unstoppable, just as AIDS appeared incurable at the time. Indeed, though successfully dispatched by the end of the film, the killer nevertheless returns in the sequel to once again stalk and kill society's sexual deviants. Thus, slasher films more accurately reflect the anxieties generated by stories of rampant drug use, uninhibited teens, and a fatal sexually transmitted disease, and this likely explains the slasher subgenre's rise and the concurrent (albeit temporary) decline of exorcism cinema.

Hence, the slasher emerged as a cultural touchstone for the 1980s. Even when yielding to the postmodern sensibilities of the 1990s, slasher films continued to thrill their youthful audiences for over twenty years. Indeed, even *The Exorcist* franchise succumbed to the slasher's influence; released during this period, *The Exorcist III* thematically combined the figure of the psychotic or supernatural serial killers with demonic possession, and much of the film's imagery reflects that found in slasher films. For instance, a killer clad in a white sheet violently dispatches a young blonde nurse in a thoroughly terrifying sequence that in many ways foreshadows the *Scream* franchise, which features a similarly attired killer (known to fans as Ghostface).

While sociocultural anxieties regarding satanism and occultism (aka "satanic panic") persisted well into the 1980s, the exorcism cinema subgenre nevertheless waned considerably in the decades immediately following the 1970s (though plenty of possession or occult films emerged during this period). In fact, aside from *Exorcist III*, only a handful of B-movies released during this period actually qualify as exorcism films. Most notable were the exorcism parodies released during this period, particularly *Repossessed* (1990, Bob Logan), in which Linda Blair reprises her role as the possessed woman. This chapter considers the slasher film's rise and the exorcism cinema subgenre's subsequent descent into parody in relation to the prevailing sociocultural anxieties of the time.

THE RISE OF THE SLASHER

While the exorcism subgenre declined during this period, slasher films rose to dominate the horror genre. Such films frequently contain a killer (usually male, though sometimes suffering from gender confusion[15]) who uses a stabbing weapon to kill victims (primarily young, sexually active women) through shocking displays of violence only to suffer defeat at the hands of the "Final Girl" (the virginal, sometimes tomboyish heroine who dispatches the killer). Petridis identifies three distinct slasher film periods: the classical (lasting from roughly 1974 to 1989), the postmodern (occurring primarily in the 1990s), and the neoslashers (which emerged near the beginning of the New Millennium).[16] Interestingly, slasher films follow a trajectory similar to that of exorcism cinema; both subgenres emerged as a dominant model within horror for a time only to subsequently decline when audiences tired of their repetitive and altogether predictable formulas.

Yet, the postmodern attitudes of the 1990s ultimately created the conditions that allowed for a slasher film resurgence, leading to self-aware but serious slasher films like *Scream* (1996, Wes Craven) and *I Know What You Did Last Summer* (1997, Jim Gillespie). These were followed by the neoslashers, which similarly deconstructed the slasher genre's most recognizable tropes, but were less tongue-in-cheek.[17] Exorcism films experienced a similar revival after the terrorist attacks of September 11, 2001. This resurgence coincided with the rise of the neoslashers, but the exorcism films produced at the turn of the century did not reflect the same sort of postmodern shift. Instead, twenty-first century exorcism films follow the same narrative conventions established by those produced throughout the 1970s, and contain many of the same themes regarding the disempowerment of women and other non-dominant groups. We discuss the twenty-first century exorcism cinema resurgence in more detail in Chapter 7.

Like the exorcism cinema subgenre, slasher films depict female sexuality as a threat to the established order. Yet, while exorcism cinema typically features a male hero subjugating feminine sexuality, slasher films often portray a virginal woman subjugating her own sexuality. This woman—termed the Final Girl—conforms to traditional sociocultural norms because she exhibits traits commonly associated with masculinity, such as intelligence, curiosity and vigilance, while simultaneously suppressing her own female sexuality.[18] She also inhabits a masculine role because she tends to have a unisex name and performs violence.[19] In a sense, then, the Final Girl represents a queer character who transgresses gendered boundaries to promote identification from male and female viewers.

Through this queering, the Final Girl resembles the possessed woman. Yet, the Final Girl clearly functions as the hero, because she oppresses her own sexuality to restore normalcy. She thwarts the sometimes queered killer, often depicted as a man confused about his own gender.[20] The Final Girl's triumph thereby denotes the "correct" form of transgression: masculinity's continued dominance regardless of the individual's biological sex. At the same time, the Final Girl remains within the boundaries of appropriate feminine behavior as determined by patriarchal values; she maintains her virginity and refuses to abuse drugs or alcohol, and these actions render her gender transgression acceptable. Read this way, the slasher film appears every bit as antifeminist as the traditional exorcism narrative. Indeed, while some scholars contend that the Final Girl reveals the slasher subgenre's pro-feminist, anti-misogynist nature,[21] we argue that the most common reading actually supports a conservative, patriarchal perspective.[22]

Whether feminist or antifeminist, the slasher subgenre's apparent focus on sexuality suggests a continuation of the concerns seen in exorcism cinema, in which patriarchal order apparently stems from the repression of female sexuality. Slasher films, however, deal more explicitly with this issue because they often link sex with violent death, and associate the chaste Final Girl's survival with her reluctance to participate in socially unacceptable behavior. Thus, slasher films reflect one of the predominant cultural anxieties of the 1980s: the AIDS epidemic and the idea that sex potentially leads to death. Exorcism cinema, meanwhile, uses possession and exorcism as allegories for the disempowerment of sexually liberated women and other "deviant" groups. In addition, the Final Girl's use of masculine violence supports patriarchy while the possessed girl uses a masculinized voice to speak out against patriarchal oppression. So while both subgenres essentially function as morality tales, slasher films present their ideological messages in a more overt and reactionary manner, and this could explain why they displaced exorcism films as the dominant paradigm in horror for a time.

In essence, the differences between 1970s and 1980s horror films appear to reflect the various sociocultural tensions that came to define each decade. The horror films of the 1970s often depict patriarchal institutions as ineffectual because they work to repress countercultural attitudes but their efforts ultimately fail, which reflects the era's widespread mistrust of masculine social structures and traditions like patriarchal ideology.[23] This theme manifests most clearly in *The Exorcist*; Fathers Karras and Merrin (both of whom represent the symbolic father) temporarily halt the incursion of subversive attitudes regarding sex and feminine propriety, but the two heroes cannot banish these ideas entirely because they fail to destroy Satan and the evil he represents. Thus, the exorcism films produced throughout the 1970s frequently convey the idea that much like the countercultural ideologies of the time, evil cannot be completely vanquished. The fear of the Other's power, metaphorically depicted in possession, continues to threaten the world despite the power of exorcism.

Conversely, the horror films of the 1980s tend to depict the restoration of the symbolic father, a theme that reflects the overall attitude of the era, which emphasized a return to conservative, patriarchal values.[24] In other words, 1980s horror routinely reaffirmed family values while 1970s horror challenged such values. Slasher films in particular reflect a conservative ideology because they often depict the violent punishment of relaxed attitudes toward female sexuality and recreational drug use. As such, the slasher figure becomes a surrogate for the restored symbolic father. This becomes significant when considering that in slasher films, the killer inhabits the role of the monster, which in turn positions the symbolic father as monstrous or undesirable.

Yet, the monsters in these films tend to achieve pop cultural longevity and lasting significance, to a much greater degree than the Final Girls who ostensibly act as the heroes in such films. This tendency indicates that slashers (both the films and the titular killers) hold more significance for audiences of the 1980s and beyond, and thus reaffirm the dominant reading that positions the monster as the defender of proper mainstream values regarding sexuality and deviant behavior. While a viewer may watch an exorcism film and remain concerned about Others gaining power in the world, that same viewer could watch a slasher film and feel confident that such deviant threats will ultimately experience defeat. In an era that desired such stability, slasher films provided what exorcism films could not.

EXORCISM AS LAUGHING MATTER

As previously discussed, the 1980s and 1990s produced few true examples of exorcism cinema. Films like *The Evil Dead* (1981, Sam Raimi), *Evilspeak* (1981, Eric Weston), *Black Devil Doll from Hell* (1984, Chester

Novell Turner), *The Devil's Gift* (1984, Kenneth J. Berton), *Demons* (1985, Lamberto Bava), *Night of the Demons* (1988, Kevin S. Tenney), *The Church* (1989, Michele Soavi), and *The First Power* (1990, Robert Resnikoff) all depict demonic possession but do not include a subsequent exorcism to abate that possession. Thus, they do not qualify as exorcism films according to our definition. Indeed, many of the occult films produced during this era depicted demonic possession, but the exorcism ritual rarely appeared on cinema screens at this time. Instead, demonic possession was depicted in such a way that it aligned more closely with slasher films, which became increasingly gory throughout the decade and ultimately led to the so-called torture porn films produced during the early years of the twenty-first century.

Two genuine exorcism films produced in the 1980s and 1990s exist at the fringes of exploitation cinema. In fact, they resemble the international rip-offs and homages of the 1970s we discuss in chapter 3. For instance, in the Hong Kong horror film *Mo Tai* (aka *The Devil Fetus*; 1983, Hung-Chuen Lau), a demonic spirit terrorizes a young couple after they purchase a possessed vase at an auction. While the film focuses more on the possession (which interestingly lends itself to a queer reading), it nevertheless includes a brief depiction of a Taoist exorcism, complete with Kung Fu action. Also from Hong Kong, *Jing hun feng yu ye* (aka *Devil Returns*; 1982, Richard Chen Yao-Chi) tells the story of a pregnant rape victim who seeks an exorcism to remove an evil spirit from her unborn child. While both films align with the traditional exorcism narrative in a variety of ways, they also feature considerable blood and gore, and thus resemble the slasher films of this period.

Other exorcism films produced at this time border on parody. For instance, in *Ninja III: The Domination* (1984, Steve Firstenberg), a young, female aerobics instructor becomes possessed by the spirit of an evil ninja intent on avenging his death from beyond the grave. The film reflects the traditional exorcism narrative because it depicts a wanton woman as a threat to patriarchal order, positions a religious man in the role of savior, and features a brief exorcism sequence. However, *Ninja III* deviates from the narrative because the threat to that order originates when the young woman becomes possessed by the spirit of a deceased man rather than a demon, which in turn implicates maleness as a threat to established order. Likewise, *The Mangler* (1995, Tobe Hooper) features a demonically possessed laundry press in place of a bedeviled human being. Based on a short story by Stephen King, the film does feature an exorcism, but it proves ineffective because the invading entity ultimately escapes and seemingly possesses a young woman. Bordering on farcical, *The Mangler* has more in common with post-9/11 horror films due to the bleak ending in which the heroes explicitly fail to stop the onslaught of evil and restore the status quo (see chapter 7 for more on post-9/11 horror films).

Two other authentic exorcism films bookend the subgenre's lean period, and while we discuss them in greater detail in chapter 6, we should at least mention them here. *Amityville II: The Possession* (1982, Damiano Damiani) depicts both a possession and a subsequent exorcism, but it nevertheless challenges the traditional exorcism narrative because it positions a young, heterosexual, white man as the possessed individual. *Stigmata* (1999, Rupert Wainwright), meanwhile, offers a postmodern and altogether complicated approach to Catholicism, which no longer functions as a straightforward solution to female empowerment. We consider how both films challenge the traditional exorcism narrative in chapter 6. In this chapter, however, our analysis concerns how the parodies produced during the 1980s and 1990s mined comedy from the traditional exorcism narrative.

As discussed earlier in regard to the slasher film, the horror films produced during the 1990s tended to exhibit a postmodern sensibility, one that questioned the terrifying nature of all horror films. Indeed, as indicated by their use of pastiche and the rise of horror-comedies, the postmodern horror movies of this period exhibited a sense of self-awareness regarding the genre's most recognizable tropes.[25] This postmodern turn produced a handful of parody films that relied heavily on audiences' knowledge of horror tropes in general and the exorcism cinema subgenre in particular (indeed, such films regularly lampooned *The Exorcist*). In other words, intertextuality represents an important characteristic of the humor in these parodies, suggesting a cultural saturation of the exorcism cinema subgenre's tropes, which in turn allowed horror fans to comprehend jokes based on these tropes.

The parodies discussed below demonstrate this postmodern approach to deconstructing narrative conventions because they satirize *The Exorcist* by primarily highlighting its artifice.[26] *L'esorciccio* (aka *The Exorcist: Italian Style*; 1975, Ciccio Ingrassia) was the first film to satirize *The Exorcist*, only two years after that seminal film's release. Similar and increasingly common lampooning occurred throughout the late 1980s through the 1990s, including in the Looney Toons short, *The Duxorcist* (1987, Greg Ford and Terry Lennon), and sketch comedy duo French and Saunders's 1990 parody of *The Exorcist*. Similarly, the horror-comedy *Beetlejuice* (1988, Tim Burton) flips the traditional exorcism script and thus ostensibly functions as a parody; the film involves the eponymous bio-exorcist's attempts to drive living beings from a house that once belonged to a young couple who were killed in a car accident and returned as restless spirits. *Scary Movie 2* (2001, Keenen Ivory Wayans), meanwhile, includes a scene clearly inspired by Regan's onscreen possession, and the unreleased anthology film *Undershorts* (1987, Bryan Michael Stoller) contains a sketch in which Linda Blair parodies her most iconic role by playing both the mother and the daughter (who has become possessed by the spirits of comedians).[27]

A parody typically uses "an ironic exaggeration of style or manner" to comment on some pre-existing text.[28] Yet, this type of deconstruction still allows filmmakers to address sociocultural and historical matters, such as the rise of the religious right in the 1980s. Such commentary occurs in both of the films analyzed in this chapter. To better understand this phenomenon, we first examine a parody that directly satirizes *The Exorcist*, and then we turn our attention to a film that lampoons the horror genre in general and exorcism cinema in particular. While parodies frequently highlight an original film's artificiality in their effort to challenge the seriousness of its premise, both *Repossessed* and *Teenage Exorcist* (1991, Grant Austin Waldman) do little to challenge the traditional exorcism narrative. Each film pokes fun at *The Exorcist* by deconstructing how it presents its narrative rather than by critiquing the narrative itself.

Distributed by New Line Cinema, *Repossessed* received a limited theatrical release in September 1990. Starring Linda Blair (essentially reprising her role as Regan in *The Exorcist*) and Leslie Nielsen, the film received consistently negative reviews upon release, with one critic writing it "goes to the devil almost as soon as it starts—though hell can't be much worse than 90 minutes of these pea soup, 'Love Boat' and Holy Evian Water gags."[29] Even the film's theme song, "He's Coming Back (The Devil)," written and performed by Chris LeVrar, received a Golden Raspberry Award for Worst Original Song. Despite its poor reception and even poorer reputation, *Repossessed* nevertheless offers some vital insight into how the traditional exorcism narrative persisted even during the subgenre's lean years.

Repossessed opens in 1973 (the same year *The Exorcist* debuted in theaters) as Father Jedediah Mayii (Nielson) exorcises a young possessed girl named Nancy.[30] Seventeen years later, Nancy (Blair) becomes repossessed while watching the religious television program "The Ernest and Fanny Miracle Hour." She turns to Father Luke Brophy (Anthony Starke) for help, and he in turn implores Father Mayii to assist with the exorcism. Mayii refuses, however, because he barely survived Nancy's previous exorcism and fears his weak heart cannot withstand another attempt. Brophy then consults the Supreme Council for Exorcism Granting, where he meets popular televangelists Ernest and Fanny Ray Weller (Ned Beatty and Lana Schwab, respectively). Ernest offers to assist with the exorcism, but only if the council allows him to televise the event. While the televangelists only care about the profits this show will generate, the council enthusiastically agrees to Ernest's terms because they believe the spectacle will convert millions of viewers. During the exorcism, however, the devil attempts to claim the souls of everyone in the viewing audience, but Father Brophy manages to cut the broadcast before the demon can achieve its nefarious goal. Shortly afterward, a reinvigorated Father Mayii arrives to exorcise Nancy. When he learns that the demon hates rock and roll music, he banishes the invading entity back to Hell by performing the song "Devil With The Blue Dress."

Repossessed maintains and reinforces the traditional exorcism narrative's most common tropes, particularly those that deal with the repression of female sexuality, even as it satirizes *The Exorcist*. While the film directly parodies cinematic depictions of possession and exorcism, its portrayal of both nevertheless reinforces the subgenre's central message: the possessed woman threatens order, and a male priest must act to cast out the demon, thus reaffirming both his faith and patriarchal authority. Prior to her repossession, Nancy occupies the dual roles of complacent housewife and perfect mother, largely because her initial exorcism encouraged her to lead a moral life. In essence, her ordeal caused her to internalize predominant societal expectations regarding proper feminine behavior, as predicted by the traditional exorcism narrative. Furthermore, she becomes distressed when she realizes she has become repossessed despite conforming to male expectations of feminine decency. When the demon repossesses Nancy, she not only becomes a threat to those around her, but also to the very notion of patriarchal order as exemplified by the domestic ideal.

Nancy jeopardizes the symbolic order primarily because her possession enables her to speak out against the confines of her domestic life. She initially hides her possession from her family—she never told them about her previous exorcism, either—and this secrecy hints at the corruption hidden just beneath the surface of her seemingly idyllic life. The demon grants Nancy the power to voice her suppressed rage and frustration, such as when she angrily reprimands her family for playing with a Ouija board (the same activity that caused Regan's possession in *The Exorcist*). In effect, possession allows Nancy to speak out against the distinctly paternal vision of the model housewife.

Significantly, possession also reveals her hidden or suppressed urges. Nancy and her family live on Sex Drive, a gag that likely refers to Nancy's own suppressed sexual impulses. Once she becomes repossessed, however, Nancy exhibits increasingly sexual behavior. For instance, during Father Brophy's initial visit, Nancy attacks the handsome young priest, tossing him on to the bed and straddling him in an overtly sexual way. This sequence suggests that possession allows Nancy to express both her anger and her sexual desires, and thus upset the traditional domestic order. The film further positions Nancy as a threat when the invading demon attempts to possess millions of other unsuspecting victims via the television screen. During this sequence, Nancy threatens society because her possession could potentially corrupt others, which in turn suggests that female empowerment threatens the established social order. Thus, the film depicts the possessed Nancy—and by extension empowered women—as a threat to her family, to those around her, and finally to the entire world.

The film further emphasizes this idea by repeatedly mocking strong women (i.e., empowered, sexually active women) to undermine the threat they pose to masculine order. Indeed, *Repossessed* utilizes recurring PMS jokes to explain away Nancy's erratic behavior. For example, when Father Brophy determines that Nancy has become repossessed, her daughter readily accepts this explanation but her son blames PMS for Nancy's unruly behavior. Later, when Brophy asks Father Mayii to help perform the exorcism, Mayii also wonders if PMS could explain Nancy's condition. Other jokes, meanwhile, portray women as both weak and domineering, which renders them undesirable and also restores them to a marginalized position. For example, during the televised exorcism the possessed Nancy screams out "Mayii!" at which point Father Mayii turns to the camera and deadpans, "And they wonder why priests never get married." Later professional wrestling announcer "Mean" Gene Okerlund declares that Father Mayii will triumph over the possessed Nancy because she is, after all, just a woman. Similarly, the demon implies that it could more easily kill Father Mayii if only he were a woman. Thus, *Reposssessed* uses misogynistic humor to disempower women and marginalize female sexuality.

In another nod to *The Exorcist*, *Repossessed* also includes the doubting priest figure. Father Brophy assumes this role because of his self-doubt and initial skepticism regarding demonic possession. During the early stages of her possession, Nancy mocks Brophy for placing so much faith in a God he has never seen, but Brophy retorts that he does not need to see God to know He exists. Despite this boast, however, Brophy suffers from doubt throughout the film. For instance, he personally witnesses the possessed Nancy performing supernatural acts, yet he still worries that he has lost his faith in a higher power. Later, Mayii suggests that God may be using Nancy's possession to test and subsequently reaffirm Brophy's faith; by saving Nancy, the young priest can save himself. This assertion leads to a satirical workout montage that parodies similar contemporary training montages in films like *Rocky IV* (1985, Sylvester Stallone) and *Bloodsport* (1988, Newt Arnold). In this sequence, Mayii endeavors to become stronger physically while encouraging Brophy to become stronger spiritually.

Yet, *Repossessed* also ridicules the religious figures by using heteronormative and non-heteronormative sexuality to reveal the priests' own deviance and incompetence. For example, Mayii is routinely aroused by women's breasts, which suggests that he harbors sexual desires that conflict with his station and thus undermine his authority. Meanwhile, in another moment that clearly references *The Exorcist*, Brophy commands the devil to leave Nancy's body and enter his, and the film uses this event to satirize male homosexuality; after the devil enters Brophy's body, Mayii pulls the younger priest into an embrace and exclaims "It's my body you want! Enter me! Enter me!" This double entendre suggests that

Mayii wishes to have homosexual intercourse with the younger priest. Then, the devil enters Mayii, whose vestments change into women's clothing (complete with pronounced feminine breasts). Thus, the film relies on sexuality and transgressive queering to undermine the religious figures tasked with upholding patriarchal order.

Repossessed similarly spoofs televangelists by portraying them as greedy and faithless. The film clearly patterns Ernest and Fanny Ray after infamous 1980s televangelists Jim and Tammy Faye Bakker.[31] Like Reverend Cotton Marcus in *The Last Exorcism* (which we discuss in chapter 8), the Rays initially use trickery and special effects to fake the televised exorcism. Moreover, they use the event as an excuse to swindle their audience, claiming the devil will only appear if viewers donate money. Thus, instead of serious, dedicated, and competent priests like Karras and Merrin, *Repossessed* depicts religious figures as incompetent sexual deviants and/or faithless swindlers, and this in turn suggests a contempt for Catholicism in particular and organized religion in general. *Repossessed*, then, departs from the traditional exorcism narrative because in that it satirizes these patriarchal figures, but it ultimately reinforces the central idea regarding the need to defend patriarchy from empowered women. In other words, *Repossessed* questions the patriarchy, but ultimately reaffirms its authority.

Teenage Exorcist similarly lampoons and reaffirms the traditional exorcism narrative. Shot in 1991 but not released until 1994, the film bypassed theatrical release and went straight to video. Written by star Brinke Stevens, the film uses lowbrow humor akin to that of other sex comedies produced during this period to satirize the demonic possession movies of the 1980s. Interestingly, Stevens originally envisioned the titular character as a cute teenage girl, but hastily rewrote the role when cult star Eddie Deezen came on board the production.[32] While the film's depiction of possession and exorcism includes elements intended for comedic effect, the underlying themes still involve a possessed woman asserting control over her sexuality and thus threatening patriarchal order.

At the same time, the film deviates from the traditional exorcism narrative because it does not include the doubting priest figure. *Teenage Exorcist*'s patriarchal representatives differ greatly from those depicted in straightforward exorcism films. For instance, the film portrays the priest as inept and incapable of saving the possessed woman and thereby restoring order. In addition, the film queers the one character who exemplifies the sort of ideal masculinity with sitcom fathers of the 1950s and 1960s, such as those appearing in *Leave it to Beaver* and *Father Knows Best*. Thus, like *Repossessed*, *Teenage Exorcist* lampoons both religion and paternal law, and thereby destabilizes patriarchal authority. Nevertheless, while *Teenage Exorcist* challenges men's roles in the traditional exorcism narrative, it still portrays a sexually liberated woman as a danger to society.

In the film, virginal young college student Diane (Stevens) rents a spacious Hollywood home haunted by an ancient demon (Oliver Darrow) summoned years earlier by the previous owner, the wicked Baron DeSade (Hoke Howell). The demon wastes no time in possessing the bookish but nubile Diane and turning her into a sex-crazed succubus. Around this time, Diane's sister, Sally (Elena Sahagun), her brother-in-law, Mike (Jay Richardson), and her boyfriend, Jeff (Tom Shell), all arrive for a visit, but the possessed Diane attacks them, prompting the trio to summon local priest Father McFerrin (Robert Quarry). After failing to drive the demon out, Father McFerrin tries to contact an exorcist, but instead calls the local pizza parlor and accidentally places an order. Soon afterward, a delivery boy named Eddie (Eddie Deezen) arrives and joins the others in their battle against the nefarious demon. Jeff eventually dispels the demon and saves the day.

Like the majority of exorcism films, *Teenage Exorcist* portrays female sexuality and empowerment as dangerous. The film immediately establishes Diane as independent and self-reliant; she even tells her would-be suitor, Jeff, that she prefers living alone. This independent streak likely renders her more susceptible to demonic possession. At the same time, however, the film initially portrays Diane as virtuous; prior to her possession, she wears a chaste white nightgown, signifying her innocence. Her sister's husband, Mike, reinforces this perception when he refers to Diane as an uptight, mousy virgin.

After she becomes possessed, however, Diane's attire changes to reflect her new, far more sexually aggressive personality. First, she lounges in a sexy black negligee, and then dons a dominatrix outfit, complete with a whip. She also drinks and smokes, much to the chagrin of Mike and Sally, and she openly flirts with all the men in the movie, explaining that she wants to experience all the pleasures she previously denied herself. While Diane appears to take pleasure in her newfound vices and promiscuity, those around her react with horror and disgust. Even Jeff recoils from her sexual advances. The film perpetuates the idea behind the virgin/whore dichotomy, which states that women become impure when they engage in hedonistic activities. Thus, *Teenage Exorcist* renders the possessed Diane as abject, and consequently implicates female sexuality as a threat to order and stability.

The film also links Diane's demonically-induced sexuality to power. At one point, Diane announces that she can feel her powers growing, and, still dressed in her dominatrix outfit, she whips a zombie and commands it to terrorize Jeff and the others. Indeed, she controls a horde of male zombies during this sequence, and thus the film suggests that Diane's newfound sex appeal grants her power over men, who become mindless brutes when faced with such uninhibited sexuality. Moreover, the exorcism fails to undermine this power. Instead, the film neutralizes Diane's threatening sexuality by revealing her as incompetent in matters of sex. First, she fails to acquire the virginal sacrifice the baron requires, and later she attempts to seduce Eddie, but he seduces her instead. Thus, much like *Repossessed*, *Teenage Exorcist* treats the idea of a smart, independent, and sexually uninhibited woman as a joke, and thereby undermines her power.

Furthermore, the film ultimately places Baron DeSade in control of Diane's power; when he dies, Diane reverts to her previous state of innocence. More importantly, perhaps, Diane's story concludes with her wrapped in Jeff's protective embrace. As such, the film reinforces the idea that Diane (aka the empowered, sexually uninhibited woman) has relinquished her power and become subservient to another man rather than return to her previous state of feminine independence. Thus, the movie ends with Diane inhabiting a far more repressed state than she did at the beginning.

Yet, like *Repossessed*, *Teenage Exorcist* offers a slight challenge to the traditional exorcism narrative, because it depicts the priest figure as incompetent. Father McFerrin arrives and attempts to exorcise Diane in a sequence that both recalls and subverts *The Exorcist*'s climactic exorcism sequence. McFerrin stands over the young woman and chants "The Power of Christ compels you to leave," but he fails to cast out the demon and free her soul. Later, he botches his attempt to call for backup when he accidentally summons a pizza delivery boy rather than an exorcist. He even highlights his own incompetence when he admits that he only knows how to perform last rites. Thus, the film positions Father McFerrin as a joke from the start.

The film also uses sexual deviance to ridicule Father McFerrin. When he arrives at the house, he mistakenly hands Mike a card from a "full service" massage parlor, suggesting that, much like Father Mayii in *Repossessed*, this supposed holy man has forsaken his vows and indulged in sins of the flesh. McFerrin does not doubt his faith, but neither does he conform to the image of the capable religious figures portrayed in other exorcism films. Both his incompetence and his sinfulness render him incapable of defeating the demonic force that inhabits the house. Thus, *Teenage Exorcist* undermines patriarchal authority by portraying the priest as both deviant and inept.

Additionally, the film ridicules and queers Mike to destabilize the image of the ideal 1950s man commonly associated with patriarchal authority. In *Teenage Exorcist*, Mike represents the patriarchal ideal complete with his pipe and his nebulous position in the business world. In a highly intertextual moment, Mike recognizes the possessed Diane as a threat because her behavior reminds him of Regan in *The Exorcist*, at which point he asserts his paternal authority; he calls Jeff "kid" and thereby positions himself as the man in charge. As the horror increases, however, the film rapidly undermines Mike's confidence and his competence in ways that suggest a queering of his character. In one scene, for instance, Mike and Jeff accidentally hold hands, but instead of panicking, they simply shrug and continue holding hands. In addition to establishing a homosexual subtext, this scene represents a turning point for the characters, with Jeff becoming the brave hero while Mike assumes the role of the cowardly victim. Indeed, Mike even tries to flee the house at one point, content to abandon Diane and the others and consign the world to its ultimate fate.

Thus, *Teenage Exorcist* casts doubts about Mike's masculinity (and masculinity in general). Later, the film further emphasizes this uncertainty; Mike becomes explicitly feminized when Diane garbs him in a white dress and straps him to a table as a sacrifice to the demon, who mistakes Mike for a virginal young woman. Diane then applies makeup to Mike's face and anoints him with perfume. Afterward, instead of rejecting his newfound femininity, Mike wonders aloud if his new look suits him. Thus, *Teenage Exorcist* portrays yet another representative of patriarchal authority as incompetent, cowardly, effeminate, and perhaps mentally broken. Such feminization serves to satirize the conservative patriarchal ideologies commonly found in exorcism films. *Teenage Exorcist* thereby destabilizes the traditional exorcism narrative by exalting a non-dominant masculine figure as heroic, even as it reinforces the narrative's central theme by promoting the repression of female sexuality and independence.

CHANGING ANXIETIES AND THE TRADITIONAL EXORCISM NARRATIVE

Throughout the 1980s and into the 1990s, fears surrounding the AIDS epidemic combined with concerns over teenage sexuality and drug use, and the United States responded to these tensions with a new wave of conservatism. The widespread backlash to sexuality manifested most overtly in the slasher film, in which only the virginal Final Girl survives the serial killer's onslaught. Indeed, such films closely aligned with the prevailing sociocultural norms of the time and therefore did not need to couch their views on sexuality in metaphorical terms. In other words, whereas the traditional exorcism narrative metaphorically reflects issues regarding the subjugation of women and non-dominant groups, slasher films use gore and jump scares to teach lessons about the dangers of sex and uninhibited female sexuality. Thus, slashers explicitly confront issues that exorcism cinema only hints at, which could explain why the latter declined as the former ascended.

Furthermore, the postmodern shift that occurred in popular culture throughout the 1990s affected both slasher films and exorcism cinema to differing degrees. Slasher films experienced a second cycle during which they became increasingly self-referential, but nevertheless remained serious. The 1990s also saw the return of more progressive social values, a shift reflected in this horror subgenre. According to Petridis, this period "helped slasher films to branch off in a new direction away from sexual punishment and [leave] behind the standardized classical conventions."[33] In other words, the postmodern slashers produced during this period reflect a more liberal view on teenage sexuality. Postmodern slasher films deconstruct the subgenre's central concern—that is, the relationship between sex and death—by suggesting that the Final Girl need not remain virginal to survive and that such films need not adhere quite so stringently to the virgin/whore dichotomy. As such, postmodern slasher films almost satirize conservative views regarding sexuality.

During this same period, few true exorcism films emerged, and those that did became increasingly self-referential. However, while slasher films remained horrific, the exorcism subgenre largely descended into parody. A more general deconstruction of exorcism cinema may not have occurred during this period because, unlike the slasher film, the subgenre had received less social and academic consideration. Until the resurgence, *The Exorcist* remained the most widely known exorcism film. The movies discussed in chapter 3 were low budget and/or foreign films with low distribution. Among mainstream audiences, such films likely remained obscure or unknown, and even horror aficionados at the time would have had a difficult time locating the films. Thus, the exorcism films produced during this period likely flew under the radar and were therefore subject to less sociocultural scrutiny, critique, and self-reflection.

A similar lack of scrutiny and introspection has thus far accompanied the films produced during the exorcism resurgence period discussed in chapter 7. When we described our conceptualization of the traditional exorcism narrative to Daniel Stamm, director of *The Last Exorcism* (2010), he expressed surprise at our reading of his film, and was concerned that he had made "such a non-feminist movie."[34] He went on to describe how even five years later, no one had approached him with this feminist reading of the film.[35] Interestingly, during the conversation, he described how the original conception of the film would have produced a more postmodern text.[36] In the original draft, the exorcist would have been revealed as a fake who modeled his exorcisms on those portrayed in *The Exorcist*; indeed, this idea called for Reverend Cotton to watch that movie in *The Last Exorcism*, suggesting a more intertextual narrative.[37] However, the producers scrapped that version in favor of one that more closely aligned with the traditional exorcism narrative.[38] If contemporary exorcism films fail to engage in such deconstruction, it should come as no surprise that the films produced during the 1980s and 1990s similarly fail to do so. Such exorcism films demonstrate a postmodernist approach only in how they ridicule and deconstruct the artifice of the best-known exorcism movie, *The Exorcist*.

Furthermore, while the parodies produced during this time did not lampoon conservative notions of sexuality in the same way as the postmodern slashers, they nevertheless poked fun at Reagan-era ideas regarding patriarchy, masculinity, and traditional religious beliefs/practices. Both *Repossessed* and *Teenage Exorcist* mock religious figures, patriarchal institutions, and paternal authority primarily because they ridicule men of faith and traditional values. For example, *Repossessed* depicts Ernest and Fanny Ray Weller as crooks and liars who use religion to gain fame and riches, and this portrayal reflects a cultural perception of disgraced televangelists like Jimmy Swaggert or the Bakkers. Thus, the film mocks televangelism, which negatively impacted how people viewed organized religion. Indeed, whereas a straightforward film like *The Exorcist* appears more respectful and reverential toward religion, parodies like *Repossessed* and *Teenage Exorcist* use irony to advance a post-Christian attitude and dismantle the concepts of faith and belief. This rhetorical positioning reflects the postmodern sensibilities of the 1990s.

Yet, these films still portrayed female sexuality as a threat. *Repossessed* mocked this idea by making Nancy the butt of jokes about women, but she still threatened her family and society at large. Similarly, *Teenage Exorcist* responded to second-wave feminism by satirizing softer masculinities and thereby undercutting the rise of the "New Man";[39] that is, the film's jokes frequently demonstrate the inadequacies of feminized men like Mike and Eddie. Thus, unlike the postmodern slasher films of the period, which deconstructed the overwhelmingly negative depiction of female sexuality during the subgenre's classical period, these exorcism parodies fail to deconstruct the recurring possessed-woman-as-threat figure. Instead, such films reaffirm this trope and reinforce the idea that women should occupy domestic and subservient roles, even as they mock religion to satirize patriarchal figures.

Ultimately, slasher films more accurately reflected the anxieties of the 1980s and 1990s because depictions of realistic serial killers provoked more immediate anxiety than the thought of supernatural forces operating in the world. The terrorist attacks of 9/11, however, inspired a whole new set of sociocultural anxieties; people around the world feared sudden, unexpected violence, and they became increasingly anxious about religion. For some, these conditions only reaffirmed the belief that the Devil exists and continues to exert influence over the modern world. Moreover, while the United States seemingly became more conservative after 9/11, sociocultural anxieties focused chiefly on terrorism rather than sex because this time gave rise to a prevailing view that racial, cultural, and religious Others threatened to topple Western civilization's stability and prosperity. The horror genre experienced a similar shift as it attempted to reflect these new fears. Indeed, as Petridis notes, the post-9/11 neoslashers decoupled sex and death, and focused more on the randomness of death by linking slashers to terror.[40] Much like the effort to understand the terrorists' motivation, then, slasher films explored questions about evil's creation by portraying killers with more psychologically realistic motivations.[41]

Exorcism films produced during the subgenre's twenty-first-century resurgence exhibited a similar shift toward realism. In the next chapter, we consider three films that predate the exorcism cinema's resurgence, but which presaged the subgenre's shift toward realism in the New Millennium. These films challenge the traditional exorcism narrative in several significant ways, but nevertheless continue to reaffirm it along the lines we have previously discussed. While the films analyzed in chapter 6 demonstrate the potential to resist the exorcism cinema subgenre's boundaries, those analyzed in chapter 7 seemingly ignore these possibilities entirely and instead reaffirm the oppressive ideologies perpetuated by the traditional exorcism narrative. Significantly, the primary difference between these films lies in the sociocultural conditions that existed at the times of their production.

NOTES

1. Isabel Pinedo, "Recreational Terror: Postmodern Elements of the Contemporary Horror Film," *Journal of Film and Video* 48, no. 1/2 (1996): 28–29.
2. Sotiris Petridis, "A Historical Approach to the Slasher Film," *Film International* 12, no. 1 (2014): 77.
3. Ibid., 77–79.
4. See Petridis, "Historical Approach," 77–79 and Harry M. Benshoff, *Monsters in the Closet: Homosexuality and the Horror Film* (New York: Manchester University Press, 1997), 239.
5. Ibid.
6. Graham Thompson, *American Culture in the 1980s* (Edinburgh: Edinburgh University Press, 2007), 9–15.
7. Ibid.
8. See Petridis, "Historical Approach," 80 and Benshoff, *Monsters*, 230.
9. Benshoff, *Monsters*, 231.
10. Thompson, *American Culture*, 21.
11. Ibid.
12. Petridis, "Historical Approach," 80.
13. Carol J. Clover, *Men, Women and Chainsaws: Gender in the Modern Horror Film* (Princeton: Princeton University Press, 1992), 26–30.
14. Benshoff, *Monsters*, 2.
15. This trend of gender confusion seems to have originated with the proto-slasher film *Psycho* (1960, Alfred Hitchcock), which features a male killer who dresses as a woman. Similarly, in *The Texas Chainsaw Massacre* (1974, Tobe Hooper), Leatherface engages in a grisly form of crossdressing when he wears the face of one of his female victims. Meanwhile, *Sleepaway Camp* (1983, Robert Hiltzik) represents another notable example of a slasher film that features a transgender antagonist; the film ultimately reveals that the female killer (a rare occurrence in slasher films) "Angela" actually has male genitalia. Other slashers that feature gender confused killers include *Dressed to Kill* (1980, Brian De Palma), *Cherry Falls* (2000, Geoffrey Wright), and the 2006 remake of *Black Christmas* directed by Glen Morgan.
16. Sotiris Petridis's taxonomy of the slasher film resembles Clover's own. For more see Petridis, "Historical Approach," 76 and Clover, *Chain Saws*, 23–26.

17. Petridis, "Historical Approach," 82.

18. Clover, *Chain Saws*, 39–40.

19. Ibid., 40.

20. Ibid., 27

21. For instance, see Nicholas Rogers, *Halloween: From Pagan Ritual to Party Night* (Oxford: Oxford University Press, 2002), 118, 120.

22. For more on how this conservative reading correlates sex and death and thus condemns female sexuality, see Clover, *Chain Saws*, Petridis, "Historical Approach," and James Kendrick, "Slasher Films and Gore in the 1980s," in *A Companion to the Horror Film*, ed. Harry M. Benshoff (Malden: Wiley Blackwell, 2014), 320.

23. Robin Wood. *Hollywood from Vietnam to Reagan . . . and Beyond* (2003, New York: Columbia University Press), 44, 78.

24. Ibid., 152.

25. Kevin J. Wetmore, *Post-9/11 Horror in American Cinema* (New York: Continuum, 2012), 194.

26. According to Bob McCabe (1999), "*The Exorcist* remains one of the most parodied movies of all time" (176).

27. Bob McCabe, *The Exorcist: Out of the Shadows* (New York: Omnibus Press, 1999), 176–77.

28. Jonathan L. Crane, "'It was a Dark and Stormy Night . . . ': Horror Films and the Problem of Irony," in *Horror Film and Psychoanalysis: Freud's Worst Nightmare*, ed. Steven Jay Schneider (Boston, Cambridge University Press, 2004), 146.

29. Michael Wilmington, "San Diego Movie Reviews: 'Repossessed': Devil Made Them Do It," *Los Angeles Times*, accessed September 24, 2015, http://articles.latimes.com/1990-09-25/entertainment/ca-1326_1_san-diego-movie-reviews.

30. Likely a reference to former First Lady, Nancy Reagan.

31. Thompson, *American Culture*, 16–17.

32. "Teenage Exorcist (1991), *buried.com*, last modified February 16, 2008, http://www.buried.com/horrormovies/teenage-exorcist-1991/4373/.

33. Petridis, "Historical Approach," 81.

34. Daniel Stamm (film director) in discussion with the authors, June 7, 2015.

35. Ibid.

36. Ibid.

37. Ibid.

38. Ibid. For more on *The Last Exorcism*, see chapter 8 in this volume.

39. For more on the concept of the New Man, see Michael A. Messner, "'Changing Men' and Feminist Politics in the United States," *Theory and Society* 22, no. 5 (1993): 723–37.

40. Petridis, "Historical Approach," 83.

41. Ibid.

SIX

Dangerous Boys and Rebellious Priests

Possessed *and the Real Story of* The Exorcist

When William Peter Blatty set out to write a story about religion in the modern world, he learned of a Maryland family allegedly involved in one of the few—if not the only at that time—documented and thus official cases of exorcism in the United States.[1] In this case, a fourteen-year-old boy known only as "Roland Doe" endured a months-long exorcism after supposedly becoming possessed by demonic forces.[2] Blatty first learned of the story while a junior at Georgetown University, after discovering the original *Washington Post* article from 1949 in the school archives.[3] Over the years, Blatty has stated that he believed this story proved the existence of angels, demons, God, and "a life everlasting."[4] He hoped that by sharing this harrowing tale, he could inspire and/or reinvigorate religious belief in others.[5] Blatty wrote *The Exorcist* a few years later.[6] According to Alexandra Heller-Nicholas, the author originally intended his story as a factual account of the Maryland boy's predicament, but when the family opted not to participate, he fictionalized the tale.[7] Thus, when it came time to actually write the story, Blatty changed the details, inventing the characters, settings, and tensions that would become immortalized in *The Exorcist*.

Most notably, at least for the purposes of this book, Blatty swapped the possessed child's biological sex from male to female. In the years after *The Exorcist*'s publication, the author remained evasive about exactly why he changed the child from a boy to a girl, claiming in interviews that it was simply a way to protect the family's identities.[8] Yet, William Paul contends that the possessed person's gender impacts how audiences experience the film, primarily because of the way society constructs masculine and feminine behaviors. *The Exorcist* (both the book and the film) suggests Pazuzu actually targets Father Merrin, and therefore any child could have served as the demon's vessel for revenge. Yet, Blatty specifically situates a young girl in the role of the possessed individual, and thus Regan's sex becomes significant, particularly when considering that in Western society and culture it is more common and acceptable for a boy to have "a bit of the Devil in him."[9] As such, Regan's demonic possession and grotesqueness renders *The Exorcist*'s narrative more exciting and disturbing primarily because a young girl exhibits unorthodox behavior. Yet, Blatty contends that the child's biological sex holds less importance than the story's religious overtones.

Blatty's novel appears to reflect his beliefs and experiences more than the facts of the case, and indeed, in many ways, his life paralleled *The Exorcist*.[10] For instance, much like Regan's mother, Blatty's own overprotective mother, Mary, ignored his emotional needs and frequently spoke ill of his absent father, who left when the author was only three years old.[11] Unlike the staunchly atheistic Chris MacNeil, however, Mary was a devout Catholic, which likely accounts for Blatty's own deeply held faith. Despite their emotional separation, Mary's death from myocardial infarction in 1967 devastated Blatty, who at that time worked as a screenwriter on such films as Blake Edwards' *A Shot in the Dark* (1964) and *Darling Lili* (1970). For a time, Blatty found that he could not mourn his mother's passing. After writing *The Exorcist*, however, he claims to have encountered various supernatural phenomena, including poltergeist activity and omens of future events, and this glimpse into the afterlife helped him come to terms with Mary's death.

While Blatty offered a fictionalized account of the Maryland possession case in his novel, a movie that purports to tell the true story behind this incident was produced in 2000. Directed by Steven E. de Souza, the telefilm *Possessed* initially premiered on the premium cable channel Showtime and was later released on DVD. Given our focus on films inspired by or in some way related to *The Exorcist*, we include *Possessed* as part of our project because the producers claim it more accurately depicts the events that inspired Blatty's novel. Interestingly, *Possessed* recalls *Amityville II: The Possession* (1982, Damiano Damiani) in that it depicts the possession and subsequent exorcism of a young, white boy, an altogether rare occurrence in the exorcism cinema subgenre. Therefore, the film raises several questions regarding why so few exorcism films portrayed demonically possessed Caucasian boys, and why the majority of exorcism films that followed maintained the focus on possessed women.

In this chapter, we examine how the depictions of possessed boys in *Amityville II* and *Possessed* both resemble and contradict those featured in *Exorcist II: The Heretic* and *Dominion: Prequel to the Exorcist*. Additionally, this chapter considers how the film *Stigmata* (1999, Rupert Wainwright) challenges prevailing contemporary dogmatic thought that situates the Church as a force for good, but otherwise maintains the traditional exorcism narrative. Indeed, much like the parodies discussed in the previous chapter, *Stigmata* offers a fairly scathing criticism of the Church. Across all three films, the depictions of possession and exorcism challenge the traditional exorcism narrative in a variety of ways, demonstrating that the lull period likely allowed for further exploration of the exorcism cinema subgenre's boundaries. Yet, while these films challenge the traditional exorcism narrative in some ways, they nevertheless reaffirm the patriarchal attitudes that tend to define the exorcism cinema subgenre.

THE "TRUE" STORY OF *THE EXORCIST*

As mentioned above, *The Exorcist* offers a heavily fictionalized account of a 1949 case of possession and exorcism that occurred in Mount Rainier, Maryland.[12] According to reports, the boy known only as "Roland Doe" shared a close relationship with his aunt, a spiritualist who claimed to have psychic abilities. She also taught Roland how to use the Ouija board to contact the spirit realm. After her death, strange noises could be heard coming from Roland's bedroom, and objects supposedly moved of their own accord whenever he entered a room. Once, he even appeared to levitate in a chair. Additionally, the boy often lapsed into long blackouts, and he suffered violent seizures. Roland's distraught parents brought him to Georgetown University Hospital for evaluation, but the doctors there could find nothing wrong with him. Eventually, the family contacted Jesuit priests, who determined that Roland had become possessed and opted to perform an exorcism.

The procedure lasted for five nights, and only ended when Roland "[pried] loose a spring from his bed and sliced one of the priest's arms open."[13] Following this incident, the word "Louis" appeared in the teenager's flesh, and the priests took this as sign to move him to a hospital in St. Louis, where a different set of Jesuit priests performed the rituals, which continued for several more weeks.[14] These priests later recalled witnessing as arrows, the word "HELL," and an image of a winged bat or devil appeared in Roland's flesh.[15] Shortly before Easter, the boy reportedly spoke with a deep, otherworldly voice and identified himself as the Archangel Michael. He then uttered the Latin words *"dominus vo-viscom,"*[16] at which point an explosive bang reverberated throughout the hospital. Roland then awoke and seemed to have no memory of his possession.

Stories of exorcisms date back centuries, but the Maryland case remains one of the most comprehensively documented incidents. Thomas B. Allen offers a historical account of this incident in his nonfiction book, *Possessed*. Published in 1993, the book allegedly chronicles the true details of the exorcism that so captivated and inspired Blatty, while still retaining the anonymity of "Roland Doe" and his family. The priests who performed the exorcism supposedly provided details about the events that led them to determine that the boy had become possessed and thus required an exorcism.[17] *The Exorcist*'s highly successful twenty-fifth anniversary rerelease generated a renewed interest in tales of exorcism (as discussed in the next chapter), so it should come as no surprise that Showtime decided to capitalize on this interest by producing an adaptation of Allen's book. Interestingly, while the book suggests a rational explanation for the possession, the movie foregrounds the supernatural explanation that so enticed Blatty and enraptured audiences around the world for decades.[18]

Set during the early 1950s, the film focuses on William S. Bowden (Timothy Dalton), a former U.S. Army chaplain who lost his faith and descended into alcoholism due to his harrowing experiences during World War II. Bowden now teaches at St. Louis University, a school on the brink of racial integration. During a riotous civil rights demonstration, Bowden attacks the police, who arrest him. Not long after, Father Raymond McBride (Henry Czerny) arrives at the jail to pay Bowden's bail and bring him to a hospital that specializes in caring for alcoholics and the mentally ill.

Meanwhile, a woman named Hanna (Piper Laurie) teaches her young nephew, Robbie Mannheim (Jonathan Malen), how to use a Ouija board to contact the "other world," much to the chagrin of Robbie's devoutly religious mother (Shannon Lawson). Hanna dies soon afterward, but Robbie continues to interact with the other world. Various supernatural events follow, and Robbie soon exhibits signs of abnormal behavior. Fearing the boy has fallen under the sway of demonic influence, his parents visit Reverend Eckhardt (Richard Waugh), a Lutheran pastor knowledgeable in such matters. The reverend agrees to meet with Robbie, and after a series of strange events he becomes convinced that demons have indeed possessed the boy.

The family eventually contacts McBride, who informs Bowden of the situation. Following a series of unsettling incidents, Bowden and McBride approach Archbishop Hume (Christopher Plummer) and ask him to exorcise Robbie. Hume refuses, because he wants to maintain the Catholic Church's reputation as a modern institution no longer beholden to ancient superstition. Instead, he instructs Bowden to perform the ritual, with the assistance of McBride and Father Walter Halloran (Michael McLachlan). Bowden reluctantly agrees, and over the course of several visits to the Mannheim home, the three priests endeavor to drive the demons from Robbie's body. After several demoralizing defeats, Bowden takes the boy to a monastery. Once there, Bowden finally musters his faith and manages to cast out the demonic spirit. Archbishop Hume then orders the room sealed.

Possessed aligns with the traditional exorcism narrative because it de-picts the doubting priest figure. Like Father Merrin in *Exorcist: The Begin-ning* and *Dominion*, Bowden's experiences during World War II shook his faith, and now he abuses alcohol to cope with his despair. Bowden's doubt informs his first encounter with the possessed Robbie. Upon enter-ing the boy's bedroom, Bowden encounters all manner of strange, super-natural occurrences; for example, objects fly around the room, and the word "HELL" appears in the flesh on Robbie's chest. Furthermore, the boy thrashes about violently, screaming and swearing in a deep, demonic voice that sounds like it belongs to an older male. Despite witnessing these events, Bowden initially doubts Robbie's possession. For instance, after hearing the boy whisper "Minister of Christ, can't you see, I'm the Devil" in Latin, he declares that Robbie likely encountered a Latin book at some point and remembered the words. However, like other doubting priest figures, Bowden's confrontation with evil ultimately reaffirms his faith in God. The exorcism allows Bowden to cast out his own inner demons—that is, his memories of World War II and his alcoholism—just as it helps Robbie expel the literal demons from his body.

While the presence of the doubting priest figure reinforces the tradi-tional exorcism narrative, *Possessed* challenges this narrative by depicting a possessed boy rather than a possessed girl. Yet, the film maintains the idea that female sexuality, agency, or voice pose a threat to patriarchal stability. It also positions non-heteronormative Others as deviant and dangerous. Robbie's possession conforms to other depictions of pos-sessed men, such as those in *Exorcist II* and *Dominion*. Like those films, *Possessed* implies that possession causes the boy to transgress established sociocultural boundaries regarding gender identities. Possession distorts Robbie's perception; he believes he hears Hanna's voice coming from his ventriloquist's dummy, and so he dresses it in her clothes. These events position the invading entity as feminine. The film furthers this position-ing during scenes in which Robbie speaks with Hanna's voice. However, the possessed Robbie also speaks with a deep, raspy, masculine voice. Thus, the film equates possession to a form of gender confusion as Rob-bie routinely inhabits both ends of the gender binary throughout the film. For instance, during the third exorcism, Robbie curses in Hanna's voice, but then sings "Ave Maria" in a soprano male voice. By transgressing gender boundaries in this way, Robbie occupies the realm of the trans-gendered, which the film positions as dangerous and abject. Therefore, the film aligns with the traditional exorcism narrative because it depicts an Other as a threat to patriarchal order.

During those times when the possessed Robbie assumes Hanna's identity, the film advances the idea that women threaten male order, a notion reinforced via Hanna's relationship with Robbie's mother. Ac-cording to Allen's account of the actual case, the family shunned the woman known as "Aunt Harriet" because of her psychic abilities;[19] in

Possessed, meanwhile, Robbie's mother considers the free-spirited Hanna
a disruptive influence, and therefore objects to her close relationship with
Robbie. Furthermore, the film implies that the possession causes Robbie
to adopt Hanna's undesirable qualities, including her independence, her
rebelliousness, her occult tendencies, and her femininity. In the context of
the film, these traits render Hanna unclean, and therefore Robbie becomes similarly unclean when Hanna's spirit possesses him.

  In horror and fantasy texts, ghosts sometimes function as metaphors
for lingering memories of the past that require expulsion or exorcism.[20]
For example, in Toni Morrison's 1987 novel *Beloved*, the protagonist experiences a haunting that functions as an external traumatic manifestation
of her "reified memory."[21] In *Possessed*, Robbie's possession serves a similar function; in the film, Hanna's spirit seemingly possesses Robbie and
causes him to act like her, which suggests that her death has left the boy
so traumatized that he assumed her personality traits out of grief. In
other words, Hanna's invasive spirit—that is, Robbie's reified memory of
his aunt and the transgression she represents—renders the boy similarly
transgressive. As with possessed girls, only exorcism can free Robbie
from Hanna's disruptive influence and restore him to his proper place
within the symbolic order.

  While the possessed Robbie clearly threatens both himself and others—for instance, he slashes Eckhardt's arm with a bedspring—*Possessed*
suggests that possessed males do not threaten order in the same way as
possessed females, and therefore do not require the same sort of suppression. Whereas Regan and other possessed girls spend the majority of
their possessions (not to mention a significant amount of screen time) tied
to their beds or otherwise restrained, the possessed Robbie remains almost entirely unbound throughout his possession. Indeed, Bowden only
secures Robbie with chains after the boy becomes excessively violent
during the third exorcism session in the monastery, thus suggesting a
need to suppress unhinged male violence. Thus, the film relates to other
exorcism films that equate possession to masculine violence, such as *Amityville II*, which we discuss in this chapter, and *Deliver Us From Evil*,
which we discuss in chapter 7.

  Additionally, Robbie does not succumb to possession to the same extent as Regan, who becomes "dragged into an overpowering dementia
which contorts both her mind and her physical features beyond recogni-
tion."[22] *Possessed* portrays Robbie as more or less lucid during the day,
yielding to possession only at night. Moreover, unlike the vast majority
of exorcism films, *Possessed* even offers the viewer a peek into the possessed Robbie's subjective experience via point-of-view shots, allowing
the viewer to empathize with his plight. Exorcism films rarely employ
such first-person perspective shots,[23] which in turn suggests that possessed women have little to no agency of their own, and therefore cannot
save themselves. By including these shots, *Possessed* suggests that Robbie

holds the power to resist the demonic possession and its negative influence. As such, he aligns with Father Karras in *The Exorcist* or *The Exorcist III*; Karras appears to maintain some agency even after he succumbs to possession, enough to throw himself out the window at the end of the first film and beg Kinderman to shoot him at the end of the third. This agency could explain why Robbie spends much less screen time tied to his bed or otherwise bound; he has some measure of control while possessed, and thus represents less of a threat. Conversely, exorcism cinema as a whole suggests that independent and sexually liberated women physically and symbolically jeopardize the patriarchal order, and therefore require both restraint and repression.

Additionally, unlike Regan, Robbie does not engage in the type of sexualized behavior that so scandalized viewers of *The Exorcist* in the 1970s, and therefore he does not sexually threaten those around him. In that respect, *Possessed* deviates from the account offered in Allen's book, which states that Roland Doe routinely behaved in a sexually deviant manner during the months-long exorcism.[24] Like Regan, he mimed masturbation and taunted those around him with graphic descriptions of sexual acts.[25] By omitting this aspect of the reported "true" story, *Possessed* reaffirms the idea that the traditional exorcism narrative chiefly concerns the oppression of female sexuality and agency. In the vast majority of exorcism films, aggressive female sexuality becomes the true threat to patriarchal order, because young girls should not exhibit such uninhibited behavior. Conversely, the possessed Robbie does not exhibit any deviant sexual behavior, which in turn suggests that male sexuality and agency do not require a negative portrayal because they do not threaten patriarchal order.

Overall, *Possessed* aligns with the traditional exorcism narrative because it reinforces the idea that disobedient women threaten patriarchal order. The film also includes the doubting priest figure, who must once again confront evil and thereby regain his faith and restore order. In addition, the film queers Robbie's gender identity, thereby positioning him as an Other that threatens mainstream sociocultural values. As such, *Possessed* aligns with other exorcism films such as *The Exorcist*, *Abby*, and *Exorcist II*, all of which conform to widespread sociocultural rhetoric that upholds the repression of marginalized individuals or ideologies. Therefore, while *Possessed* initially appears to challenge to the traditional exorcism narrative, it ultimately aligns with that narrative.

EMERGING CHALLENGES IN THE TRADITIONAL EXORCISM NARRATIVE

As discussed in chapter 5, the 1980s and 1990s produced few serious exorcism films, as many filmmakers opted to instead parody *The Exorcist* or find humor in the idea of possession and exorcism. During this lull period, however, two films offered somewhat realistic and horrific takes on possession and exorcism, while simultaneously challenging the traditional exorcism narrative. First, *Amityville II* depicts a teenage boy becoming possessed. However, unlike other exorcism films that position a boy as the possessed individual, *Amityville II* does not queer the possession. *Stigmata*, meanwhile, once again features a possessed woman, but the true nature of her possession and the film's overall negative depiction of the Catholic Church suggests a challenge to the traditional exorcism narrative.

Like *The Exorcist*, *The Amityville Horror* (1979, Stuart Rosenberg) had a long-lasting cultural impact, spawning numerous sequels, prequels, sidequels, TV references, and a high-profile remake in 2005 (directed by Andrew Douglas and starring Ryan Reynolds). Inspired by a true story, the original film focuses on a family threatened by their increasingly unstable patriarch, who is seemingly driven mad by the malevolent spirits haunting their recently purchased house. While the father's insanity likely results from possession, *The Amityville Horror* does not depict an exorcism. The film's sequel, however, does include a depiction of the ritual and therefore merits inclusion in this study.

According to *Amityville II*'s marketing campaign, the film reveals the events that led to the murder portrayed in the original film's opening sequence. While *Amityville II* does not allege any basis in reality (a direct contrast to *The Amityville Horror*, which uses superimposed text to present the facts of the case), its story nevertheless originated with Austrian-American parapsychologist and self-proclaimed ghost hunter Hans Holzer.[26] Credited as the first person to investigate the potentially supernatural cause behind the gruesome Amityville murders, Holzer wrote the book *Murder in Amityville*, which in turn inspired *Amityville II*.[27] Holzer speculates that a Native American spirit compelled Ronald Defeo, Jr. to murder his entire family. Of course, Holzer's tale includes descriptions of events that no one (not even Holzer himself) witnessed directly, and these details call the book's legitimacy into question. Nonetheless, Holzer's account resonated with the popular imagination of the time, despite the fact that such rampant theory, conjecture, and lack of verification likely reveals his book as a work of fiction.

Perhaps because of the book's questionable nature, the makers of *Amityville II* opted to forego the realism angle, and the film takes numerous liberties with the story that inspired it. For instance, the script changes the characters from the Defeos to the Montellis. Furthermore, while *Amityville II* ostensibly functions as a prequel, its relationship to the original film remains vague at best, because the filmmakers fail to clearly establish whether the events depicted onscreen take place before or after the events of *The Amityville Horror*. The sequel/prequel opens with the dysfunctional Montelli family moving into their dream home and discovering a mysterious tunnel in the basement. Soon after, the family experiences a series of unsettling paranormal events that culminate in a tense showdown between eldest son, Sonny (Jack Magner), and his abusive father, Anthony (Burt Young). These events allow the evil spirit that lurks within the tunnel to possess Sonny in a sequence that recalls a sexual assault; Sonny lies in his bed when his shirt suddenly rips open and some unseen force presses down on his stomach, as though a great weight has settled there. Sonny struggles against the assault, but he nevertheless succumbs to the possession.

The next day, Sonny's mother, Dolores (Rutanya Alda), implores Father Frank Adamsky (James Olson) to bless the house, but Anthony angrily chases the priest out the door. Meanwhile, Sonny seduces his younger teenaged sister, Patricia (Diane Franklin), and the guilt causes her to confess to Father Adamsky. Sonny tries to isolate himself in an effort to protect the others, but the invasive entity eventually compels him to kill his family. Unable to resist the demon's influence, Sonny uses his father's shotgun to execute his parents and his siblings. Afterward, the police arrive to arrest Sonny, who claims to have no memory of his homicidal actions. Suspecting that Sonny has become possessed, Father Adamsky seeks permission to perform an exorcism, but the Church refuses his request. Adamsky ignores the decree and sets out to free Sonny from the demon's influence. He breaks Sonny out of jail and takes him to the church, but the boy flees when he sees the crosses on the doors. Adamsky follows Sonny back to the Montelli house and successfully casts the demon out of the young man's body. Afterward, the exhausted Adamsky beseeches his superior, Father Tom (Andrew Prine), to care for Sonny. Tom agrees and takes the boy away. The film ends by revealing that the demon has possessed Father Adamsky.

Unlike the majority of exorcism films, *Amityville II* situates a white, heterosexual male as the victim of possession. Moreover, it positions Sonny's sexuality as dangerous, and thereby challenges the traditional exorcism narrative. Prior to the possession, Sonny appears to flirt with Patricia when they arrive at their new home, and his possession accelerates this sexual deviance and causes him to becomes far more sexually aggressive. He seduces Patricia, and though she initially finds Sonny's advances off-putting, she nevertheless consents to sleep with him. While the film renders Sonny's sexuality as dangerous because he initiates this relationship with his own sister, the film ultimately shifts the focus of deviant sexuality onto her. Indeed, while the possessed Sonny cannot control his actions, Patricia agrees to sleep with him of her own accord. Thus, the film absolves Sonny's actions and implicates Patricia's sexuality as deviant because it upsets traditional familial relations, which in turn positions female sexuality as a dangerous threat to the established order.

Patricia initially experiences a great deal of guilt as a result of the incest and confesses her sin to Father Adamsky. The next day, however,

she tells Sonny that she does not regret sleeping with him, which reinforces the idea that she harbors an aberrant and altogether dangerous
sexuality. The film further depicts her as a wanton woman during the
exorcism during the scene in which the possessed Sonny attempts to
seduce Father Adamsky by assuming Patricia's image. Dressed provoca-
tively and slathered in makeup, the girl accuses Adamsky of lusting after
her. Thus, while *Amityville II* uses gender transgression to queer Sonny
and position him as a threatening Other, this does not represent a central
motif in the film. Ultimately, *Amityville II* portrays Patricia as a rebellious
and sexually aggressive young woman whose feminine wiles openly
challenge patriarchal institutions. Thus, the film codes the feminine as
monstrous.

While *Amityville II* absolves Sonny of his deviant sexuality by shifting
the focus of deviant sexuality onto his sister, the film does condemn his
increasingly violent tendencies, which ultimately lead him to murder his
entire family. Even then, however, it pardons his actions because they
only intensify once he succumbs to possession and loses control. Adrian
Schober notes that Sonny's violent tendencies mirror his father's violence. However, rather than blame Anthony for the family's predicament,
the film lays the blame on a so-called crisis of patriarchy that supports
this sort of familial violence, particularly when perpetrated by a father
figure.[28] Sonny's violence far exceeds Robbie's in *Possessed*, yet *Amityville
II* does not queer Sonny in the same way. Instead, the film links Sonny's
violence to his father, and by extension implicates a patriarchal order that
permits such masculine violence. The possession, then, merely exacer-
bates Sonny's pre-existing tendencies, and the film thereby offers a metaphorical condemnation of patriarchy itself, which challenges the traditional exorcism narrative. This linking of possession and masculine violence recurs in the exorcism films produced during the resurgence period, as discussed in the next chapter.

The film also deviates from the traditional exorcism narrative because
it lacks the doubting priest figure. Father Adamsky's faith appears much
stronger than the priests depicted in other exorcism films, who initially
express skepticism toward demonic possession. In fact, Adamsky so
steadfastly believes that Sonny has become possessed, he breaks the boy
out of jail, in defiance of both the wishes of his superiors and earthly law.
The priest's unwavering conviction allows him to dismiss any fear he
might feel for his own professional life or freedom. In fact, the only time
Adamsky really suffers from a possible lack of faith occurs during the
exorcism sequence when Sonny assumes Patricia's form and tries to
tempt the priest. Even then, however, Adamsky ultimately resists this
temptation and saves Sonny's soul, at which point the boy rises into the
air with his arms and legs cruciform. The film uses this crucifixion imagery to portray Sonny as Christ-like and thereby absolve him of his sins

while simultaneously reaffirming Adamsky's decision to disregard both the Church and the Law in his efforts to accomplish God's work.

Thus, the film challenges the traditional exorcism narrative because it does not portray a male protagonist reaffirming his spiritual faith by oppressing a woman's agency. Instead, the film appears to critique patriarchal structures by metaphorically linking possession to masculine violence. Furthermore, Sonny's possession disrupts the traditional family structure, which in turn destabilizes the paternal symbolic order. Andrew Tudor observes that the *Amityville* films focus more on an invasive force that threatens to destabilize the traditional family structure, and that unlike in *The Exorcist*, "it is our *social* lives that are invaded here, and rather less the fabric of our bodies and minds."[29] Sonny's threat, then, appears to reflect fears regarding the dissolution of the nuclear family that persisted in the United States during the time of the film's release.[30] Yet, the exorcism occurs too late to save the family, which in turn suggests that the Church has lost its power and can no longer maintain the familial institution. The film reinforces this notion when it reveals that Father Adamsky has become possessed. Thus, *Amityville II* does not depict a return to patriarchal stability, and this failure to reestablish order ultimately suggests that the film represents a challenge to the traditional exorcism narrative.

While *Amityville II* premiered at the beginning of the lull period, *Stigmata* emerged near the end and further undermined the Church's role in stabilizing society and culture. Douglas E. Cowan called *Stigmata* "*The Exorcist* for an MTV generation," in reference to the countercultural sensibilities used to market the film.[31] Yet, this phrase could also refer to the tensions and cultural anxieties of the late 1990s as the era's dominant youth culture—dubbed Generation X by author Douglas Coupland[32] — increasingly turned away from organized religion. In many ways, *Stigmata*'s message seemingly supports this cynicism toward the patriarchal institution of the Church.

The film opens with Father Andrew Kiernan (Gabriel Byrne)—a former scientist turned Jesuit priest charged with investigating supposed miracles—arriving in the Brazilian village of Belo Quinto to examine a statue of the Virgin of Guadalupe that locals claim wept blood during the funeral of excommunicated priest Father Paulo Alameida (Jack Donner). During the investigation, a young boy steals Alameida's rosary and sells it to a woman who mails it to her atheist daughter, Frankie Paige (Patricia Arquette), in Pittsburgh, Pennsylvania. That night, a supernatural entity assaults Frankie in the bath, leaving her with deep wounds on both of her wrists. Learning of the incident, the Vatican dispatches Father Kiernan to investigate.

Father Kiernan believes that Frankie's injuries result from stigmata, an affliction that causes the deeply devoted to manifest wounds similar to those suffered by Christ during his crucifixion. Frankie dismisses this idea, because she does not believe in God. Yet, after she leaves the hospital, bloody gashes that resemble those caused by Christ's crown of thorns appear on her head. Confused and terrified, Frankie flees into the night. Kiernan eventually finds her hiding in an alley, but when he tries to approach her she curses at him in another language, which he later identifies as Aramaic, the language of Christ.

Frankie soon exhibits more signs of possession: she speaks Italian in a deep, male voice and becomes more sexually aggressive. She scrawls Aramaic words on the walls of her apartment and tries to seduce Father Kiernan. He rejects her, which causes her to attack the priest and denounce his faith with her demonic male voice. Later, she levitates and weeps tears of blood, at which point Father Dario (Enrico Colantoni) and Cardinal Houseman (Jonathan Pryce) intervene and attempt to exorcise the young woman. Meanwhile, Father Kiernan meets with a historian named Marion Petrocelli (Rade Serbedzija), who reveals that the words Frankie wrote on her apartment walls come from the recently discovered Gospel of Thomas, supposedly written by Jesus Christ. The Vatican assigned Petrocelli and a team of scholars to translate the controversial document, but Houseman ordered them to stop, so Father Alameida stole the document and continued translating it in secret. Petrocelli also divulges that Father Alameida also suffered from stigmata.

Realizing that Father Alameida's spirit has possessed Frankie, Father Kiernan races to free her from the invasive entity. He arrives in time to stop Houseman from strangling the young woman, just as the room bursts into flames. Kiernan pulls Frankie from the fire and implores Alameida's spirit to leave in peace. The entity departs, and Kiernan then returns to Belo Quinto, where he finds the lost gospel hidden in Alameida's church. The film then dissolves to a title card stating that the Catholic Church refuses to recognize the Gospel of Thomas, because they consider it a heretical document.

Stigmata challenges the traditional exorcism narrative largely because it uses a young woman's possession to rightly challenge the Catholic Church's corrupt power and authority. The film establishes that the Church suppresses information when officials at the Vatican falsely claim that they kept no records on Alameida's parish in Brazil. Thus, much like Dan Brown's 2003 novel, *The Da Vinci Code, Stigmata* portrays the Church as a secretive organization involved in a vast conspiracy to withhold sensitive information from the public in an attempt to control the truth and maintain power. The film further reinforces this perception by having the Vatican send Father Kiernan to investigate a seemingly unimportant case, but then proceeds to hamper his investigation at every turn. For instance, Kiernan photographs the words scrawled on Frankie's wall and sends the pictures to a friend back at the Vatican, who suggests that Kiernan abandon this line of questioning in response. Later, the film again references a conspiracy when it reveals that the Vatican wants to suppress the Gospel of Thomas because it reveals that God's power resides in people and nature rather than in holy buildings and institutions. Such information could effectively undermine the Church's power, and thus the organization acts to bury the document.

Frankie's possession allows her to access this secret knowledge, however, and thus she holds the power to dismantle the Church's patriarchal authority. *Stigmata* thereby positions her as both a literal and figurative threat to the Church, which in turn does everything in its power to quash that threat (including employing lethal force, if necessary). By positioning the Church as a clandestine, conspiratorial, and almost villainous organization, the film therefore situates the possessed girl as a heroic figure by default, because her possession provides her with the knowledge, agency, and voice to halt this conspiracy. While possessed, Frankie speaks and writes in Aramaic, revealing the truth that her oppressors do not want others to know. Additionally, instead of silencing her through exorcism, Kiernan ultimately aligns with Frankie and helps reveal the truth; he "overcomes the powers of repression in the church"[33] that would continue to marginalize people like Frankie. As such, *Stigmata* challenges the traditional exorcism narrative, which commonly positions a representative of the Church as the hero who must confront the possessed girl or woman who threatens patriarchal order.[34]

Furthermore, while the film establishes Frankie as a sexually rebellious woman who refuses to conform to patriarchal ideals of feminine behavior, her possession nevertheless positions her as the only person capable of speaking the truth that could potentially change the world. Frankie assumes the role of the whore who becomes the virgin—indeed, rather than the Virgin Mary's story, *Stigmata* portrays Mary Magdalene's tale of redemption. Initially, the film appears to condemn uninhibited female sexuality as deviant and dangerous. *Stigmata* introduces Frankie by intercutting images of her drinking and having sex with strangers with images of holy iconography. Chumbawamba's song "Mary Mary (Stigmatic Mix)"—which includes the line "whatever happened to Mary?"—accompanies this opening montage. By contrasting Frankie's lustful behavior with sacred imagery, the film suggests a disconnect between the way women behaved in the days before women's liberation, and how they conduct themselves in a more uninhibited era that exalts sex, drugs, and rock-and-roll over God. *Stigmata* further reinforces this view of Frankie by having her attempt to seduce Kiernan during the possession, and thus the film aligns with other exorcism films because it positions the possessed woman's uninhibited sexuality as a threat to patriarchal order.

Yet, the possession ultimately saves both Frankie and Christianity. Frankie's possession causes her stigmata, which normally affects truly holy individuals. Such wounds reflect an inner spiritual battle, and represent a physical manifestation of an individual's struggle against evil.

Moreover, the Church regards stigmata as a gift from God. However, Frankie does not believe in God, and therefore her body should not exhibit the wounds of Christ, as this would imply an existential contradiction. As such, Frankie's possession functions as a form of redemption that absolves her lack of belief and her sexual promiscuity. Graham Ward suggests that when Frankie acquires the rosary, she begins to formulate a faith that disrupts "the layers of secular assumption and surmise" that previously defined her life.[35] Indeed, the film even portrays her dressed in a diaphanous white gown after the exorcism to imply a newfound saintliness. As such, the film depicts Frankie's journey in a way that recalls other possessed women, who end up "saved" by the exorcism.

At the same time, however, Frankie's possession potentially redeems the Church, because it grants her a voice that allows her to convey Jesus's message to the world. By portraying a sexually deviant woman ascending to the position of a holy figure, the film thereby positions traditional norms—particularly those informed by patriarchal institutions like the Church, which had become tainted—as incorrect. In other words, much like Mary Magdalene, Frankie's sins did not prevent her from redeeming herself, which in turn suggests that the criteria for redemption (i.e., traditional patriarchal values) can potentially change. The film suggests that while Frankie needed saving, so did the Catholic Church. Thus, *Stigmata* once again deviates from the traditional exorcism narrative, because it depicts a woman taking an active role in redeeming the Church rather than the other way around.

While the majority of exorcism films metaphorically depict women as threats to the patriarchal order, *Stigmata* depicts women as a literal danger to the Church, because Frankie's possession threatens to undermine the patriarchal institution's authority and credibility. In the end, though, Frankie redeems the Church, and her possession acts to save Catholicism's soul as much her own. Thus, like *Amityville II*, *Stigmata* implies the Church lost touch with the modern world. Of course, the former film suggests this institution cannot defend families, while the latter advances the idea that the institution itself requires fixing. As such, both represent a stark contrast to *Possessed*, which aligns with the traditional exorcism narrative established by *The Exorcist*. Thus, *Amityville II* and *Stigmata*, the two films that bookend exorcism cinema's lull period, demonstrate that exorcism films can do more than just metaphorically depict the oppression of non-dominant groups.

THE REAL STORY AND THE
TRADITIONAL EXORCISM NARRATIVE

The exorcism films discussed in this chapter offer a variety of challenges to the traditional exorcism narrative at both ends of the lull period, even as they mostly uphold this narrative. While *Possessed* maintains the traditional exorcism narrative's central tropes—that is, the doubting priest figure and the idea that female sexuality threatens patriarchal stability— it nevertheless portrays a boy as the possessed individual in direct contrast to the vast majority of other exorcism films. Similarly, *Amityville II* portrays a possessed boy, but the film uses his possession as a metaphor for how male violence threatens the family unit. As such, *Amityville II* challenges the traditional exorcism narrative, which routinely reaffirms male power and dominance. *Stigmata*, meanwhile, portrays the possessed woman as a threat to patriarchal authority, but the film complicates this portrayal by positioning her as a potential savior because her possession allows her to speak out against the Church's corruption. Thus, the films produced at either end of the lull period challenge the traditional exorcism narrative even as they maintain or advance its central tropes.

Of the films discussed in this chapter, *Possessed* aligns most closely with the traditional exorcism narrative developed by *The Exorcist*, because it features the doubting priest figure and ultimately reinforces the idea that female sexuality threatens patriarchal order. *Amityville II* and *Stigmata* challenge both of these conventions, primarily because each film abandons the doubting priest figure; Adamsky and Kiernan both differ from this figure because they do not lack faith. Of course, the films complicate these characters by portraying them or the institution they represent as corrupt. Indeed, both films explore the tensions and doubts regarding religion's role in society. For instance, *Stigmata* retains the possessed-woman-as-threat figure, but it also portrays the Church as corrupt and thereby positions her as both a justifiable and necessary threat to its authority. Meanwhile, *Amityville II* maintains the idea that female sexuality represents a threat to order, but the film ultimately challenges the traditional exorcism narrative because it suggests the Church becomes corrupted when Father Adamsky succumbs to demonic possession. Thus, these films challenge the standard tropes and conventions of the traditional exorcism narrative even as they incorporate them. In this way, they recall the parodies discussed in chapter 5, which maintained the possessed-women-as-threat trope while satirizing the religious individuals tasked with exorcizing them.

Possessed, on the other hand, upholds all of the narrative's central tropes, from the doubting priest figure to the possessed-Other-as-threat to the idea that uninhibited female sexuality threatens traditional order, even as it positions a boy as the possessed individual. This becomes significant when considering that *Possessed* claims to tell the true story of *The Exorcist*. Blatty contends that changing the possessed character's biological sex from a boy to a girl has no bearing on the story. Yet, this decision has a profound impact on the gender dynamics of possession and exorcism, particularly as other films copied this narrative conceit and also portrayed girls or young women as the possessed individuals. By routinely portraying men confronting and repressing possessed women, exorcism films position female sexuality as a dangerous threat to patriarchal order. This idea becomes the central concern of the traditional exorcism narrative, and even those exorcism films that focus on a possessed boy, such as *Possessed* or *Amityville II*, still tend to position unconventional women as the true threat to order. Furthermore, even when the Church itself poses a danger, as in *Stigmata*, the possessed woman still threatens sociocultural stability—while corrupt, the Church still constructs and maintains patriarchal stability.

This possessed-woman-as-threat trope then became extended to position other marginalized people as threats, and Robbie represents that extension. Robbie's threat involved a transgression of gendered identities, because a feminine entity possessed him. This queering aspect of Robbie's character did not occur in the book that inspired *Possessed*, which indicates the influence of the traditional exorcism narrative on the film. Although *Possessed* maintained the gender identity of the possessed person from the real story, the film nevertheless uses possession to queer him. Therefore, the possessed-Other-as-threat in the film still relies on the fear of a feminine entity, which in turn aligns the film with *The Exorcist* and the traditional exorcism narrative. Even without Regan, the supposedly "real story" still positions women as dangerous.

Thus, even exorcism films that appear to, or in some way do, challenge the traditional exorcism narrative nevertheless uphold the idea that women and female sexuality pose a threat to traditional patriarchal order. As we discuss in the next chapter, this depiction recurs even as exorcism films become increasingly concerned with conveying a sense of realism. Released in 2000, *Possessed* foreshadowed the subgenre's shift toward realism during its resurgence in the years after 9/11. Indeed, the films produced throughout this resurgence period focus far more on the trope of the possessed-woman-as-threat than on the possessed-Other-as-threat figure. Furthermore, the need to portray possession and exorcism as real can potentially become problematic, most notably when it reinforces a narrative that hinges primarily on the oppression of marginalized identities.

NOTES

1. Simon Tomlinson, "The Devil in Roland Doe: How the 1973 Horror Film *The Exorcist* was Based on a Real-life Possession in Missouri," *Daily Mail*, last modified October 8, 2013, http://www.dailymail.co.uk/news/article-2449423/Devil-Roland-Doe-The-Exorcist-based-real-life-Missouri-possession.html.

2. "Roland Doe" was a pseudonym given to the teenager to protect his identity. For more, see Tomlinson, "Roland Doe."

3. For more, see Mark Kermode, *The Exorcist: Revised 2nd Edition* (London: British Film Institute, 2003), 11–12.

4. Kermode, *The Exorcist*, 12.

5. Bob McCabe, *The Exorcist: Out of the Shadows* (New York: Omnibus Press, 1999), 18–19.

6. For more, see "Exorcising *The Exorcist*" and Mark Opsasnik, "The Haunted Boy of Cottage City: The Cold Hard Facts Behind the Story That Inspired 'The Exorcist,'" *Strangemag*, accessed August 8, 2015, http://www.strangemag.com/exorcist-page1.html.

7. Alexandra Heller-Nicholas, "'The Power of Christ Compels You': Moral Spectacle and The Exorcist Universe" in *Roman Catholicism in Fantastic Film: Essays on Belief, Spectacle, Ritual and Imagery*, ed. Regina Hansen (Jefferson: McFarland & Company, Inc., 2011), 65–80.

8. William Paul, *Laughing Screaming: Modern Hollywood Horror and Comedy* (New York: Columbia University Press, 1994), 296.

9. Ibid.

10. Bruce Ballon and Molyn Leszcz, "Horror Films: Tales to Master Terror or Shapers of Trauma?," *American Journal of Psychotherapy* 61, no. 2 (2007): 211–30.

11. Ibid., 219.

12. For more detailed information on this case, see Tomlinson, "Roland Doe," Kermode, *The Exorcist*, 11–22, and "'The Exorcist' fairly close to the mark," *National Catholic Reporter*, Sept. 1, 2000.

13. "'The Exorcist' fairly close to the mark."

14. Ibid.

15. Ibid.

16. Latin for "Lord, be with us." From "Exorcising *The Exorcist*."

17. Mark Kermode (2003) notes that Father Raymond J. Bishop's diaries largely inspired Allen's account (11).

18. "Exorcising *The Exorcist*."

19. Kermode, *The Exorcist*, 13.

20. For instance, many of director Guillermo Del Toro's films feature lingering ghosts that double for some past indiscretion. For more, see Tasha Robinson, "The Theme That Ties All of Guillermo del Toro's Movies Together," *io9*, last modified October 20, 2015, http://io9.gizmodo.com/the-theme-that-ties-all-of-guillermo-del-toros-movies-t-1737615770.

21. Daniel Erickson, *Ghosts, Metaphor, and History in Tony Morrison's* Beloved *and Gabriel Garcia Marquez's* One Hundred Years of Solitude (New York: Palgrave MacMillan, 2009), 28.

22. Kermode, *The Exorcist*, 17.

23. Notable examples of exorcism films that feature such point-of-view shots include *The Last Exorcism* (2010, Daniel Stamm), which we discuss in chapter 8, and *Grace: The Possession* (2014, Jeff Chan), which we discuss in chapter 7.

24. Kermode, *The Exorcist*, 14.

25. Ibid.

26. For more, see William Grimes, "Hans Holzer, Ghost Hunter, Dies at 89," *The New York Times*, last modified April 29, 2009, http://www.nytimes.com/2009/04/30/books/30holzer.html?_r=2&.

27. Tracy Allen, "This Week in Horror Movie History—*Amityville II: The Possession* (1982)," *Cryptic Rock*, last modified September 26, 2014, http://crypticrock.com/this-week-in-horror-movie-history-amityville-ii-the-possession-1982/.

28. Adrian Schober, *Possessed Child Narratives in Literature and Film: Contrary States* (New York, Palgrave, 2004), 83.

29. Andrew Tudor, *Monsters and Mad Scientists: A Cultural History of the Horror Movie* (Cambridge: Basil Blackwell, Ltd., 1989), 176. Italics in original.

30. Schober, *Possessed Child Narratives*, 82.

31. Douglas E. Cowan, "Horror and the Demonic" in *The Routledge Companion to Religion and Film*, ed. John Lyden (New York: Routledge, 2009), 405.

32. Douglas Coupland, *Generation X: Tales for an Accelerated Culture* (New York: St. Martin's Press, 1991).

33. Graham Ward, *True Religion* (Malden: Blackwell Publishing, 2003), 149.

34. *L'ossessa* (1974, Mario Gariazzo) also depicts the possessed woman suffering from stigmata, but the film ultimately reveals the she has become possessed by the devil and therefore aligns with the traditional exorcism narrative.

35. Graham Ward, *True Religion*, 149.

SEVEN

True Stories and Found Footage

The Exorcism Cinema Resurgence

Two major events—only one of which was cinematic in nature—signaled the end of exorcism cinema's lull period: first, the rerelease of a newly restored and re-edited version of *The Exorcist* and second, the terror attacks of September 11, 2001. While the latter had a profound impact on horror (not to mention the world), the former reminded audiences and movie producers that exorcism films could be both terrifying and lucrative. These dual events arrived at a time when many people believed that horror had become stagnant. For instance, Steffen Hantke notes that the glut of horror remakes produced during the early 2000s indicated a lack of originality.[1] Yet, this period also saw the resurgence of exorcism cinema. This new wave of exorcism films consisted primarily of original stories that stressed the "reality" of possession and exorcism. This resurgence likely occurred because the sociocultural atmosphere of the time enabled a revival of supernatural horror. The slasher films of the 1980s and 1990s reflected prevailing sociocultural anxieties regarding sex, AIDS, and morality, and therefore they no longer resonated with audiences faced with terrorism, perpetual war, natural disasters, climate change, and global economic collapse. Post-9/11, an overwhelming sense of hopelessness, paranoia, pessimism, dread, fatalism, and vulnerability defined the prevailing social mood.

Kevin J. Wetmore contends that after 9/11, many horror films reflected the widespread anxieties and tensions aroused by the terrorist attacks on the U.S. Pentagon and the World Trade Center.[2] Following these attacks, the world at large entered a period of fear, mistrust, and hopelessness.[3] The United States in particular "became dominated by fear [. . .] out of proportion to the genuine threat."[4] This fear fostered a culture of paranoia that led to widespread mistrust in institutions like the government, mass media, and science, and the films produced during this period reflect, and even confirm, that paranoia.[5] Moreover, the mainstream political rhetoric and sociocultural discourse of the time positioned terrorism as an abstract and existential threat, one that unscrupulous individuals used to legitimize existing power structures and/or reify traditional modes of thought and behavior. The 9/11 terror attacks and the Bush administration's subsequent fearmongering also stoked sociocultural anxieties about religion; Eastern and Western ideologies clashed, thereby creating the conditions that allowed for a resurgence of supernatural horror.[6] If, as Wetmore proposes, "the purpose of horror is to generate fear in the audience," then post-9/11 horror films function as "one of the best vehicles for allowing our culture to process the experience of terror" precisely because they reflect and confront the widespread concerns that emerged in the wake of the 9/11 terror attacks.[7]

In many ways, the possessed individual seems perfectly suited for the post-9/11 atmosphere. Indeed, of the 127 exorcism films produced since 1937, eighty-two of them—almost two-thirds—emerged after the September 11 terror attacks.[8] From a metaphorical standpoint, exorcism films can function as an allegory for terrorism in numerous ways. First, as discussed in previous chapters, they reflect the tensions between Eastern and Western religions. Furthermore, such films depict an individual becoming invaded and occupied by a vague, abstract force that destabilizes the status quo. Finally, at its most basic level, possession inspires terror, the core tenet of terrorism. In addition, following the attacks, many people believed that killers lurked everywhere and could strike without warning; exorcism films similarly suggest that anyone can become possessed at any time. As these horrors became more commonplace and the resulting fears mounted, exorcism cinema capitalized on this paranoid atmosphere by endeavoring to depict realistic tales of possession and exorcism.

While such sociocultural anxieties likely helped stimulate exorcism cinema's return, the successful rerelease of *The Exorcist* no doubt had a more direct impact on the studios' decision to produce and exhibit new, original exorcism films. In interviews, William Peter Blatty stated that he felt the original theatrical version had no moral center, nor did it sufficiently explain why events occurred as they did and therefore only offered shock value.[9] William Friedkin eventually came around to this point of view, admitting that his original version was colder while the recut felt much warmer.[10] Thus, after a financially successful twenty-fifth anniversary theatrical rerelease of *The Exorcist* in the United Kingdom,[11] Friedkin worked to reproduce the film's "first cut," and in 2000 the studio released this re-edited version of the film to theaters around the world as *The Exorcist: The Version You've Never Seen.*

This cut offered viewers—even those intimately familiar with the film—an almost entirely different viewing experience. For instance, Friedkin reinstated a sequence in which Karras and Merrin sit on the staircase outside Regan MacNeil's bedroom and discuss the implication of her possession, a scene Friedkin initially considered unnecessary because he trusted the audience to understand that the demon targeted Regan's loved ones rather than Regan herself.[12] However, Blatty believed this point remained unclear in the original cut. With the help of digital effects, Friedkin also restored the infamous "spider walk" sequence, which he cut because the physical effects appeared unconvincing.[13] The new version also restored the original ending, wherein Chris MacNeil offers to give Father Merrin's St. Joseph medal (first seen at the archaeological dig site in Iraq) to Father Dyer, but he refuses and tells her to keep it. Mark Kermode argues that this ending hints at Chris's blossoming faith.[14] Finally, the new cut also reinstated a fleeting glimpse of Regan smiling and waving goodbye as the car pulls away from their Georgetown home, followed by a brief sequence in which Kinderman strikes up a friendship with Father Dyer (a relationship explored further in *The Exorcist III*).

While *The Exorcist*'s successful rerelease undoubtedly encouraged studios to greenlight other exorcism cinema projects, the subsequent success of many of these original projects actually propelled the exorcism cinema subgenre's resurgence during the early part of the twenty-first century. Many of these films reflect the widespread anxieties that defined the tumultuous post-9/11 sociocultural atmosphere, because they portray possession and exorcism as something that can affect anyone at any time (though possession appears to afflict Caucasian women more than anyone else in these films, which we discuss further in chapter 9). Furthermore, these films sometimes aim for a sense of verisimilitude by employing production techniques that replicate the look and feel of the increasingly common recording technologies people use to document their own lives, such as webcams, GoPro cameras, smartphones, etc. This chapter considers how the exorcism cinema resurgence and its shift toward depicting realistic horrors impacts the traditional exorcism narrative.

THE EXORCISM CINEMA RESURGENCE AND THE SHIFT TOWARD REALISM

The postmodern and intertextual horror films of the 1990s frequently deconstructed long-standing horror film tropes, thus downplaying their potential to frighten by revealing the artifice behind the monsters, situations, and gore. To counter this period of deconstruction, horror films employed different tactics, such as a documentary aesthetic meant to increase viewers' suspension of disbelief. At the dawn of the New Millennium, found footage horror films emerged as a viable subgenre due to the massive financial success of a handful of films that used the technique, beginning with the smash hit, *The Blair Witch Project* (1999, Daniel Myrick and Eduardo Sánchez).[15] Found footage horror films succeed primarily because horror becomes more frightening when it obliterates the lines between fantasy and reality.[16] Thus, found footage films and other movies that allege a basis in reality became increasingly common as horror entered the twenty-first century, and these techniques influenced exorcism cinema during this resurgence period. Post-9/11 horror films frequently attain a sense of credibility by claiming a basis in true events, or by utilizing the found footage aesthetic to frame the narrative as something that actually occurred.

Exorcism cinema frequently relies on a similar tendency toward realism, and actually has since the beginning. Scholars observe that purportedly true stories from Eastern Europe and Russia inspired playwright Shloyme Zanvl Rappoport to write the stage play *The Dybbuk*, later adapted for the screen by director Michal Waszynski (as discussed in chapter 1). Furthermore, as discussed in chapter 6, Blatty based *The Exorcist* on a supposedly real case of exorcism, later portrayed in the telefilm *Possessed*. *The Exorcist*'s marketing extended this realism, as the film's producers encouraged the spread of rumors about the cursed production.[17] Linda Blair recalled that news media attempted to portray her as deranged, much like her character. She claimed that such stories likely helped audiences view the film as real and thus more genuinely frightening.[18] Indeed, some critics contend that *The Exorcist* succeeded primarily because audiences perceived it as authentic, and the film may have had a more profound effect on those who subscribed to the Catholic faith because they believed it portrayed a real case of possession.[19]

Observations such as these provide a possible explanation for the popularity of "realistic" horror films that blur the lines between fiction and reality; such films suggest that the "dark and eerie landscapes, the threatening shadows and noises" exist in the supposedly "safe" real world the audience inhabits.[20] Viewers who perceive the cinematic threat as real may experience more dread, but they also derive more pleasure from "surviving" the horror.[21] The majority of films produced during the post-9/11 period use these techniques to achieve a sense of authenticity and thus strike a chord with audiences seeking realistic horrors portrayed onscreen. In the following sections, we consider how the production methods employed by some of these films serve to reinforce the ideological positioning of the traditional exorcism narrative.

TRUE STORIES OF EXORCISM

Thus far, fifteen exorcism films claiming to be based on true stories or events have emerged during the first two decades of the twenty-first century. These include *Requiem* (2006, Hans-Christian Schmid), *Costa Chica: Confession of an Exorcist* (2006, David Heavener), *Semum* (2008, Hasan Karacadag), *Chronicles of an Exorcism* (2008, Nick G. Miller), *The Rite* (2011, Mikael Håfström), *The Possession* (2012, Ole Bornedal), *The Conjuring* (2013, James Wan), *The Exorcism of Anna Ecklund* (2015, Andrew Jones), *The Conjuring 2* (2016, James Wan), and *The Crucifixion* (2016, Xavier Gems). Each film allegedly adapts some "true" story of possession and exorcism. Additionally, these films hail from a variety of nations, and this indicates a global tendency to portray true exorcism stories onscreen. For example, the German film *Requiem* loosely retells the true story of Anneliese Michel, changing the young woman's name to Michaela Klingler but taking a straightforward, almost documentarian approach to depicting the events of her case. This true story has inspired several productions, including one of the films analyzed in this chapter.

Regardless of whether or not the incidents actually occurred, all of the films listed above rely on that connection to generate a sense of realism.[22] In a world in which the news consistently broadcasts stories about horrific events, the stories portrayed in such films feel much more plausible. In this section, we consider how *The Exorcism of Emily Rose* (2005, Scott Derrickson) and *Deliver Us from Evil* (2014, Scott Derrickson), two films allegedly based on actual events, reflect and maintain the traditional exorcism narrative.

In 1975, a young woman named Anneliese Michel supposedly succumbed to demonic possession and was subjected to a series of Catholic exorcism rites. She died a year later due to malnourishment and dehydration. Author Felicitas D. Goodman chronicled Anneliese's story in the nonfiction book *The Exorcism of Anneliese Michel* (1981), which in turn served as the basis for the documentary *Anneliese: The Exorcist Tapes* (2011, Jude Gerard Prest). In 2005, director and co-writer Scott Derrickson fictionalized the account in *Emily Rose*, bringing renewed attention to the events leading up to Michel's death. During preproduction, Derrickson extensively researched real cases of possession and exorcism, so he could more realistically portray them onscreen.[23] Furthermore, like Blatty, the devoutly religious Derrickson wanted his film to inspire audiences to experience both psychological terror and a spiritual reawakening.[24] *Emily Rose* earned over $144 million worldwide against a $75 million budget,[25] and this success helped spur the production of other exorcism films.

Despite the title, the film actually centers on the plight of Father Richard Moore (Tom Wilkinson), a priest arrested and charged with the death of nineteen-year-old Emily Rose (Jennifer Carpenter). The film opens as Father Moore performs an exorcism on Emily, who dies before he can complete the ritual. Wishing to cover up the incident, the archdiocese instructs Father Moore to plead guilty, and they hire atheist lawyer Erin Bruner (Laura Linney) to negotiate the plea deal. Father Moore insists on pleading innocent, however, and the case goes to trial, where the events surrounding Emily's death slowly emerge through a series of flashbacks.

Upon arriving at college, Emily apparently suffered a seizure, and afterward experienced hallucinations, loss of bodily control, and extreme hysteria. Fearing that their daughter had become possessed, Emily's parents contacted Father Moore, who immediately attempts to exorcise the girl. During the ritual, Emily speaks in tongues and performs superhuman physical feats, and declares that six demons have possessed her. Eventually, the Virgin Mary appears to inform Emily that the demons will never leave, and she offers the young woman an immediate and painless death to alleviate her suffering. Emily declines, however, saying she would rather endure the possession so the world will once again believe in demons. She dies soon after.

Throughout the trial, the skeptical Bruner experiences a variety of unsettling supernatural phenomena: objects move of their own accord and she hears strange noises in her apartment late at night. She nevertheless remains determined to win the case. She manages to evoke some sympathy among the jury, who find Father Moore guilty of neglect and wrongful death but recommend the judge sentence him to time served. The film ends with Bruner sitting in bed, plagued by a newfound sense of doubt and fear.

Emily Rose exemplifies the traditional exorcism narrative's central theme, which concerns the silencing of women. Indeed, the film silences Emily from the beginning, because the main narrative takes place after her death. As the district attorney points out, Emily cannot speak for herself during the trial, and thus her experience with possession unfolds only through other people's flashbacks and recollections, thereby stripping the young woman of agency, even before the exorcism. The film conveys Emily's experience primarily via Father Moore's subjective reminiscences; he narrates the flashbacks, which in turn suggests that a man must speak for Emily. In fact, Emily's agency only manifests in her decision to attend college against her devoutly religious parents' wishes, and the film suggests this independence ultimately leads to her downfall. Otherwise, Emily has no agency and, most significantly, no voice; in the flashbacks, she rarely speaks until after the demons possess her, at which point she becomes simultaneously threatening and helpless. As in other exorcism films, the Church represents the girl's only hope of salvation. Father Moore uses exorcism to save Emily's soul and thereby restore her to her prescribed place within the symbolic order. This process leads directly to Emily's death, which silences her completely.

Furthermore, *Emily Rose* prevents the viewer from knowing Emily before she becomes possessed; unlike other onscreen depictions of possessed individuals, audiences only witness the horrific spectacle of Emily's possession and consequently cannot identify with the pain she experiences while possessed. Derrickson cast dancer-turned-actress Jennifer Carpenter as Emily because she could contort her body in extreme ways, and therefore more dramatically visualize the effects of possession.[26] Emily's body therefore becomes her sole means of expression, her way of giving voice to her experience. She literally becomes objectified for the viewer's pleasure, exemplifying Laura Mulvey's concept of the male gaze as combined with Kristeva's concept of abjection: viewers are meant to enjoy the oddity of Emily's body rather than empathize with her plight.[27]

Furthermore, while the possession sequences are told from Emily's perspective, she nevertheless only conveys her true feelings or thoughts by screaming in pain and/or terror. Many exorcism films commonly depict women "speaking" their possession by "moaning, vomiting, [. . .] swaggering"[28] and so forth, but they also often swear, taunt, and speak truth to power while possessed. Emily's subjectivity generally emanates from the painful expressions her body uses to "speak" for her. Thus, the flashbacks effectively deny Emily's agency, and thus serve the viewer's pleasure. Ultimately, Emily's possession does not lead to the same type of empowerment that occurs in other films, primarily because *Emily Rose* pre-emptively silences the title character through an exorcism that leads to her death, and takes place prior to the film's central narrative.

Furthermore, Emily's possession causes Bruner to reconsider her own lack of faith. The film does grant Emily power, but this power aligns with patriarchy. Due to her possession, Emily experiences a vision of the Virgin Mary, an act that suggests she harbors a holiness that recalls Regan in *Exorcist II: The Heretic*. According to Derrickson, he wanted Emily's plight to inspire the faithless to discover their belief and follow the teachings of the Church[29] (and by extension the patriarchy). The film depicts Bruner potentially falling victim to the unseen demonic evil. *Emily Rose* establishes Bruner as a single, fiercely independent, atheistic career woman who does not believe in possession or exorcism. She only takes the case because her law firm pressures her to make the Church look good, and Bruner subsequently risks demonic attack by agreeing to defend Father Moore. Yet, as the trial continues and she experiences events she cannot fully explain, Bruner reconsiders her original position. Thus, she essentially assumes the role of the doubting priest figure, and faces spiritual danger because of that doubt. Furthermore, she experiences a sort of spiritual awakening following her brush with possession and exorcism. Yet, the film does not position her as the protagonist tasked with saving the possessed woman and thus society. Instead, Father Moore assumes that role because he confronts the demon possessing Emily. Therefore, the film's plot focuses on Bruner's conversion, which in turn serves to reaffirm the Church's righteousness because an atheist woman comes to believe in the traditions of patriarchal order, thereby legitimizing the continued repression and silencing of women who threaten that order.

A few years after *Emily Rose* became a box office success, Derrickson produced another exorcism film supposedly based on a true story. *Deliver Us* offers a fictionalized account of former NYPD police sergeant Ralph Sarchie's allegedly real encounters with the supernatural.[30] Producer Jerry Bruckheimer purchased the rights to Sarchie's story, and hired Derrickson to oversee a big screen adaptation. According to the DVD special features, Derrickson wanted to produce a film that portrayed possessed people as more calculating and thus more threatening to others as well as themselves.[31] Bruckheimer, on the other hand, wanted a more realistic and grounded depiction of the paranormal, and envisioned the film as a cross between *The Exorcist* and *Serpico* (1973, Sidney Lumet).[32] *Deliver Us* therefore resembles *The Exorcist III*, because it merges the tropes of exorcism cinema with those of serial killer films.

In *Deliver Us*, Sarchie (Eric Bana) investigates a series of paranormal incidents occurring throughout the Bronx. Like *The Exorcist*, Derrickson's film opens in Iraq as a platoon of marines engage enemy forces somewhere in the Diyala Province in 2010. During the battle, three marines retreat into a cavern and uncover some terrifying and unknown thing. Roughly three years later, Sarchie and his partner, Butler (Joel McHale), respond to a domestic disturbance call at the Bronx apartment of former marine Jimmy Tratner (Chris Coy), who draws a knife on Sarchie before fleeing the house on foot.

Afterward, Sarchie and Butler respond to another call at the Bronx Zoo, where a woman named Jane Crenna (Olivia Horton) supposedly threw her toddler into the lion enclosure. The cops find Jane hiding in the monkey pen, frantically clawing at the ground and muttering incoherently. As they apprehend her, Sarchie notices a mysterious man painting the rear wall of the lion enclosure. Sarchie tries to question this man, but a lion attacks Sarchie, who barely escapes with his life. Sarchie and Butler return to the station, where they meet a Jesuit priest named Mendoza (Édgar Ramírez), sent to check on Jane by her family. Before Sarchie and Butler can learn more, however, they must respond to yet another domestic disturbance call, this time from a family dealing with a series of bizarre events in their house. While there, Sarchie stumbles on the rotting corpse of a retired marine named David Griggs in the family's basement. The two cops then visit Griggs' apartment, where they find a photograph of him with Jane Crenna and their child, and another picture of Griggs in uniform alongside Tratner and a third marine named Santino (Sean Harris). Sarchie and Butler recognize Santino as the mysterious man from the zoo.

Back at the station, Sarchie once again bumps into Mendoza, who explains that Jane has succumbed to demonic possession. Sarchie initially dismisses this idea, but when he and Butler review the surveillance footage from the zoo, Sarchie sees and hears things that Butler does not. Returning to Tratner's apartment, Sarchie notices that one of the walls was recently painted. He scrapes off the paint to reveal a message written in Latin words and Persian pictographs. He also discovers a recording from the cavern in Diyala that shows the soldiers discovering the same message carved into the wall of the cave. Returning to the basement where he found Griggs' body, Sarchie finds the message yet again. He returns to the station and reviews the surveillance footage from the zoo, only to see Santino painting over the same message.

Mendoza identifies the message as a mixture of Christian and pagan theology designed to grant demons access to the human world. Mendoza accompanies Sarchie and Butler as they search for more clues, but they run into Santino and Tratner, who attack the trio. Sarchie and Mendoza manage to subdue Tratner, but Santino kills Butler and escapes. Despondent over the death of his partner, Sarchie returns home, where he discovers Santino waiting for him. Santino claims to have abducted Sarchie's wife and daughter, so Sarchie arrests him and brings him to the station for questioning. Mendoza arrives to assist Sarchie with the interrogation, which eventually turns into an exorcism. Sarchie and Mendoza successfully exorcise Santino, and a short while later, the police locate Sarchie's wife and daughter. The film ends with the baptism of Sarchie's second child.

In many ways, *Deliver Us* reaffirms the traditional exorcism narrative, particularly in that it features a man struggling with doubt or a loss of faith. The film also depicts a possessed woman who threatens the lives of the men around her. Additionally, much like *The Exorcist* and *Abby*, the film includes a Babylonian demon, meaning a non-white entity possesses individuals and threatens the stability of Western civilization. Thus, *Deliver Us* metaphorically portrays the oppression and repression of non-dominant groups, and it accomplishes this primarily by promoting a white, heteronormative, patriarchal status quo. Like the majority of exorcism films, Jane Crenna inhabits the role of monster and helpless victim. Yet, like *Exorcist III*, *Deliver Us* positions white, heterosexual male Santino as the main possessed individual who can spread demonic possession to other individuals (including another white, heterosexual male). As such, while a possessed woman threatens patriarchal order and normality in *Deliver Us*, the film's true threat emerges in the form of uncontrolled or destructive masculinity.

In the context of the traditional exorcism narrative, possessed women become dangerous because possession grants them access to a traditionally masculine form of power that allows them to act violently, behave sexually, and speak openly about their desires. *Deliver Us* uses Jane's possession to reinforce this idea, because she threatens the symbolic order through her newfound willingness to kill or harm men; first, she throws her son to the lions, then she viciously bites Sarchie's already wounded arm, and finally she kills a male orderly while escaping from the psychiatric hospital. Thus, like other exorcism films, *Deliver Us* maintains the central trope of the traditional exorcism narrative, that is, that women and female sexuality threaten patriarchal order.

Yet, *Deliver Us* ultimately reveals Jane's threat as secondary; like *Exorcist III*, the true threat manifests in the form of a possessed man, even as the narrative appears to advance a male worldview. Throughout the film, violence—particularly male violence—functions as a way to solve problems, suggesting a masculine approach to conflict resolution. At the same time, *Deliver Us* only endorses violence performed in the service of upholding traditional patriarchal institutions such as law or religion—in other words, righteous violence. The film portrays any violence committed outside the confines of these masculine institutions as unacceptable or harmful, particularly when perpetrated against women. For instance, when Sarchie and Butler respond to the domestic abuse call, Tratner's wife explains that he "just went crazy," a claim seemingly supported by his lack of prior arrests. Thus, the film appears to condemn uncontrolled violent masculinity as a dangerous aberration that does not align with patriarchal notions of chivalrous manhood.

In the film, faith functions as a metaphor for an individual's ability to control such violent masculine impulses. Men who lack faith or become corrupted by demonic influence can no longer control their violent impulses. As such, they threaten a traditional patriarchal order that only condones the use of violence as a last resort, such as in cases of self-defense or enacting justice. Despite grappling with their own crises of faith, Sarchie and Mendoza both hold (or eventually discover) the requisite belief in God, which in turn allows them to control their own destructive male impulses. Yet, the film still features the doubting male figure that recurs throughout the exorcism cinema subgenre. In *Deliver Us*, Sarchie assumes the role of the man who doubts both himself and God. At the same time, his links to the supernatural and his active attempts to control his anger mark him as a man who has not lost his faith entirely. Similarly, the film depicts Mendoza as flawed and grappling with his own inner demons. Yet, he believes in true evil, and therefore quickly accepts the idea that Jane has become possessed. The film portrays alignment with the patriarchy (i.e., Catholicism) as proper male behavior.

While spiritually protected from the possession and the destructive masculinity it represents, the film nevertheless portrays both men as complex figures whose struggles with faith and confrontation with supernatural evil ultimately cements their faith in God. For instance, Mendoza admits to Sarchie that he once fell from grace; after exorcizing a young possessed girl, Mendoza embarked upon an affair with her mother. The woman became pregnant with Mendoza's child but opted to abort it (or at least claimed to), and the grief caused Mendoza to abuse drugs. However, he cleaned up by choosing to serve God, and this decision aligns him with Father Karras and other doubting priest figures whose confrontation with demonic evil ultimately reaffirmed their faith.

Sarchie, meanwhile, recounts an incident from his childhood in which he saved his mother from a heroin addict who broke into their home. Whereas Mendoza's experiences reaffirmed his faith, Sarchie's served to cement his atheism; he contends that God had nothing to do with saving his mother. Sarchie says that over time he simply outgrew the idea of God, and the horrible things he routinely experienced as a cop only intensified his lack of faith. For instance, Sarchie once beat a child murderer to death, and afterward became plagued by visions of the man he killed. Thus, the film reveals Sarchie as a man haunted by his own personal demons, which result from his inability to control his anger and his fear that he might harm his family. It would take an experience with possession and exorcism to finally defeat these inner demons, which recalls how Bowden overcame his lack of faith in *Possessed*.

Beyond just reflecting the doubting priest figure, the film's central theme reaffirms patriarchal dominance primarily through its depiction of destructive masculinity.[33] Tanya Krzywinska terms the masculine demonic force as the "monstrous masculine," and argues that it represents a primal, anarchistic, and dreadful force.[34] While Krzywinska was writing about *The Exorcist*, this idea applies to *Deliver Us*, in which this monstrous masculine manifests primarily through the actions of the possessed marines, though Sarchie also exhibits such traits. Yet, he demonstrates an awareness of the destructive tendencies that reside within him, and actively works to control them. For instance, Sarchie confesses to Mendoza that he sometimes neglects his family, but only because he has difficulty controlling his anger and thus displays an attempt to control his destructive masculine impulses. In many ways, the possessed marines resemble men who cannot even recognize, much less control their violent or destructive impulses, not unlike soldiers suffering from post-traumatic stress disorder. In *Deliver Us*, Santino's possession stands in for destructive masculinity, and the film positions this extremely violent and aggressive form of maleness as harmful to both the individual and society.

The film ultimately reaffirms traditional and appropriate masculine power because it imbues the possessed Santino with enough agency to free himself from the demonic possession. During the exorcism sequence, Mendoza holds a saint's medallion and approaches Santino, who takes the priest's hands in his own and places them on his head. This action indicates a desire on Santino's part to assist in the exorcism and ensure its success, as though he desires to participate in his own salvation. In essence, the film suggests that Santino's masculine power grants him the ability to save himself, whereas possessed women commonly appear incapable of asking for help due to a lack of agency and require a man's intervention to free them from possession. Santino seems to recognize his potential for extreme violence and aggression, and his actions realign him with traditional patriarchy because he manages to bring his destructive masculine impulses under control. Santino maintains some level of agency during his possession, a common occurrence among possessed men (see also Karras in *The Exorcist* and *Exorcist III*, Sonny in *Amityville II: The Possession*, and Robbie in *Possessed*). Possessed women, on the other hand, cannot save themselves from possession, and often seem to revel in the power granted by their possession. Therefore, a member of the patriarchy must act to restrain, silence, and oppress them and thereby restore order.

FOUND FOOTAGE EXORCISM FILMS

In this section, we consider how the found footage movie *[Rec]* [2] (2009, Jaume Balagueró and Paco Plaza) and the first person perspective film *Grace: The Possession* (2014, Jeff Chan) both reflect the traditional exorcism narrative. Since 9/11, nineteen movies have thus far utilized the found footage narrative and aesthetic style. These include *Home Movie* (2008, Christopher Denham), *The Last Exorcism* (2010, Daniel Stamm), *The Devil Inside* (2012, William Brent Bell), *[REC]³: Génesis* (2012, Paco Plaza), *The Vatican Exorcisms* (2013, Joe Marino), *The Taking of Deborah Logan* (2014, Adam Robitel), *The Possession of Michael King* (2014, David Jung), *The Atticus Institute* (2015, Chris Sparling), and *Paranormal Activity: The Ghost Dimension* (2015, Gregory Plotkin).

Found footage horror films often imply that ordinary people or would-be documentary filmmakers (i.e., amateurs) shot the onscreen footage while experiencing the unusual circumstances that led to their demise. Such films mimic footage shot on handheld recording equipment and/or surveillance cameras to replicate documentary-style aesthetics and narrative tactics to give the impression that the events depicted onscreen actually happened; filming with these techniques produces a "fly-on-the-wall" effect and creates an observational tone that blurs the lines between reality and fiction.[35] For instance, *The Devil Inside* features a documentary film crew encountering a demonic presence while documenting a young woman's quest to vindicate her mother. Similarly, *The Atticus Institute* presents itself as a documentary, using the found footage from a scientific institute to tell the "real" story of an attempt to weaponize a possessed woman for military purposes.

Other found footage films reflect the increased preponderance of video recording devices in people's everyday lives and the constant surveillance that occurs elsewhere in the culture. Aside from those framed as documentaries, such films rarely clarify who found the footage and what led them to edit it together into a feature-length film. For example, *Paranormal Activity: The Ghost Dimension*—the fifth film in the highly successful franchise—furthers the stylistic conceits of the previous films, this time using surveillance style footage to uncover a young girl's possession. *[REC]³*, meanwhile, features an outbreak of demonic possession at a wedding as recorded by the attendees, using recording devices commonly found at contemporary weddings, such as smartphones and video cameras. Thus, the found footage aesthetic lends an amplified sense of authenticity to cinematic depictions of supernatural events.

According to Alexandra Heller-Nicholas, the found footage subgenre achieved prominence because its "particular brand of filmmaking aesthetics have opened it up to a range of production budgets."[36] Similarly, film critics Keith Phipps and Scott Tobias observe that found footage films increased in popularity after *The Blair Witch Project* became a massive hit;[37] following a wildly successful and innovative Internet marketing campaign, the film grossed $248 million worldwide against a reported $60,000 production budget.[38] However, the subgenre did not truly take off until *Paranormal Activity* grossed $193 million worldwide against a reported production budget of only $15,000.[39] These two films not only demonstrated the technical and narratological feasibility of the found footage conceit, but also proved that it held great commercial potential as well. When combined with the increased affordability and availability of high-end commercial filmmaking equipment, it makes sense that many directors opted to construct their horror films using the found footage, pseudo-documentary narrative conceit.

Indeed, the post-9/11 social atmosphere that stimulated the horror genre in general and exorcism cinema in particular also likely encouraged the rise of these innovative filmmaking techniques. Wetmore notes that amateur video has emerged as the primary trope of post-9/11 horror, because it resembles both the footage of the attacks (i.e., primarily shot on consumer digital video equipment) and the "terrorist-made, internet-dispersed video of real torture and death."[40] These practices led directly to the proliferation of found footage or pseudo-documentary horror films, which use verisimilitude and immediacy to suggest that the events depicted onscreen actually occurred and thus generate an enhanced sense of fear in the viewer.[41]

Found footage became a global phenomenon as filmmakers around the world used such techniques to portray a variety of culturally specific horrors onscreen. For instance, the Spanish found footage movie *[Rec]* (2007, Jaume Balagueró and Paco Plaza) made enough of an impact at the box office that Hollywood quickly remade it as *Quarantine* (2008, John Erick Dowdle). Both films depict essentially the same sequence of events: a news team follows a crew of firemen as they deal with an emergency at an apartment building where the residents have become infected with a mysterious disease that seemingly turns them into zombies. Both films end with an unseen monster dragging the surviving female reporter into the darkness. Interestingly, each film spawned sequels, but only one would align the franchise with exorcism cinema. *[Rec]²* reveals demonic possession as the source of the affliction rather than a mutant strain of rabies, as proposed by the original film and its Hollywood remake. Furthermore, *[Rec]²* suggests the Catholic Church played a role in the demonic outbreak, and the film clearly blames the apocalyptic events engulfing Spain on a viral form of demonic possession.

In *[Rec]²*, Madrid's Ministry of Health orders Dr. Owen (Jonathan Mellor) and a special ops team equipped with video cameras to investigate the quarantined apartment building from the first film. Upon entering, an infected resident attacks and seemingly kills one of the officers. The rest of the team retreat to safety, where Owen reveals himself as a priest sent by the Vatican to obtain a blood sample from a demonically possessed girl named Tristana Medeiros (Nico Baixas). The surviving members of the special ops team reluctantly agree to help Owen complete his mission, and they set off to explore the apartment complex. Officer Larra (Ariel Casas) finds a vial of Tristana's blood, and Owen performs a religious rite over it, causing the blood to combust. Startled, commanding officer Jefe (Óscar Zafra) drops the vial which shatters, meaning they now have to retrieve a sample from the girl herself. This necessitates further exploration of the building, during which the crew encounters several other possessed individuals.

During the course of their investigation, the team meets up with Ángela Vidal (Manuela Velasco), the reporter from the previous film. She helps them locate the possessed Tristana, who immediately attacks them. Ángela kills the girl with a shotgun, and then attacks Owen without warning and kills the special ops cameraman. The film then reveals that Ángela has become possessed, and the demon wants nothing more than to escape from the quarantined building. The possessed Ángela kills Owen and steals his radio; speaking in his voice, she contacts the police outside and tricks them into letting her go free, thus unleashing a demonic plague upon the world.

[Rec]² aligns with the traditional exorcism narrative because it portrays both a possessed woman as a threat to order and a doubting priest who must reaffirm his faith and halt the threat. Throughout the film women become possessed and assault others. For instance, while searching the apartment complex, Owen and his team discover a young possessed girl who attacks them. However, they also encounter a possessed teenage boy, and while this initially seems like a challenge to the traditional exorcism narrative, it ultimately proves otherwise because the boy provides the group with vital information. Thus, the possessed boy proves useful, whereas possessed girls prove dangerous. Indeed, the infection began when a girl became possessed. Furthermore, the film's ultimate threat arrives in the form of the female reporter from the first film; the now possessed Ángela tortures and/or kills each member of the team in her effort to escape the building and infect others. Thus, she not only threatens Owen and the special ops team, but the entire world (as seen in *[REC]³: Génesis*). In the end, Ángela escapes because she mimics the

priest's voice to call for retrieval. Indeed, the possessed woman's voice represents the deadliest threat in the film, because it allows the demon to engulf the world in the same sort of death and destruction that afflicted the apartment complex.

Unlike other exorcism films, *[Rec]²* features no sustained attempt to exorcise the demon; instead, Owen uses exorcism rituals to interrogate possessed individuals rather than free them from demonic influence, and his actions ultimately allow the infection to spread. The film introduces Owen as a man of science sent to investigate the outbreak, and does not identify him as a priest until he uses prayer to confront an infected officer. Following this reveal, Owen admits that the Vatican secretly dispatched him to study the possessed girl and gain a better understanding of demonic possession. Owen's predecessor, Father Albeda, believed the cure for this infernal infection lies with science, and this misplaced belief apparently caused the initial outbreak. Owen shares this belief, but when faced with his own death, he realizes that he has mistaken his faith in science rather than God. Had Owen exorcised Ángela, her corruption would not have spread beyond the apartment building. Owen's doubt allows the demon to succeed, and the film thereby aligns with the traditional exorcism narrative because Owen exemplifies the doubting priest figure and a woman threatens patriarchal order.

At the same time, *[Rec]²* offers a slight challenge to the traditional exorcism narrative because it blames the Church for causing pain and suffering even as it reveals that a possessed girl caused the outbreak depicted in the first film. Eleven-year-old Tristana showed signs of possession, which in turn prompted the Vatican to send Father Albeda to study the physiological symptoms of her condition. The film then reveals that Church officials wanted to isolate her chemical essence so they could use it to create an antidote to possession, essentially equating demonic influence to a virus. The film posits a medical explanation for a supernatural affliction, and thus represents an interesting combination of religious dogma and scientific inquiry, which serve as the backbone for two different patriarchal institutions. At the same time, however, *[Rec]²* also challenges the traditional exorcism narrative in a way similar to *Stigmata* (discussed in the previous chapter); while the danger originates with a woman, it increases due to the Catholic Church's sense of its own infallibility. Indeed, *[Rec]²* clearly establishes that the Church caused the outbreak and, more heinously, it did so by experimenting on children.[42] Thus, the film challenges the traditional exorcism narrative because it portrays the Church as a clandestine and altogether dishonest organization.

Yet, *[Rec]²* also suggests that religion held the power to end the possessed woman's threat if only Albeda had exorcised Tristana, or if Owen had exorcised Ángela. So while *[Rec]²* challenges the Church's role and power, it nevertheless reinforces its necessity; Owen's words of prayer and muted attempts at exorcism function as the only means to stop the possessed people (outside of a bullet to the head, which references *Exorcist III*). Owen could have fulfilled his role as protagonist if he had performed the full rites of exorcism, but his lack of faith ultimately dooms the entire world.

Grace similarly suggests that a priest's failure endangers the world, while offering another innovative variation on the found footage style of storytelling. As discussed above, found footage films typically depict the onscreen events in a way that implies the footage was collected from numerous cameras—often recovered after some mysterious and/or terrifying event—and then edited together to provide the viewer with a cohesive narrative. *[Rec]²* conforms to this approach, for instance. Other times, a found footage movie will employ documentary techniques such as narration, talking head interviews, voiceovers, inserts of official documents, and first person camera footage to create a sense of verisimilitude. In both cases, the film restricts the audience's perspective to that of the characters who capture events with their cameras. While *Grace* does not conform to either of these standard approaches, it nevertheless portrays a first-person point of view account of a young woman's possession and subsequent exorcism. Thus, while not a found footage film per se, it recalls such aesthetic conventions because it similarly restricts the audience's viewpoint, as the character of Grace becomes the camera through which the audience experiences her story.

The film opens with eighteen-year-old Grace (Alexia Fast) arriving at college, in a sequence that resembles other conventionally-shot horror films (i.e., the camera assumes a more or less omniscient perspective). Yet, as soon as the pious young woman settles into her dorm room, the camera glides behind Grace and seemingly enters the back of her head. From that point on, the film adopts a first person perspective, and the audience views the world through the young woman's eyes. This first person perspective necessarily limits how the film depicts possession, but it also offers more insight into the possessed person's subjective experience than any other exorcism film produced up to that point. While the film's portrayal of possession and exorcism allows the audience to experience Grace's subjective experiences and thus empathize with her, it nevertheless aligns with the traditional exorcism narrative because it depicts her as a threat to others.

Shortly after arriving at Middleton State University, Grace experiences all manner of stranger phenomena, including terrifying nightmares and unsettling visions. One night, she attends a house party where she meets a young man named Brad (Brett Dier) and encounters more supernatural phenomena. At one point, Grace suffers a hallucination in which she kills her roommate, Jessica (Alexis Knapp), by shoving her off the second story balcony. This vision proves so distressing that Grace faints. She wakes up in the hospital a few hours later to find her devoutly

Catholic grandmother, Helen (Lin Shaye), at her bedside. Helen takes Grace back to their home to speak with Father John (Alan Dale) and Deacon Luke (Joel David Moore). Afterward, Helen forbids Grace from returning to school.

That night, Grace hears strange noises coming from her dead mother's old room. She attempts to investigate, but Helen prohibits her from entering. The next day at church, Grace coughs up blood after taking communion. She returns home and sneaks into her mother's room, where she finds an old keepsake box. Grace then locks herself in her room and opens the box to discover a bottle of old sleeping pills hidden inside. She swallows a handful of the pills and falls into a deep sleep. Grace wakes several hours later and masturbates while fantasizing about Brad. Helen enters and catches Grace in the act, and whips the young woman as punishment. The next day, Grace attends one of Deacon Luke's youth group meetings, but she blacks out and attacks another girl. Horrified, Grace flees into the woods and has a vision of her mother, Mary (also played by Alexia Fast in flashbacks). Afterward, Grace returns home and has yet another vision, this time of Father John raping her mother.

At that point, Grace succumbs fully to demonic possession; she attacks Helen and then returns to the church. There, she attempts to seduce Deacon Luke, but he rebuffs her. Enraged by his rejection, the possessed Grace attacks the young holy man, but Father John intervenes and knocks her unconscious. Sometime later, Grace awakens to find herself bound to a table in the church's basement. Just then, Father Michael (Clarke Peters) arrives to help Father John and Deacon Luke exorcise Grace. However, she manages to escape her bonds and kill Father Michael. Grace then chases Father John into the church and drowns him in the basin of holy water. Luke confronts the possessed Grace, and convinces the demon to enter his body. Afterward, the now possessed Luke accepts a position as the new parish priest.

Over the course of the film, Grace goes from an innocent, virginal girl striving to navigate the oppressive conditions of her home life, to a defiant and deadly young woman who threatens those around her. Moreover, while the film essentially justifies her deviant behavior by blaming it on Father John's actions, Grace nevertheless submits to repression like other possessed woman. Significantly, the film links the possession directly to Grace's sexuality when Grace attends a fraternity "angels and demons" party in spite of her grandmother's wishes. This act of disobedience apparently renders the young woman susceptible to possession. Indeed, the demon enters Grace when she prepares for the party; she stands in front of the mirror wearing a modest but revealing outfit, and as she applies her lipstick a dead-eyed, demonic visage suddenly flashes across her face. Thus, the film suggests that by embracing her sexuality, Grace rendered herself susceptible to demonic influence, thereby aligning female sexuality with the abject.

At the party, Grace meets and becomes infatuated with Brad, and her desire only seems to accelerate her possession because her sexual urges increase at that point. For instance, the morning after she breaks into her mother's old room, Grace wakes to find Brad lying next to her in bed. He initiates intercourse, and though shocked to find him in her bed, Grace nevertheless submits to his advances. Yet, when she glances over at the mirror, she discovers that she is actually alone and masturbating. By depicting Grace's burgeoning sexuality as a side effect of her possession, the film links the female sex drive to demonic evil and thus renders it deviant and abject, which in turn aligns *Grace* with the traditional exorcism narrative.

The film does challenge this narrative, however, particularly in how it portrays the Church as a flawed institution. While *Grace* depicts Deacon Luke as the holy man who finally halts the threat posed by the possessed woman, the film also positions Father John as the ultimate cause of the threat when it reveals that he raped Grace's mother and subsequently unleashed the demonic spirit into the world. Moreover, when Grace finally confronts Father John about her mother's assault, he stabs her. His actions indicate an attempt to silence Grace and prevent her from speaking the truth about his indiscretion, which would tarnish the Church's reputation and thereby call its patriarchal authority into question. Thus, Father John recalls Cardinal Houseman from *Stigmata*, because his actions again indict the Church itself as a corrupt institution.[43]

Furthermore, while Grace's exorcism serves to redeem both her and the Church, the latter remains tainted in the end. After killing Fathers Michael and John, the demon compels Grace to slit her own throat, but Luke intervenes and demands the entity leave her body and enter his instead (much like Father Karras in *The Exorcist*). Luke's willingness to sacrifice himself to save Grace appears to redeem the sanctity of Church, which initially become fouled by Father John's actions. Notably, when the demon possesses Luke, the viewer leaves Grace's subjectivity and enters Luke's perspective. This change in viewpoint suggests that Grace has lost the power and agency granted by the possession, but it also implies that she has realigned with the symbolic order. At the same time, however, Father Luke remains alive and possessed, and afterward assumes a position of increased power within the Church, an act that aligns patriarchal power with corruption. Thus, while the film reaffirms the traditional exorcism narrative by advancing the idea that only a holy man can suppress the threat posed by a possessed woman, it nevertheless raises doubts about the appropriateness of such action by having the priest succumb to possession himself.

As in other exorcism films, Grace's possession grants her the power to speak the truth and resist her oppression, but also positions her as a threat in the process. Though Father John's actions essentially caused Grace's possession and subsequently sullied the Church's reputation,

Grace nevertheless emerges as the true threat because of her newfound ability to speak truth to power. Similarly, when she passes the demon to Luke, she remained a threat, because her possession and thus the truth behind it ultimately taints Luke. Indeed, Luke's actions both redeem and damn the Church because he willingly sacrifices himself to save Grace, but he also becomes contaminated by an evil that could potentially dismantle the organization from within. Grace, meanwhile, functions as the conduit that linked these two men; if Father John had refrained from assaulting her mother, Grace likely would not have become empowered to speak the truth, and thus she would not have threatened the Church or the patriarchy. Therefore, while the film indicts the Church's oppressive treatment of women, it also reinforces the idea that women endanger patriarchal authority when they transition from virgin to whore.

REALISM AND THE TRADITIONAL EXORCISM NARRATIVE

Following the terrorist attacks of 9/11, exorcism cinema roared back to life. Many of the films released during this period depicted possession and exorcism in a realistic manner. Some of these films challenged the traditional exorcism narrative, while others reaffirm its ideological positioning. *Emily Rose* and *Deliver Us* largely align with the traditional exorcism narrative, while *[REC]²* and *Grace* offer challenges. These last two films, however, ultimately align with the possessed-woman-as-threat trope even as they challenge the doubting priest or male savior tropes. Despite how they differ the traditional exorcism narrative, the films analyzed in this chapter all offer realistic portrayals of possession and exorcism. This realism angle potentially serves to marginalize women and other non-dominant groups to an even greater extent than exorcism films produced before 9/11. Using realism to add authenticity to stories that thematically represent oppression could further stigmatize individuals seeking to assert their voice.

Wetmore argues that post-9/11 horror does not situate death as a force for morality, but rather as something random and senseless. Slasher films commonly moralized the deaths of the young victims by suggesting that "engaging in negative behavior such as drinking, doing drugs, having premarital sex are often forerunners to being killed by the killer(s)."[44] Horror films of the twenty-first century, according to Wetmore, tend to suggest that death can affect anyone at any time, meaning that it has nothing to do with their behavior, good or bad. Thus, while good behavior often functions as a form of protection from the serial killers and slashers of films produced during the 1980s and 1990s, post-9/11 horror films offer no similar guarantee.[45] Wetmore observes that horror films of this era tend to reflect the sense of hopelessness that emerged after 9/11.[46] From Wetmore's perspective, possessions become random events in post-

9/11 exorcism cinema, and thus reflect the real-life terrorism facing the films' audiences.

Yet, these seemingly random possessions serve the same kinds of metaphorical purposes as the pre-9/11 films. The films discussed in this chapter demonstrate how the exorcism cinema resurgence incorporates the traditional exorcism narrative established by *The Exorcist*, because the films produced during this period retain their metaphorical focus on oppressing non-dominant groups, particularly women. In these films, the women become possessed to provide morality tales regarding appropriate and inappropriate behavior, either for the women or for the male priests tasked with saving them. For instance, Emily Rose's possession allowed her to serve as an example for the world, and thereby the possession aligns her with patriarchal notions of feminine propriety. Even Santino's possession demonstrates the dangers that hyperviolent masculinity pose to society, much like Sonny's possession in *Amityville II* or Karras's in *Exorcist III*. Thus, these possessions reaffirm a traditional patriarchal ideology. Meanwhile, Ángela's and Grace's possessions challenge the Church's inviolability, much like Frankie's possession in *Stigmata*. If the religious figures had acted in accordance with proper patriarchal traditions, neither woman would have become possessed, much less a threat to those around her. All four films depict proper patriarchal values that should be followed to prevent moral decay. Thus, while the possessions in post-9/11 exorcism films may seem random because the demon does not have a clear motive,[47] the portrayals of possession and exorcism nevertheless tend to reflect widespread sociocultural concerns about patriarchal authority and thereby reaffirm the traditional exorcism narrative.

As such, these films function as morality tales, discursively depicting the boundaries of appropriate and inappropriate behavior. The most problematic aspect of these films, then, lies in the insinuation that they reflect the "real" terror of possession. The realistic aesthetic reinforces the possibility of possession and the metaphorical reasons for it, which could in turn further reaffirm the legitimacy of the exorcism required to remove the threat. As such, post-9/11 exorcism films further reinforce the idea that oppressing these marginalized voices represents the correct action; since these voices could potentially threaten traditional order, oppressing them becomes the legitimate course of action to prevent or stop such societal or cultural upheaval. As Wetmore notes, horror suggests that viewers should "be afraid, suspicious and even paranoid and, by extension, to be violent and aggressive" toward those causing fear, and position violence as the only defense because the monstrous Other(s) "will not stop trying to kill you until you are forced to kill it or them."[48] Therefore, portraying non-dominant groups as a threat to the established order could potentially lead to the increased stigmatization of marginalized Others, an experience common in the hypermediated post-9/11 world.

More and more, people come to know reality only through mediated experiences, and therefore audiences can more readily accept the idea that a mediated narrative reflects reality, particularly those that contain and reinforce prevailing stereotypes. Cultivation theory,[49] the perceived reality concept,[50] and the postmodern concept of the simulacrum[51] come into play at this point; if individuals accept the signs of reality and the simulated experience as real, then any narrative that strives to replicate reality could impact the individual to a greater degree. When people can no longer distinguish between a mediated reality and reality itself, they could potentially accept the lessons imparted by the mediated reality. As discussed in chapter 1, research into media effects that arise from watching horror movies suggests the possibility of this type of incidental learning, even if the viewer has no awareness of this impact. Thus, any film that uses narrative and aesthetic techniques to reinforce the reality that lies behind the traditional exorcism narrative's tropes could potentially lead viewers to more readily believe in the reality of those tropes, including the idea that societal order depends on the oppression and marginalization of certain groups of people. This message becomes even more persuasive in the post-9/11 period, as people perceive the world as increasingly unstable, and seek any means to stabilize it once more.

The majority of films produced during this post-9/11 period reify the traditional exorcism narrative, and in fact focus more on the possessed-woman-as-threat trope rather than its subset, the possessed-Other-as-threat. With so many films focusing on women as threats, it becomes important to examine those that do not align completely with the traditional exorcism narrative. In the next chapter, we analyze two films that, when considered together, not only challenge the narrative, but appear to destabilize its ideological messages of feminine repression. Such challenges may reflect the state of feminism in Western civilization two generations removed from the emergence of second-wave feminism. As such, they reflect contemporary tensions regarding the limits of female empowerment.

NOTES

1. Steffan Hantke, "Academic Film Criticism, the Rhetoric of Crisis, and the Current State of American Horror Cinema: Thoughts on Canonicity and Academic Anxiety," *College Literature* 34, no. 4 (2007): 191–202.

2. Kevin J. Wetmore, *Post-9/11 Horror in American Cinema* (New York: Continuum, 2012), 142.

3. Ibid., 5.

4. Ibid., 168.

5. Ibid.

6. Ibid., 142.

7. Ibid., 12.

8. This includes films already released, as well as those currently listed as "in development" or "in production."

9. Mark Kermode, *The Exorcist: Revised 2nd Edition* (London: British Film Institute, 2003), 95.

10. Ibid.

11. Bob McCabe, *The Exorcist: Out of the Shadows* (New York: Omnibus Press, 1999), 179.

12. Kermode, *The Exorcist*, 95.

13. Interestingly, a similar, more extensive spider walk sequence occurred during the exorcism scene featured in *Il demonio* (1963, Brunello Rondi), a full ten years before the aborted attempt in *The Exorcist*.

14. Kermode, *The Exorcist*, 104.

15. Critics often cite *Cannibal Holocaust* (1980, Ruggero Deodato) as the first true found footage film. For more on the found footage subgenre, see Alexandra Heller-Nicholas, *Found Footage Horror Films: Fear and the Appearance of Reality*, (Jefferson: McFarland & Company, Inc., 2014) and Chris Eggertson, "From 'Blair Witch' to 'Project Almanac': A History of the Found Footage Genre," *Hitfix*, last modified February 2, 2015, http://www.hitfix.com/news/from-cannibal-holocaust-to-project-almanac-a-history-of-the-found-footage-genre.

16. For more, see Heller-Nicholas, *Found Footage*.

17. For more on *The Exorcist*'s production and marketing, see Kermode, *The Exorcist*, 73–77 and Alexandra Heller-Nicholas, "'The Power of Christ Compels You': Moral Spectacle and The Exorcist Universe" in *Roman Catholicism in Fantastic Film: Essays on Belief, Spectacle, Ritual and Imagery*, ed. Regina Hansen (Jefferson: McFarland & Company, Inc., 2011), 68.

18. Kermode, *The Exorcist*, 73.

19. Richard Deutch, *Exorcism: Possession or Obsession?* (London: Bachman & Turner, 1975), 31.

20. J. P. Telotte, "Faith and Idolatry in the Horror Film," in *Planks of Reason: Essays on the Horror Film*, eds. Barry Keith Grant and Christopher Sharrett (Lanham: Scarecrow press, Inc., 2004), 22.

21. Ibid.

22. Of course, contemporary audiences can easily go online and learn the truth behind each of these films, and a few savvy marketers have even incorporated such awareness as part of their marketing campaigns.

23. Jeffrey Overstreet, *Through a Screen Darkly: Looking Closer at Beauty, Truth and Evil in the Movies* (Ventura: Regal Books, 2007), 278–79.

24. Peter T. Chattaway, "Devil in the Details?: Horror-Flick Director Seeks to Confront Postmodern Culture With Ultimate Issues," *Christianity Today*, 49 no. 11 (2005): 102.

25. "The Exorcism of Emily Rose," *Box Office Mojo*, accessed August 6, 2016, http://www.boxofficemojo.com/movies/?id=blairwitchproject.htm.

26. "Story Notes for *The Exorcism of Emily Rose*," *AMC.com*, accessed February 19, 2016, http://www.amc.com/talk/2011/10/story-notes-trivia-the-exorcism-of-emily-rose.

27. For more on the male gaze, see Laura Mulvey, "Visual Pleasure and Narrative Cinema," in *Film Theory and Criticism* (6th Ed.), eds. Leo Braudy and Marshall Cohen (New York: Oxford University Press, 1975/2004).

28. Carol J. Clover, *Men, Women, and Chain Saws: Gender in the Modern Horror Film* (Princeton: Princeton University Press, 1992), 109–10.

29. Peter T. Chattaway, "Devil in the Details?: Horror-Flick Director Seeks to Confront Postmodern Culture With Ultimate Issues," *Christianity Today*, 49 no. 11 (2005): 102.

30. In his book, *Beware the Night: A New York City Cop Investigates the Supernatural* (written with Lisa Collier Cool and published in 2001), Sarchie allegedly chronicles his various encounters with the paranormal during his time as a police officer in the

1970s. Sarchie also claims to have worked with paranormal investigators Ed and Lorraine Warren, who gained fame after investigating the Amityville haunting. For more, see Samantha Cheirif, "Former NYPD Officer Ralph Sarchie Talks DELIVER US FROM EVIL, Having His Life Story Made into a Movie, and His Experiences with the Paranormal," *Collider.com*, last modified July 2, 2014, http://collider.com/ralph-sarchie-deliver-us-from-evil-interview/.

31. Scott Derrickson, "Illuminating Evil: Making *Deliver Us from Evil*," *Deliver Us from Evil*, Blu-ray, directed by Scott Derrickson (Culver City: Screen Gems, 2014).

32. Jerry Bruckheimer, "Illuminating Evil: Making *Deliver Us from Evil*," *Deliver Us from Evil*, Blu-ray, directed by Scott Derrickson (Culver City: Screen Gems, 2014).

33. This recalls Barry Keith Grant's (2011) assertion that in conventional horror films, "the male hero must defeat the masculine monster, who may be seen to embody an uncontrollable phallic sexual aggression [. . .] and so assume his proper place within the prevailing patriarchal order" (285).

34. Tanya Krzywinska, "Demon Daddies: Gender, Ecstasy and Terror in the Possession Film," in *The Horror Film Reader*, eds. Alain Silver and James Ursini (New York: Limelight Editions, 2000), 256.

35. Heller-Nicholas, *Found Footage*, 13–14, 18.

36. Ibid., 3.

37. Keith Phipps and Scott Tobias, "The Present and Future of Found-footage Horror," *The Dissolve*, last modified October 30, 2014, https://thedissolve.com/features/movie-of-the-week/804-the-present-and-future-of-found-footage-horror/.

38. "The Blair Witch Project (1999)," *Box Office Mojo*, accessed August 10, 2015, http://www.boxofficemojo.com/movies/?id=blairwitchproject.htm.

39. "Paranormal Activity (2009)," *Box Office Mojo*, accessed August 10, 2015, http://www.boxofficemojo.com/movies/?id=paranormalactivity.htm.

40. Wetmore, *Post 9/11 Horror*, 59.

41. Ibid., 63–65.

42. A possible reference to the Catholic Church's involvement in various child abuse scandals throughout the 1990s and beyond.

43. Two other films from 2015 also feature a similar indictment of the Catholic Church. Directed by Steven R. Monroe, *The Exorcism of Molly Hartley* reveals officials within the Catholic Church as the Satanists behind Molly's possession. Meanwhile, in Marcus Nispel's *Exeter*, the possessed woman seeks revenge on her father, a Catholic priest who sought to hide his illicit offspring.

44. Wetmore, *Post 9/11 Horror*, 83.

45. Ibid., 86.

46. Ibid., 144.

47. Except in *Grace*, which clearly identifies why the demon chose to possess the title character.

48. Wetmore, *Post 9/11 Horror*, 190.

49. George Gerbner, Larry Gross, Michael Morgan, Nancy Signorielli, and James Shanahan, "Growing Up with Television: Cultivation Processes," in *Media Effects: Advances in Theory and Research* (2nd Ed.), eds. Jennings Bryant and Dolf Zillmann (Hillsdale: Lawrence Erlbaum Associates, 2002), 43–66

50. W. James Potter, "Perceived Reality in Television Effects Research," *Journal of Broadcasting and Electronic Media* 32, no. 1. (1988): 23–41.

51. For more on the concept of simulacra, see Jean Baudrillard, *Simulacra and Simulation* (Ann Arbor: University of Michigan Press, 1981), 1–42.

EIGHT

From Reaffirming to Challenging Tradition

The Last Exorcism *and* The Last Exorcism Part II

The fear and anxiety that defined the post-9/11 era ushered in a new era of horror films, including many that dealt with possession and exorcism. At the same time, the rise of smartphones and social media allowed people a greater ability to document their own lives, and horror films increasingly reflected this tendency through their aesthetics and storytelling techniques. In addition, this period experienced an increase in sociocultural tensions as subcultures and non-dominant groups clashed with traditional cultures and ideologies. According to Kevin J. Wetmore, the events of 9/11 rejected any sort of gender bias, and likely reshaped gender politics and empowered women on a global scale because the terror attacks ignored any sort of gender bias and affected both men and women alike.[1]

At the same time, contemporary media coverage of these events often advanced an agenda that negated feminism's continued relevance in the wake of such male-perpetrated horrors, and in many ways blamed the feminist ideology for the attacks. Some critics even alleged that feminist philosophy served to feminize men in the United States while promoting multiculturalism at the expense of traditional values.[2] Such hyperbolic media coverage indicates a continued demonization of feminism in the wake of 9/11; indeed, during this period feminist thought became positioned as either irrelevant or as an active threat to order and stability. Certain anti-feminist and anti-women discourses in online forums like /r/MensRights and /r/TheRedPill advance the idea that feminism victimizes men and masculinity.[3] In such spaces, men actively silence marginalized voices.[4] Such activity reflects widespread conceptualizations of dominant masculinity, which often seeks to control such voices and prevent them from upholding or enacting a specific way of life.

Various post-9/11 horror films perpetuate this negative portrayal of women and female empowerment, but as discussed in the previous chapter, exorcism cinema in particular perpetuates this way of thinking. Yet, some exorcism films do challenge or at least problematize the notion that female liberation leads to strife, and therefore align with the sort of empowering thematic content that Wetmore describes. In particular, two films produced during this period work together to reaffirm and challenge the traditional exorcism narrative. First, the found footage horror film *The Last Exorcism* (2010, Daniel Stamm) reflects and perpetuates the embedded conservative ideology that appeared in *The Exorcist*. Like that seminal film, *Last Exorcism* portrays a savior priest using exorcism to save the soul of a young woman whose possession renders her both monstrous and helpless. In contrast, *The Last Exorcism Part II* (2013, Ed Gass-Donnelly) follows a traditional narrative structure, but its portrayal of exorcism subverts the traditional exorcism narrative; the main character embraces the power offered to her by the demonic entity, and thus her feminine power, sexuality, and agency remains unchecked at the end of the film.

This chapter considers how these two films work together to destabilize the traditional exorcism narrative by reflecting and responding to prevailing contemporary discourses surrounding feminism and female empowerment. While *Last Exorcism* reaffirms the traditional exorcism narrative because it portrays a member of the patriarchy working to repress an unruly woman, *Last Exorcism II* subverts it by depicting the possessed woman as an empowered individual who overthrows her oppressors and fully embraces her power, her sexuality, and her agency. Moreover, the sequel's ending reflects potential changes in Western society and culture that occurred at the time of the film's production and reception, and involved an increased tolerance toward individuals who assert some measure of control over their own lives and identities.

THE LAST EXORCISM AND ITS SEQUEL

Last Exorcism follows the exploits of Reverend Cotton Marcus (Patrick Fabian), a troubled evangelical minister who abandoned his faith and now seeks to expose exorcism as a fraudulent and dangerous belief. Early in the film, Reverend Marcus receives a letter from an evangelical farmer in rural Louisiana named Louis Sweetzer (Louis Herthum), who believes his shy daughter, Nell (Ashley Bell), has become possessed. Reverend Marcus sees this as an opportunity to expose yet another incidence of fake demonic possession, but he and a pair of documentarians named Iris

(Iris Bahr) and Daniel (Adam Grimes) instead become involved in a larger supernatural conspiracy.

After making a show of investigating the details of Nell's case, Marcus promptly announces that the girl has become possessed by a powerful demon named Abalam. Marcus performs a sham exorcism ritual—complete with elaborate special effects—designed to dupe the family into believing that he cast out the demon. Afterward, Marcus and the documentary crew return to their hotel, but Nell appears in Marcus's room later that night, acting strangely. Marcus takes her to the hospital for testing, but doctors can find nothing wrong with the girl. Nell returns home with her father the next morning, but she loses control once more and slices her brother Caleb's (Caleb Landry Jones) face with a knife, prompting Louis to chain the uncontrollable girl to her bed.

Marcus, Ira, and Daniel return to the Sweetzer farm to check on Nell, and they decide to stay when they learn of her condition. That night, while everyone else sleeps, Nell steals Daniel's camera, and uses it to beat a cat to death in the barn. She returns to the house and tries to attack Marcus with the camera, but the crew manages to stop her. They then discover two paintings in Nell's room, one of Marcus standing before a large bonfire while holding his crucifix high above his head, and another of Iris and Daniel both hacked to pieces.

The next day, Marcus and the documentary crew learn that Nell is pregnant. They accuse Louis of incest, but he denies any involvement in her condition and insists that Abalam violated his little girl. Marcus and the film crew confront Nell about the pregnancy, but she attacks Marcus once again before fleeing from the house. Upset, Louis orders Marcus and the documentary crew to leave, but on their way out they find Nell sitting on the porch. Marcus tries to approach her and she attacks him yet again. Louis retrieves his shotgun and threatens to shoot Nell, but Marcus stops him by announcing that he will attempt a second (this time legitimate) exorcism.

During the ritual, Nell breaks down and admits that she was not impregnated by a demon, but rather by a local boy named Logan. She worried what her overprotective father would do once he learned of her indiscretion, and her anxiety caused her to suffer a mental collapse. Following Nell's confession, Marcus asks Pastor Joseph Manley (Tony Bentley) to look after the girl, and then departs with Iris and Daniel. On the road back into town, they encounter Logan and ask him about the events that led to Nell's pregnancy. Confused, the boy explains that he is gay and therefore did not sleep with Nell. Shocked by this revelation, Marcus and the documentary crew rush back to the Sweetzer home, where they discover occult symbols scrawled on the walls, but find no trace of either Nell or Louis.

Searching the woods behind the farmhouse, Marcus and the others soon stumble upon a congregation of hooded cultists led by Pastor Manley, who stands before an altar atop which the now visibly pregnant Nell lies bound. Nell screams in pain and terror as she births an inhuman child. Manley promptly tosses the child into a huge bonfire that has been built near the altar, and the flames erupt with a demonic roar. His faith now restored, Marcus rushes forward to confront the evil with his cross held high. The documentary crew flees the scene, but a member of the congregation tackles Iris and kills her with an axe. Daniel continues to run, but when he stops to make sure that no one is following him, Caleb emerges from behind a tree and decapitates the cameraman. Daniel drops the camera to the ground and the screen cuts to black.

Released nearly three year later, *Last Exorcism II* begins where the first film ends, immediately following the satanic ritual that seemingly unleashed the demon Abalam into the world. The sequel abandons both the documentary crew from the first film and the character of Reverend Cotton, all of whom presumably died at the hands of the demon or its worshipers. Furthermore, *Last Exorcism II* replaces the found footage approach with a more traditional cinematic narrative structure. These structural modifications accompany differences in the film's representation and metaphorical treatment of possession and exorcism, and our analysis focuses on these metaphorical differences.

In *Last Exorcism II*, Nell wakes from a catatonic state and finds herself in a hospital. She then moves into a home for wayward girls in New Orleans and takes a housekeeping job at a local hotel. Dismissing her possession as "bad dreams," Nell now wants nothing more than to lead a normal life. She quickly befriends the other girls at the home, and they convince her to attend the upcoming Mardi Gras parade with them. Nell reluctantly agrees, but soon finds herself unprepared for the many strange things she witnesses there. Following the parade, Nell's personality undergoes a gradual shift, indicating that the demon Abalam has returned.

Nell soon learns that a secret society known as the Order of the Right Hand has been monitoring her. Around the same time, Nell's friends discover a video of her exorcism on YouTube, suggesting that someone uploaded the "documentary" footage shot during the previous movie to the Internet. After watching the video, Chris (Spencer Treat Clark), a young man who works at the hotel who has a crush on Nell, slits his own throat. Afterward, the Order of the Right Hand introduces Nell to Calder (David Jensen) and Jeffrey (E. Roger Mitchell), who explain that Abalam has fallen in love with her. They attempt an exorcism, but the demon proves too powerful for them. Fortunately, Nell's former nurse, Cecile (Tarra Riggs), arrives and reveals herself as a practicing New Orleans voodoo priestess. She tries to transfer Abalam's spirit into a chicken that she will then sacrifice, but the exorcism fails once more. In a last ditch effort to stop the demon, Calder attempts to inject Nell with a lethal dose of morphine, but Abalam convinces Nell to accept its power. She agrees, and the house bursts into flames, killing the secret society members. Nell then sets the girls' home on fire and kills her former friends. Finally, she steals a car and drives off as the town erupts in flames around her.

From a critical standpoint, *Last Exorcism* received generally good notices; according to the aggregation site *Rotten Tomatoes*, critics certified the film 72 percent fresh based on a total of 151 reviews culled from various online sources.[5] In contrast, as of this writing, only 34 percent of 73,203 users liked the movie,[6] indicating that general audiences (at least, those who use RottenTomatoes.com) did not care for it as much. Yet, this did not stop *Last Exorcism* from grossing over $67 million against a reported $1.8 million budget.[7] This substantial commercial success inspired the studio to rush a sequel into production. Unfortunately, *Last Exorcism II* did not fare nearly as well as its predecessor with either critics or audiences. *Rotten Tomatoes* deemed the sequel 16 percent rotten based on a total of 68 reviews from a variety of online critics, while its audience score currently stands at 26 percent based on more than 21,000 user ratings.[8] Furthermore, the film's box office take reflects this widespread critical and audience rejection, as *Last Exorcism II* only grossed $15 million worldwide against a reported $5 million budget.[9]

Both films approach similar material in decidedly different ways, and they contrast not only in terms of stylistic conventions and box office success (or lack thereof), but also in how they depict exorcism and the possessed woman. *Last Exorcism* directly aligns with the traditional exorcism narrative, particularly in how it explores issues of female rebellion and the subsequent repression of female sexuality. *Last Exorcism II*, meanwhile, thematically and symbolically positions demonic possession in such a way that the entire film serves to potentially subvert the traditional exorcism narrative. This positioning becomes particularly significant given the thematic significance of the film's final shot, which appears to represent an overt depiction of female rebellion and sexual liberation.

THE DAMSEL IN DISTRESS

Last Exorcism's plot aligns with the traditional exorcism narrative primarily because it situates a young woman as a monster that threatens patriarchal order. Furthermore, the film situates Reverend Marcus as the central character, and provides more insight into his motivations as a man who purports to preach the word of God but does not appear to actually believe his own rhetoric. His motivation essentially consists of his desire to prove the falsity of demonic possession and exorcism. Like Father Damien Karras in *The Exorcist*, Marcus lost his faith in God, and therefore seeks to uncover an earthly reason for Nell's behavior. Thus, he exemplifies the doubting priest figure that recurs throughout the exorcism cinema subgenre.

At first, Marcus seems to want to empower Nell and liberate her from her oppressive father. While his efforts initially appear well-intentioned, he nevertheless acts as the savior while Nell assumes the role of damsel in distress. At the same time, the film positions Nell as a monster by implying that her possession threatens those around her primarily because her pregnancy will allow a demon to enter this world. Nell occupies the role of the victim because she did not choose to become pregnant, but the pregnancy's demonic nature nevertheless positions her as a threat. Indeed, the film renders female sexuality dangerous largely because it links Nell's pregnancy to her possession by the demon Abalam. With Nell situated as both victim and antagonist, Marcus assumes the role of the protagonist who endeavors to banish the demon and thereby suppress the threat posed by the possessed Nell. Thus, the film's central conflict revolves around Marcus and his struggle to defeat Abalam and save this woman whose sexuality renders her both monstrous and abject.

Last Exorcism establishes Nell as a shy, sweet, and soft-spoken sixteen-year-old girl who lost her mother two years earlier. Nell's characterization foregrounds her innocence as a way of highlighting the differences between her pre- and post-possession selves. While Nell does not completely succumb to Abalam's demonic influence in this film, she nevertheless exhibits increasingly unusual behaviors that recall those exhibited by Regan in *The Exorcist* or the eponymous character in *Abby*. As Abalam's influence grows, Nell swears, contorts her body in inhuman ways, and becomes increasingly violent and aggressively sexual. The film contrasts these behaviors against Nell's innocence to underscore the notion that possession represents an abnormal state, and to reinforce the idea that normal or proper female behavior does not include such violent and/or erotic impulses. By highlighting Nell's innocence, the film textually and metaphorically positions her as a non-threatening, sexually inexperienced young woman. When she exhibits signs of possession, however, Nell assumes the role of an empowered young woman who has found her voice and seemingly desires to take control of both her life and her sexuality. Thus, Nell threatens the established patriarchal status quo because she acts in ways that challenge or subvert traditional notions of feminine propriety.

Nell's burgeoning empowerment reveals itself as threatening most prominently during the sequence in which she steals the documentary crew's camera. The viewer's ability to know the world of the film comes primarily through the camera's subjectivity; in other words, whoever controls the camera controls how the viewer experiences the world of the film.[10] During this sequence, Nell gains the power to see the unseen, and to gaze upon that which the regular cameraman cannot. Thus, for a time, the film focuses exclusively on her subjectivity. Significantly, this sequence reveals the true extent of Nell's possession, because it represents the first time the viewer witnesses her commit an act of violence (i.e., when she kills the cat).[11] From a metaphorical standpoint, *Last Exorcism* suggests that Nell has taken control of her newfound power and demonstrates that she now poses a physical threat to those around her.

During this sequence, the camera comes to represent Nell's agency, much like it represents Reverend Marcus's agency throughout the rest of the film as it documents his efforts to expose exorcism as a dangerous fiction. Her ability to control what the viewers provides insight into her subjective experience. Furthermore, this sequence represents one of the few times that an exorcism film actually grants the viewer access into the possessed individual's subjective experience, aligning it with *Possessed* (discussed in chapter 6) and *Grace: The Possession* (discussed in chapter 7). This subjective experience nevertheless directly relates to her violent impulses; while Nell gains and manifests power in this sequence, that power ultimately positions her as a deadly threat. Without the camera, Nell has no power, and she remains silent, controlled, and oppressed by the men around her. Indeed, throughout the film, Nell allows the men in her life to dictate and control her actions, and her agency only emerges when a male demon enters her body.[12]

To contain the threat posed by her burgeoning sexuality and agency, *Last Exorcism* frequently strips Nell of power or actively silences her. For example, during the second exorcism sequence, Reverend Marcus views Nell as a genuine threat and therefore performs a more authentic ritual in an active attempt to banish the demon. During this confrontation, however, Nell makes awkward sexual advances toward Reverend Marcus, and he questions the authenticity of these advances and accuses the girl of speaking falsely. By denying her advances, the film indicates that Reverend Marcus does not believe Nell capable of such deviant desires. Instead, he implies that she says these things only because she thinks he wants to hear them. Thus, Marcus effectively silences Nell without even successfully completing the exorcism.

Furthermore, this sequence exemplifies Nell's positioning as a vessel for the wishes of others, specifically her father, the demon, and/or the cult. The film suggests that Nell has always lacked power or control over her own body because other people routinely stifle her voice and her ability to speak truth. In other words, she lives only to please others, and endeavors to embody all the qualities of the proverbial "good little girl." Indeed, she experienced repression long before becoming possessed; after her mother's death, Nell's father imposed his oppressive religious beliefs on her in his attempts to repress her sexuality and agency. In the context of the film, however, this repression becomes perfectly acceptable because it turned Nell into an obedient, virginal, and non-threatening young woman. Like the title characters in *The Exorcism of Emily Rose* and *Grace*, Nell's possession disrupts, challenges, and threatens this repressive religious environment, and thus the film suggests that a woman's

agency threatens prevailing patriarchal structures that dictate appropriate feminine behavior.

In the traditional exorcism narrative, the priest not only saves the
possessed girl or woman, but also the entire world. Like Father Karras in
The Exorcist, however, Marcus comes to consider Nell's salvation as the
key to his own redemption. *Last Exorcism* repeatedly positions Nell as a
helpless damsel in distress, with Reverend Marcus assuming the role of
the hero who rescues her. Throughout the film, Marcus makes it his
mission to free Nell, first from her father, then from the satanic cult, and
lastly from Abalam. In a sense, Marcus not only tries to protect Nell from
those who seek to harm her, but also from her own dangerous urges.
Only at the end, however, does Marcus fully embrace his role as priest-
turned-savior when he confronts Abalam during the demon's attempt to
enter this world through Nell. At this point in the narrative, Reverend
Marcus clearly acts to defend the world (and patriarchal order) from the
demonic threat posed by the possessed woman. Thus, the film situates
Marcus as the priest-savior standing against the possessed Nell, with
only his crisis of faith preventing him from seeing the truth all along.
Unlike the priest in *[REC]²*, however, he manages to rediscover his faith
in time to address this lacking.

Metaphorically, Marcus assumes the role of a guardian who works to
maintain and protect this world's traditions, values, and institutions from
the threat of a sexually active and empowered woman. Narratively, *Last
Exorcism*'s ending resembles other horror films like *Rosemary's Baby* (1968,
Roman Polanksi), *Constantine* (2005, Francis Lawrence), and *Devil's Due*
(2014, Matt Bettinelli-Olpin and Tyler Gillett), in which a woman becomes an unwitting conduit through which a satanic cult seeks to un-
leash a demon upon the world. As a result of the possession, then, Nell's
pregnancy represents the real danger to mankind. Pregnancies in horror
films metaphorically reflect anxieties about women's natural reproduc-
tive capabilities, as the woman's offspring potentially poses an unknown
threat.[13] In other words, the indeterminate space of the womb generates
anxieties over what could emerge from it. Thus, *Last Exorcism* mines tension from the idea that while a woman can bring life into the world, that
life could potentially reveal itself as destructive. The film implies that
leaving such power unchecked may result in dire consequences for the
entire world. Furthermore, only the male priest-savior can suppress this
power. Reverend Marcus draws on a renewed sense of faith when he
rushes to face Abalam during *Last Exorcism*'s climax, and the film ends as
he strives to halt the threat posed by Nell's burgeoning sexuality and
empowerment.

We should note that *Last Exorcism* did not originally conclude with
Marcus's heroic actions. Director Daniel Stamm told us that in the initial
version of the script, Marcus would have revealed Nell's possession as
false and her father as manipulative.[14] Initially, Marcus did not confront

Abalam at the end of the film, but rather revels in his newfound adulation after exposing demonic possession and exorcism as bogus superstitions.[15] However, the studio worried that this ending would cause audiences to reject the film. According to Stamm, a good genre film gives audiences "eighty percent of something that they know and know what to do with, and twenty percent new and original."[16] Conversely, when filmmakers give audiences "eighty percent new and original stuff and twenty percent old stuff, then they don't know what to do with it."[17] Therefore, to ensure the film's success, *Last Exorcism*'s ending was rewritten so that Marcus's doubts prove incorrect.[18] Interestingly, if the studio had maintained the original ending, the film's portrayal of the doubting priest figure likely would have challenged the traditional exorcism narrative. Indeed, Louis's repressive behavior would have become positioned as inappropriate, thereby dismantling the sort of patriarchal values that dictate feminine propriety. Instead, the film aligns with the exorcism cinema subgenre's prevailing generic formula.

Through the rhetoric of female innocence and the triumph of the male savior, *Last Exorcism* thematically reinforces the notion that sexually liberated women threaten the patriarchal status quo maintained by systemic and institutionalized notions of feminine propriety. The film's central tension focuses on the threat posed by Nell's burgeoning sexuality and power, and contrasts this with the order and safety that Reverend Marcus represents. The film's decidedly ambiguous ending does not provide for an easy resolution of the tensions regarding female empowerment, because the final shot cuts to black before Marcus actually defeats Abalam. Thus, the film conforms to Wetmore's assertion that "[i]n post-9/11 horror cinema, there is no God, there is no authority figure that can fix the situation, nothing saves us and everybody or almost everybody dies."[19] *Last Exorcism* encapsulates this idea, because the sequel reveals that Abalam ultimately triumphs over Marcus, who seemingly does not survive their encounter. However, the film's thematic importance resides in the final shot of Marcus stepping forward, empowered by his renewed faith in God, which indicates that his actions at least represent a correct step toward restoring order. As with other depictions of the doubting priest figure, starting with Fathers Karras and Merrin, Marcus exhibits the all-important masculine trait of bravery, and the determination to stand up to the evil that threatens the world.[20] Win or lose, his conviction and his faith in the traditional order serve to reaffirm the traditional exorcism narrative.

THE EMERGENCE OF THE EMPOWERED WOMAN

While *Last Exorcism* reinforces the traditional exorcism narrative, *Last Exorcism II* actively subverts it by focusing primarily on the possessed individual's subjectivity and agency. This time around, Nell assumes the role of the protagonist, and the narrative centers on her attempts to establish and claim a sense of agency over her own life and sexuality. The film does not concern a priest who struggles with his loss of faith and uses the woman's unfortunate dilemma to fortify his belief in God and the power of the Church (and by extension the validity and power of the patriarchy). Instead, the narrative focuses mainly on Nell's decision to lead what she considers a good life even as she realizes that the demon Abalam desires her for far more sinister reasons. Instead of allowing others to dictate her actions, as she did in the previous film, Nell actively chooses to succumb to Abalam's influence by the end of this film. In other words, she appears to welcome the power that comes with possession. As a result, *Last Exorcism II* represents an overtly feminist portrayal of a woman struggling with demonic possession. Unlike the vast majority of exorcism films, *Last Exorcism II* foregrounds the innocent woman's subjective experience as she succumbs to and ultimately accepts possession and, in doing so, subverts the traditional exorcism narrative.

In a sense, *Last Exorcism II* positions a possessed woman as both the protagonist and the antagonist, as the possession reflects Nell's internal struggle to define or develop a sense of self. Nell appears to have repressed the memories of the horrific events from the first film and now seeks to establish and take control of her own identity. Essentially, she has at last attained the sort of control over her life that Reverend Marcus tried to help her achieve during the early part of the first film, before realizing exorcism was the only option. Yet, *Last Exorcism II*'s central conflict concerns Nell's increasing demonic possession, as Abalam attempts to merge with her once more. At first, Nell fears the possession, because she believes it would remove her agency and identity. Yet, over time, she also comes to enjoy the power that possession grants her. Ultimately, the possession undoes her repression, and therefore Nell chooses to embrace the power Abalam offers her rather than return to that repressed state.

The sequel initially restores Nell to a state of innocence, and she actively attempts to maintain this innocence during the film's first half by portraying herself as a normal girl. Yet, her new life offers plenty of temptations, as she now resides in a group home in New Orleans with several other uninhibited teenage girls. This setting offers the potential for corruption, both from the other girls at the home and from the young man with whom Nell becomes infatuated. Additionally, Abalam's continued attempts to possess Nell represent yet another form of sexual temptation. For example, while cleaning one of the hotel rooms, Nell overhears people having sexual intercourse in the adjacent room, which causes her to become acutely aware of her own latent desires. Visually, the film depicts Nell's burgeoning sexuality as a form of corruption; she hugs the wall and black tendrils seep out from her body while a dark figure watches her from the doorway. The film portrays Nell's increasing sexual awareness and desire as a symptom of Abalam's return, because the demon inspires these urges in its attempts to seduce her; thus, *Last Exorcism II* links Nell's sexual awakening to demonic possession and thus to evil or deviance.

In addition to becoming more aware of her sexuality, Nell grows more assertive as she struggles to convince non-believers of her oncoming possession. She uses her voice to tell others about the supernatural events she experiences, but they refuse to listen and thus render her powerless. Nell even turns to a priest for help at one point, but her confession only seems to increase her possession. In other words, Nell's demonic possession does not grant her a voice, at least not at first, and therefore it does not initially appear to represent an empowerment. Unlike the possessed individuals in other exorcism films, Nell uses her own voice to try and repress the possession, indicating her desire to stave off the demon's influence. Furthermore, she actively seeks assistance from others because she initially rejects the possession and the power that comes with it. In a sense, then, Nell uses her voice to try and align with dominant patriarchal notions of feminine propriety; indeed, to maintain order through tradition, the patriarchy demands Nell strive to prevent the possession from occurring, because surrendering to it would indicate a desire to embrace immoral and altogether disruptive behavior. In other words, Nell's choice to seek an exorcism indicates a desire to return to a state of innocence and obedience, which would in turn mitigate the threat she poses to order and realign her with patriarchal authority.

Yet the film's patriarchal representatives refuse to listen to Nell, and her voice remains powerless until heard by another marginalized individual: a female, African American practitioner of a non-Christian religion. *Last Exorcism II* portrays a female exorcist—an immensely rare occurrence in exorcism cinema. More often than not, exorcism films focus on the plight of the male protagonist as he strives to save the girl and dispel the demon. As a result, the possessed girl tends to occupy a secondary position as both the monstrous antagonist and the damsel in distress. *Last Exorcism II*, however, grants Nell far more agency; she assumes the role of the protagonist seeking to cast out the demon, and the priestess (a practitioner of voodoo) endeavors to help her achieve this goal. Thus, two women endeavor to maintain patriarchal order. Their attempt to perform the exorcism fails, which in turn suggests that only men hold the power to maintain symbolic social order. This sequence implies that such attempts to assert female agency challenge traditional patriarchal values or attitudes, and reinforces the idea that women cannot access the power required to stop the horror threatening this social order largely because their empowerment threatens that order.

While Nell initially attempts to prevent her possession and align with patriarchal values, she nevertheless chooses to accept the power Abalam offers her and thus speaks out in defiance of patriarchal oppression. If Nell was a "good girl," she would have allowed Calder to kill her and thus end Abalam's threat. Doing so would have aligned Nell with other martyrs of the exorcism cinema subgenre, such as Emily Rose. Instead, Nell defies this oppressive (and fatal) conclusion. As such, Abalam comes to represent Nell's inner desire for power, which she fully embraces at this point in the film. By allowing Abalam to completely possess her, Nell gains the freedom to indulge her desires and to express herself in ways often considered harmful or improper within the confines of paternal or patriarchal values. The film reinforces this idea when Nell licks a female friend's face and says "I know who I am now, and I know who I was meant to be," which indicates that Nell has finally embraced and asserted her agency and her sexuality.

Furthermore, Nell destroys anyone who upholds the forces of patriarchy and oppression: doctors, religious figures, and even the sisterhood of teenage girls who seek to lead good and normal lives that conform to patriarchal notions of feminine conduct. Nell actively asserts her right to at last take charge of her own life, regardless of what others might think. By retaining the phallus, Nell's possession aligns her with possessed women featured in several of the European rip-offs discussed in chapter 3; like them, she becomes "a defiant example of unrecuperated primal, anarchic, hyper-feminine energy." [21] Unlike many of those women, however, Nell remains possessed and empowered at the end of the film. In the final shot, Nell smiles as she gazes into the rearview mirror of a stolen car. Earlier in the film, Nell gazed into a cracked mirror and her reflection appeared fractured. By the end, however, her reflection has become unified and clear. This visual contrast implies that by accepting Abalam and embracing the power offered by the demon, Nell at last accepts her own sense of self and her true nature. She directs her gaze at the viewer, and challenges them to accept her choice.

While *Last Exorcism II* does not depict the doubting priest figure striving to repress the possessed woman and thereby halt the threat she poses to order, the narrative nevertheless reflects the underlying themes of the traditional exorcism narrative. Although it focuses on Nell's empowerment and her decision to make her own choices, the film also depicts her struggles regarding her loss of power and control as she slowly succumbs to Abalam's influence. To save herself from this threat, Nell seeks out an exorcism, which would return her to a state of innocence by removing the rebellious entity that threatens to topple patriarchal society. Had Nell sought a male priest's assistance, the exorcism likely would have succeeded, and thus the film would align with the traditional exorcism narrative. Instead, the climactic sequence subverts this narrative and the resolution it commonly offers by having the woman consciously accept the power that comes with possession.

Ultimately, Nell's decision to accept Abalam challenges the traditional exorcism narrative's central theme of female oppression and repression. Even movies that end with the woman still possessed, such as *[REC]²*, make it clear that the woman did not choose to become possessed. Nell willingly embraces and accepts the power that demonic possession offers, and as a result she remains empowered and able to assert her voice and embrace her ability to choose. Thus, Nell actively defies patriarchal desires and values, and thereby remains a threat to the established social and symbolic order.

CHALLENGING THE TRADITIONAL EXORCISM NARRATIVE

Last Exorcism and its sequel demonstrate the range of tensions found throughout exorcism cinema. In these two films, the most prominent tension involves the emergence or awakening of female sexuality, agency, and voice. In addition to this tension, however, the *Last Exorcism* films explore related conflicts such as those between liberation and oppression, and the tension that arises when a girl or young woman finds her voice and chooses to embrace it rather than remain silent. As we have repeatedly demonstrated in this book, exorcism films support readings that situate possession as a metaphor for female empowerment, while the exorcism ritual stands in for the sort of systemic and institutionalized patriarchal values that seek to dictate how women should behave and act. In exploring these tensions, *Last Exorcism II* offers a major challenge to how these tensions have been commonly addressed through the traditional exorcism narrative.

Thus, while exorcism films routinely reflect the traditional exorcism narrative, challenges to this narrative do occur. While *Last Exorcism* offered no real challenges, *Last Exorcism II* challenged it entirely. Typically, though, films tend to challenge only one component at a time, because challenging more would likely result in a film that no longer conforms to the conventions of the exorcism cinema subgenre. Other contemporary films offer challenges similar to those in *Last Exorcism II*, but only to the possessed-woman-as-threat trope or the doubting priest and male savior tropes.

The majority of exorcism films situate male priests as saviors, while relegating women to a position of both victim and monster. It therefore becomes important to identify instances in which the woman assumes the role of the protagonist by attempting to end another woman's possession. Until the exorcism cinema resurgence, women performing this role were extremely rare, with the British film *I Don't Want to Be Born* (1975, Peter Sasdy) representing the sole exception; in that film, a Catholic nun exorcizes a newborn baby to cast out the vengeful spirit of an evil dwarf theater performer. Even during the resurgence period, these films remain rare, with *The Conjuring* series depicting perhaps the most successful sub-version of the male savior trope while still retaining the oppressive nature of the exorcism ritual.

Though set in the 1970s, *The Conjuring* (2013, James Wan) challenges prevailing post-9/11 discourses regarding feminism because it depicts a woman as the exorcist, as opposed to the doubting priest figure that recurs throughout exorcism cinema. Based on the experiences of real-life paranormal investigators and married couple Ed and Lorraine Warren (played in the film by Patrick Wilson and Vera Farmiga, respectively)—who also investigated the case that inspired *The Amityville Horror*[22] — *Conjuring* chronicles an investigation into the mysterious happenings at a Rhode Island family's newly purchased house. The film advances a pro-feminist rhetoric because it centers on the power of sisterhood and female empowerment.

Conjuring's resolution hinges on the notion that women share a common bond that can ultimately help them negotiate and cope with traumatic events, including demonic possession. In *Last Exorcism II*, a woman works to save another woman from possession, thus providing another example of a woman attempting to assume the role of empowered saviors,[23] an act also seen in *Exorcist II: The Heretic*. A parallel narrative conceit occurs in *The Conjuring 2* (2016, James Wan), wherein Lorraine once again performs the exorcism to free a teenage girl from the clutches of an evil spirit. Thus, recent exorcism movies have portrayed successful female exorcists, which counters the traditional exorcism narrative's focus on the male savior trope acting to protect patriarchy.[24] However, since their actions remove the power from the possessed-woman-as-threat, they merely stand in for the male savior by fulfilling the same narrative and metaphorical function.

Other films depict possessed women working to save themselves from possession. In *The Unborn* (2009, David Goyer), college student Casey Beldon (Odette Annable) fears that she has become possessed,[25] and she asks Rabbi Sendak (Gary Oldman) to perform an exorcism. This film challenges the traditional exorcism narrative because the young woman asserts her agency by actively endeavoring to end her own possession. Of course, Casey's salvation ultimately relies on the efforts of the skeptical rabbi and a priest (played by Idris Elba), and thus the film aligns with the traditional exorcism narrative. Like Nell in *Last Exorcism II*, Casey recognizes that her possession renders her a threat, but she actively works with the two holy men to successfully end her possession. Thus, the film does not include the same sort of subversive ending as seen in *Last Exorcism II*.

Meanwhile, in *The Exorcism of Molly Harley* (2015, Steven R. Monroe), Molly becomes possessed thanks to the machinations of a satanic cult posing as Catholics. During one of their ceremonies, the demon exits Molly's body and takes possession of the cult leader, whom Molly then kills. Thus, Molly enacts revenge on those who caused her pain, but also prevents the demon from terrorizing the world, if only temporarily (as the film's ending suggests). In opposition to Casey in *Unborn*, Molly does not work to save herself throughout the film, and only has the agency to prevent others, hopefully, from experiencing the same possession. Nevertheless, both *Unborn* and *Molly Hartley* portray a young woman struggling against demonic possession and playing a part in her own salvation, and therefore challenge aspects of the traditional exorcism narrative, which frequently situates women as passive figures in need of rescue while also hosting the threat to the world. However, both films thereby reaffirm this narrative as they participate in their own repression, with Molly even participating in the possible repression of other women.

Furthermore, these four films perpetuate the trope of the possessed-woman-as-threat. Even in films that feature female exorcists or possessed women striving to save themselves, exorcisms serve to remove the possessed woman's power, which threatens the stability of patriarchal order. For instance, *Unborn* and *Molly Hartley* feature possessed women aiding in their own exorcisms, working alongside their male saviors to cast out the invasive demonic entities that have transformed the women into abject monsters. Thus, these women assist patriarchal authority figures to perpetuate their own oppression. In chapter 5, we discussed the lack of postmodern exorcism films that demonstrate an awareness of the exorcism cinema tropes and an attempt to actively deconstruct them. While these four films demonstrate challenges to the traditional exorcism narrative, they do not represent an active deconstruction of that narrative.

One film, however, does suggest such a deconstruction, and aligns with *Last Exorcism II* in how it portrays women choosing possession as a form of empowerment. In *Ava's Possessions* (2015, Jordan Galland), demonic possession has become commonplace and institutions exist to help individuals recover their lives after their exorcisms. It begins with Ava's exorcism, which aligns with the traditional exorcism narrative, and then follows her as she struggles to recover her memories of what happened during her possession. Because she committed crimes while possessed, the government forces Ava to attend a recovery program, metaphorically aligning her possession with drug addiction. At the recovery program, Ava meets Hazel, who professes to love her demonic invader and therefore wants to become repossessed. Ava helps her achieve this goal, and Hazel embarks on a demon-fueled rampage. Later, on the verge of incarceration due to her actions, Hazel says the repossession was worth it, because the demon makes her stronger and she makes it stronger in return. This characterization aligns with the notion of possession as a form of empowerment, and it inspires Ava later in the film, when she willingly becomes repossessed to stop a killer. Ava uses her possession to force a confession from the killer, thereby situating the power as a force for good, and she demonstrates an ability to control the possession before it turns evil. Thus, the film reveals an awareness of the meanings behind the tropes of exorcism cinema. At the same time, the film does not allow Ava to remain possessed and continue to use the empowerment, suggesting that society still prefers women who repress their urges.

Both *Last Exorcism* and its sequel become immensely interesting and important to our consideration of the role and relationship exorcism films play within society and culture at large primarily because of how they resolve the conflict between Nell and Abalam. In *Last Exorcism*, Reverend Marcus's confrontation with Abalam appears to free Nell from possession at the end of the film, but the demon nevertheless pursues her and attempts to merge with her in the sequel. Furthermore, given its resolution, *Last Exorcism II* indicates that throughout the first film, Reverend Marcus effectively prevented Nell from receiving and asserting her power and her agency. As such, Reverend Marcus comes to represent the sort of patriarchal values and systemic male oppression that prevents young women from embracing their power and establishing their own sense of self, which in turn allows them to reach their full potential. The sequel's ending suggests that viewers should fear the newly empowered Nell, as she dispatches her friends and those trying to help her. Yet, the film also situates her in such a way that viewers could potentially identify with this young woman who finally gains the power she needs to take charge of her own life.

In any event, by situating Nell as the protagonist, *Last Exorcism II* leaves audiences with a character who initially experiences fear and helplessness, but by the end emerges as self-assured and fearless. As global societies and cultures struggle with the achievements of feminist ideology, women's empowerment remains a central concern on a global scale, and here, at the conclusion of *Last Exorcism II*, Nell exemplifies the empowered woman. In this way, the film subverts the traditional exorcism narrative while still representing contemporary anxieties about the parameters of appropriate female behavior. Audiences could potentially read Abalam's empowerment of Nell as a metaphor for the perceived harm that empowered women and feminist ideologies cause to men and society at large. On the other hand, audiences could view this empowerment as a suggestion that women should be allowed to control their own lives and act according to their own impulses. Whichever reading wins out over time might suggest how far feminism has come, and how far it has yet to go.

NOTES

1. Kevin J. Wetmore, *Post-9/11 Horror in American Cinema* (New York: Continuum, 2012), 195.

2. Ibid., 15.

3. Adrienne L. Massanari, *Participatory Culture, Community, and Play: Learning from reddit* (New York: Peter Lang, 2015), 136–7.

4. Ibid., 129–30.

5. "The Last Exorcism (2010)," *Rotten Tomatoes*, accessed August 6, 2016, http://www.rottentomatoes.com/m/last_exorcism/.

6. Ibid.

7. "The Last Exorcism," *Box Office Mojo*, accessed August 10, 2015, http://www.rottentomatoes.com/m/last_exorcism/.

8. "The Last Exorcism Part II (2013)," *Rotten Tomatoes*, accessed August 6, 2016, http://www.rottentomatoes.com/m/the_last_exorcism_part_ii_2013/.

9. "The Last Exorcism Part II," *Box Office Mojo*, accessed August 10, 2015, http://www.boxofficemojo.com/movies/?id=lastexorcism2.htm.

10. Adam Charles Hart (2014), however, writes that "Unlike the mastering, sadistic gazes of the monsters and villains of previous generations of horror films, the found footage film's diegetic camera is always in a position of either utter vulnerability (the handheld camera) or passive, unresponsive surveillance" (341). Nell's use of the camera suggests power more than passivity or vulnerability.

11. Alexandra Heller-Nicholas, *Found Footage Horror Films: Fear and the Appearance of Reality*, (Jefferson: McFarland & Company, Inc., 2014), 157.

12. Heller-Nicholas, *Found Footage*, 157.

13. Kelly Oliver, *Knock Me Up, Knock Me Down: Images of Pregnancy in Hollywood Films* (New York: Columbia University Press, 2012), 111, 137.

14. Daniel Stamm (film director) in discussion with the authors, June 7, 2015.

15. Ibid.

16. Ibid.

17. Ibid.

18. Ibid.

19. Wetmore, *Post-9/11 Horror*, 118.

20. According to Charles A. Baker (1976), films such as *The Exorcist* seem to imply that evil "can be dealt with by a few good men possessing courage, determination and the will to see a perilous situation through to its conclusion" (24).

21. Ian Olney, "Unmanning *The Exorcist*: Sex, Gender and Excess in the 1970s Euro-Horror Possession Film," *Quarterly Review of Film and Video* 31, no. 6 (2014): 564.

22. For more on the Warrens' involvement in the Amityville case, see "Amityville," *Warrens.net*, accessed August 10, 2005, http://www.warrens.net/Amityville.html.

23. *Last Exorcism* also hints at such kinship between women, particularly during the scene in which Iris gives her boots to Nell, much to the girl's delight. However, this kinship does not save Iris, just like it does not save the women in Nell's life in *Last Exorcism II*. For more, see Heller-Nicholas, *Found Footage*, 157–58.

24. Another recent movie from Spain, *Asmodexia* (2014, Marc Carreté), also featured a female exorcist, but her power ultimately leads to the apocalypse, thereby rendering her the biggest threat in the film.

25. Interestingly, similar to *Last Exorcism*, this possession also relates to matters of the womb, because Casey learns that her own dead twin and her grandmother's dead twin both became dybbuk spirits. Additionally, at the end of the film, Casey learns that she herself has become pregnant with twins. As Kelly Oliver suggests, the film suggests that the unborn children haunt and threaten the living, and thus female sexuality becomes positioned as a threat. For more, see Oliver, *Knock Me Up*, 140.

NINE
Conclusion

The Resiliency of Tradition

Throughout this book, we have demonstrated that exorcism films tend to reflect the narrative structure established by *The Exorcist*. This narrative primarily involves the interplay between two archetypal figures: the possessed-woman-as-threat—which eventually expanded to portray other marginalized individuals as threats—and the doubting priest, most often depicted as a holy man who reaffirms his faith by exorcising the possessed Other. Furthermore, by considering how these tropes have occurred in the portrayal of possession and exorcism over time, we have discussed how exorcism films often function as allegories for the sociocultural tensions of different historical periods. Possession represents the empowerment of marginalized individuals while exorcism stands in for the oppression, suppression, and repression of those same individuals. Analyzing representation allows for an understanding of how ideologies become constructed, maintained, and contested onscreen, and how they in turn could shape the way people engage with one another and the world around them. Thus, analyzing textual representations can contribute to an understanding of how power circulates through a society and culture,[1] and how this circulation legitimizes certain states of being while marginalizing others. Our analysis of the traditional exorcism narrative demonstrates how exorcism films can reflect the struggle for power between dominant and marginalized groups in a given society or culture.

Cinematic portrayals of possession and exorcism highlight issues of oppression, specifically those regarding women, people of color, and the non-heteronormative. Exorcism films frequently rely on stereotypes constructed and maintained throughout history by the oppressive forces of patriarchy (i.e., colonialism, racism, and heteronormativity) to position

167

such marginalized individuals as a danger to traditional order and stability. Such films demonstrate Andrew Tudor's contention that horror films function as a "safety valve" because they highlight the "fearful consequences" that often occur to those marginalized individuals who dare to challenge tradition.[2] These morality tales thereby allow audiences to experience the repressed while simultaneously assuring viewers that traditional values will ultimately be restored.

Indeed, films that align with the traditional exorcism narrative tend to return any revolutionary components to their previous state of repression. This rhetorical construction could potentially impact how viewers think about feminist, postcolonial, and queer ideologies. Robin Wood has argued that horror films reflect sociocultural events that occur at the time of their production and distribution, and that each horror film includes "a potentially (and paradoxically) revolutionary component [. . .] since that which erupts is always that which has been repressed."[3] In exorcism films, possession grants repressed and/or marginalized individuals power, and allows them to temporarily subvert the systemic oppression of patriarchal society. At the same time, such films routinely disempower these unruly Others, and restore them to a state of innocence and subservience. Thus, rather than challenge stereotypes and systems of oppression, the traditional exorcism narrative often functions as a way to reaffirm them.

Furthermore, the majority of exorcism films align with this recurring narrative structure, and few films challenge these discourses. Exorcism films can therefore reveal "connections between the visible and the hidden, the dominant and the marginalized, ideas and institutions," and analyzing such films exposes "how power works" in narratives that reflect the "language, literature, culture and the institutions which regulate our daily lives."[4] Discourses of oppression circulate throughout the films that align with the traditional exorcism narrative. Exorcism films that seek to question or satirize religion frequently stray from this narrative convention, but even those films rarely offer any sort of substantive deconstruction and/or critique of discourses that oppress marginalized groups or individuals. This reluctance to challenge the traditional exorcism narrative and its oppressive ideologies should come as no surprise, especially since heteronormative, white, male filmmakers tend to produce the majority of exorcism films and may view the "us-versus-them" binary as a necessary component of their success (financial or otherwise).[5] Regardless of when they were produced, exorcism films routinely suggest that empowered Others threaten order and stability and therefore require suppression by the forces of patriarchy, colonialism, and heteronormativity.

FROM *THE EXORCIST* TO TODAY

In writing about slasher films, Richard Nowell put forth a model that explained the formation of a film cycle. In his words, a film cycle contains a pattern of cinematic output distinguishable by several "chronologically distinct phases" that begin when a film stands out from others produced during the same historical period and performs well at the box office.[6] Other "textually similar films" follow this commercially successful film.[7] By discussing the political economic, sociocultural, and historical material aspects of a film cycle, Nowell's model aptly applies to exorcism cinema. Based on this definition, exorcism cinema has occurred thus far in two cycles: the 1970s and the early twenty-first century. In each cycle, one film emerged as a "trailblazer hit" that then led to the production of other, similar films.[8] During the 1970s, *The Exorcist* filled this role, and was followed by a series of homages and rip-offs that Nowell might label as "prospector cash-ins."[9] This cycle was followed by the lull period of the 1980s and 1990s, which did not truly end until *The Exorcism of Emily Rose* emerged as the "Speculator Production," which is a specific type of trailblazer hit.[10] This second cycle has proven more productive than the first, as the prospector cash-ins have been followed by "carpetbagger cash-ins" that expanded and perpetuated this cycle.[11] As we discuss in the remainder of this section, our analysis reveals a possible reason for the exorcism subgenre's cyclical nature: the repetition of sociocultural fears in these two historical periods.

As discussed in chapter 2, *The Exorcist* first impacted global popular culture roughly one year after Pope Paul VI delivered a speech urging people around the world to remain wary of the devil's influence. To those outside the Catholic Church, the speech seemed to confirm criticisms that the institution no longer provided a useful model for dealing with the spiritual concerns of the more enlightened twentieth century.[12] *The Exorcist*, meanwhile, confronted audiences around the world with a graphic depiction of exactly how the devil could impact modern society. Indeed, although entirely fictitious, the film portrayed evil not as some intangible thing but rather as an actual agent acting through and against humanity. More importantly, *The Exorcist* managed to blur the lines between the fictional and the real largely because it was supposedly based on factual events and featured a marketing campaign that posited a "curse" as a real phenomenon. In any event, the film encouraged discussion regarding the need to understand evil in all its forms, not just from psychological, psychiatric, and medicinal viewpoints, but also from the perspective of traditional religious doctrine; even in the modern, technologically advanced, and rational world of the 1970s, old beliefs still held sway.

Perhaps these old, superstitious beliefs allowed people of the time to cope with the sociocultural upheaval that resulted from the civil rights and youth movements of the late 1960s and early 1970s, disruptions that

impacted various longstanding social institutions. In a time of such turmoil, when people struggled to make sense of the horrors they witnessed
via their TV screens on a daily basis, a belief in the existence of demons
and evil spirits may have offered a powerful sense of comfort, because it
implied that dogmatic rituals could expel such evil. Instead of acknowl-
edging that complex disruptions required equally complex solutions, the
belief in a more simplistic (though somewhat scarier) explanation may
have helped people cope because at least then it appeared as though the
problems they faced had a tangible explanation and concrete solution.

As time passed, however, the dust from the decade's disruptions
seemed to settle, especially as the economy rebounded and the Cold War
abated, allowing people to settle into new patterns of everyday life.
Throughout the 1980s and 1990s, the anxieties of the previous decades
seemed to wane even as others escalated, particularly those concerning
crime, drug use, and teenage sexuality. Religion's role also changed during this period, as a more conservative mindset arose to overtake the
cultural landscape, particularly in the United States. A return to traditional values appeared to provide the solution to the cultural upheaval
that defined the previous decade, and thus the 1980s saw the rise of the
Moral Majority.[13] During the 1990s, however, these conservative values
encountered various challenges, and they increasingly became the subject
of criticism and jest throughout popular culture. Around this time, exorcism cinema entered a lull period, because audiences faced new problems
and therefore no longer feared the same abstract evils in the world
around them. For example, AIDS seemingly resulted from sexual behavior that could be controlled and curtailed rather than from any existential
or ideological forces. As the twentieth century came to a close, it seemed
like the old beliefs and anxieties that contributed to the exorcism cinema
subgenre's success had at last given way to a new age that emphasized
the rational, the technological, and the modern (if not postmodern).

That all changed on the morning of September 11, 2001, when terrorists attacked the World Trade Center and the Pentagon and gave rise to a
new era of paranoia and sociocultural instability. Of course, the 1970s
also experienced a period of high profile terrorism, much of it stemming
from the Iranian Revolution. Furthermore, the 1980s and 1990s experienced comparable conflicts, such as the Soviet-Afghan War, the U.S. invasion of Panama, the Gulf War, and the World Trade Center bombing. Yet,
the Western world became increasingly economically stable during this
period, or at least appeared to thanks to a cultural narrative that down-
played the skirmishes occurring around the globe and emphasized so-
called American exceptionalism in a way that recalled the prevailing discourses of the 1950s. Many of the films produced during this period
reinforced this perception, particularly the action movies of the 1980s and
1990s, which routinely positioned Islamic terrorists as the villains. In
such films, the hard-bodied American male hero would swagger on-

screen and defeat the bad guys, thus making the world safe once again for truth, justice, and the American way.[14] In the process, he also managed to dispel the audience's lingering fears of terrorism.

The events of 9/11 shattered that hero's power, however, just as it shattered many ordinary people's assumptions that they would never experience such horrific and seemingly senseless tragedy. The 9/11 terror attacks disrupted daily life and challenged many people's assumptions about reality, and allowed a new set of sociocultural anxieties to take root around the world but particularly in the United States. News media and online discourses frequently portrayed terrorists as unknowable Others acting on irrational impulses and operating to undo the world's order and stability. Moreover, this evil could strike anywhere at any time; even the friendliest neighbor could suddenly attack others in the community for reasons few could understand.

Such fear facilitated a resurgence of exorcism cinema, as superstitions and stereotypes emerged once more to explain away evil and comfort those who found it difficult to cope with the world's complex problems. Exorcism cinema seemed fitting for this period; indeed, demonic possession can function as a metaphor for terrorism, especially since demons frequently emerge without warning and cause terrifying disruptions within the ordinary world. At the same time, people grew to fear their own lack of control over their present and future lives in a variety of other ways. Both the global economic recession that started in December 2007 and a growing concern over climate change helped fuel this sense of unease and uncertainty. Kevin J. Wetmore argues that the horror films of the 1990s focused on earthly serial killers, while post-9/11 films "returned supernatural horror to the forefront."[15] Furthermore, Father Richard Woods has argued that "we should expect possession to precede and accompany crises in society such as war, civil discord, widespread fear, suspicion and slander."[16] While Woods was referring to actual cases of possession, his prediction applies to cinematic depictions as well. Thus, it seems that the post-9/11 and post-recession period encouraged a prevailing sociocultural atmosphere that resembled the dark oppressiveness that eventually came to define the 1970s, and therefore facilitated a resurgence of exorcism cinema.

Indeed, this sociocultural atmosphere might explain why Pope Francis opted to reiterate his predecessor's message in a 2014 speech warning people that Satan still held sway over the world. With this speech, Pope Francis sought to "rekindle the devil's image as a supernatural entity with the forces of evil at his beck and call."[17] The Holy See praised the International Association of Exorcists, and even reportedly laid his hands on a possessed man in an effort to cast out an invasive demon.[18] Much like his predecessor, Pope Francis urged the world to remain ever vigilant against the devil and his minions.[19] Notably, the Pope's stance refutes the longstanding Catholic tradition of viewing Satan not as a physical entity but rather as an allegory for evil.[20] The Vatican even reported a massive increase in requests for exorcisms during the early part of the twenty-first century. To meet this surge in demand, cardinals expanded the number of exorcists available in their dioceses.[21] Roughly 500 to 600 Vatican-sanctioned exorcists operate around the world at the time of this writing.[22] Indeed, cases of real exorcisms continue to be reported on a global scale.[23]

Thus, the cultural mood in the early part of the New Millennium seemed ripe for a resurgence of exorcism cinema, because this period resembles the sociocultural conditions of the 1970s, and therefore shares many of the same widespread anxieties regarding evil's impact on the state of the world. Both eras experienced economic stress and a widespread uncertainty about the future inspired by prevailing discourses surrounding the negative effects of gay rights, women's liberation, and the emancipation of racial and ethnic minorities, all of which suggested a clash of "minority cultures against white protestant populism."[24] Therefore, a surge in exorcism cinema during these two periods makes sense, because such films depict evil emerging to upset the order of everyday life and therefore tend to reflect such widespread sociocultural anxieties.

THE POWER OF OPPRESSION COMPELS YOU

Based on our research, the bulk of exorcism cinema occurred in two key time periods: the 1970s and post-9/11. These time periods resemble one another in terms of the presence and impact of similar sociocultural anxieties. Both periods experienced economic turmoil and involved challenges to the idealized middle-class nuclear family, which was seemingly threatened by the forces of feminism, gay rights, multiculturalism, and economic instability. These two periods also experienced a pronounced uptick in terrorist activity—which in turn inspired fears of unexplainable evil—and a resurgence of religious dogma. Furthermore, like the 1970s, a paranoid distrust of government and corporate institutions came to define the first fifteen years of the twenty-first century.[25]

Of course, it becomes difficult to determine and demarcate the exact reasons for the emergence and resurgence of the exorcism cinema subgenre, largely because such cycles result from numerous disparate factors working together. Nevertheless, the anxieties described above undoubtedly contributed to this cinematic subgenre's renaissance because horror films in general and exorcism films in particular tend to reflect and inspire prevailing sociocultural fears. As Stephen King notes, the horror genre waxes and wanes in relation to "periods of fairly serious economic and/or political strain," largely because horror stories allow audiences to deal with "free-floating anxieties (for want of a better term) which accompany such serious but not mortal dislocations."[26] During those periods when exorcism films thrived, traditional culture routinely clashed with the countercultural. Such films reflect the idea that traditional culture often worries that non-dominant or marginalized people will find their voice and speak out against their oppression, thereby destabilizing a system of order that privileges certain states of being (i.e., white, heteronormative, male) over others. Thus, traditional culture continues to assert itself in an effort to maintain its dominant position. The tensions between these two opposing ideologies manifest in exorcism narratives, and in many ways this conflict represents the exorcism cinema subgenre's defining feature.

The traditional exorcism narrative appears to allow producers and audiences to create allegories that enable them to find and relieve these "national phobic pressure points."[27] From the perspective of textual analysis, whether the entire audience agrees or disagrees with the allegorical message remains beside the point; the films themselves reflect those anxieties the audience may not be able to fully articulate or understand. When read in the ways suggested by this book, exorcism films could facilitate a dialogue about these anxieties and their impact, particularly with regard to the oppression of non-dominant groups or marginalized individuals. Scholars frequently argue that horror movies depict the restoration of the status quo after the hero confronts the monster/threat. However, upsetting the status quo does not necessarily imply a negative outcome if the status quo was undesirable to begin with. Movies that challenge the traditional exorcism narrative demonstrate how the status quo often disregards or oppresses non-dominant groups or individuals; thus, dismantling the status quo exemplified by the dominant ideology may represent the best course of action for these oppressed Others. The fact that this so rarely happens in exorcism cinema suggests that the people who make such films and the audiences who consume them are not aware of the problem, or perhaps do not wish to challenge or upset the dominant status quo.

This maintenance of the status quo manifests in the exorcism cinema subgenre's most stable trope, the possessed-woman-as-threat figure, whose repeated appearance throughout these films suggests an unconscious desire to maintain dominant patriarchal ideologies and values. The recurrence of the male protagonist charged with saving the possessed woman's soul and ending the threat she poses to stability and order further reinforces this metaphorical reading. Yet, while the figure of the possessed woman varies little across these films, the male hero does not always manifest as the doubting priest figure exemplified by Father Karras in *The Exorcist*. While the doubting priest most commonly assumes the role of the hero in exorcism cinema, several variations on this figure do exist. For example, some films depict the hero as a man struggling with his masculinity as he endeavors to live up to positive societal ideals regarding manhood, such as Sarchie in *Deliver Us from Evil*.

Whereas the exorcist frequently appears as a more complex figure with a richer and deeper emotional life (while often conforming to the doubting priest figure), exorcism films regularly construct the possessed person through the lens of various stereotypes that largely focus on sexual behavior. Indeed, it often seems as though exorcism films use the possessed woman—or the possessed non-dominant Other—solely as a way to help men navigate notions of masculinity in a variety of sociocultural settings and historical periods. The onscreen construction of the possessed women not only positions her as abject and a threat, but also dehumanizes her while simultaneously confirming the man's humanity, which in turn reinforces his status as a defender of tradition.[28] Exorcism films, therefore, address the crisis of masculinity often said to affect white, heterosexual males—particularly in the twenty-first century—because they ultimately reassure men of their dominant roles within society and culture.[29] Thus, much like the horror genre as a whole, exorcism cinema reflects traditional masculine values, and therefore targets a primarily male audience, despite the fact that female fans increasingly comprise a large percentage of the horror audience.[30]

Overall, horror films continue to reflect a conservative or traditional ideology, which advocates for the silencing and oppression of women and members of other non-dominant groups. Exorcism films routinely advance such ideology by depicting women and other marginalized individuals as threats to patriarchal order, and only the act of exorcism (i.e., repression) can restore this order. Yet, some significant differences emerge in the exorcism films produced in the 1970s and those produced during the post-9/11 resurgence period. Post-9/11, the rise of social media allows countercultural voices to be heard. These non-dominant groups have taken strides to make their voices heard during the post-9/11 period, which has slowly but surely witnessed the production of films that challenge such regressive portrayals. Indeed, based on our analysis, post-9/11 horror films appear to grant women and members of other marginalized groups a greater sense of agency than their 1970s counterparts, and allow them to assume a much more active role in undoing or embracing their possession and exorcism. Thus, films like *The Last Exorcism Part II*, *The Conjuring*, *The Unborn*, and *American Exorcist* (2016, Tony Trov and Johnny Zito) directly challenge the oppressive ideologies advanced by the traditional exorcism narrative.

The true challenge to the traditional exorcism narrative may not lie in these films' production but in their reception. Exorcism films appear to allow members of both dominant and marginalized groups to identify with the characters and metaphors that validate their worldview, which likely explains the subgenre's success during times of strife. As Andrew Scahill argues, such films allow for both oppositional and dominant identifications and readings;[31] people who fear the changes occurring in the world around them may align with the film's dominant ideological messages while those interested in promoting such changes would subscribe to a more oppositional identification. Whether engaging in a dominant or oppositional reading of these films, this complicated engagement with exorcism films could explain their popularity in two tumultuous time periods, when traditional and subcultural ideologies clashed. In both the 1970s and post-9/11 periods, those desiring stability could find reassurance in the outcomes of these films, while those seeking change could at least take pleasure in seeing stability challenged for a time.

Thus, viewers can choose to reject the dominant reading, which encourages them to identify with the doubting priest figure as he heroically confronts and eliminates the threat posed by the possessed woman or Other. Meanwhile, viewers concerned with the implications of personal responsibility may find pleasure in identifying with a character who seemingly cannot control his or her actions.[32] Indeed, viewers might identify with the possessed person because doing so allows them to vicariously experience an abject state without actually transgressing established societal boundaries. Similarly, viewers may adopt a non-dominant viewing position and identify with the struggles of the possessed Other because such portrayals mirror their own struggle to gain and retain a sense of empowerment.[33] Fans of slasher films often identify with the monster more so than the survivors,[34] and it may be that viewers of exorcism films similarly identify with the possessed individual and receive pleasure through such identification. Brigid Cherry argues that this type of reading and identification implies an affinity for subversion and resisting social expectations.[35] A person who inhabits a similar marginalized state may engage in such identification with the possessed Other,[36] and thus the act of resisting the film's dominant reading and its ideological messages of oppression could indicate a rejection of the systems of oppression that operate in a society or culture.

Yet, oppositional reception alone may not effectively end the perpetuation of the oppressive ideologies that manifest in the traditional exorcism narrative. Michel Foucault argues that "dominant structures legitimize themselves by allowing a controlled space for dissidence—resistance, in this view, is produced and then inoculated against by those in power."[37] Meanwhile, Linda Williams argues that women who watch horror films tend to identify with the monster, but do not find such affinity pleasurable,[38] which in turn renders the spectator less likely to indulge revolutionary impulses. Indeed, given that the possessed woman becomes oppressed once more when returned to her "normal" state, any identification only serves to further the female spectator's own repression. As such, the perpetuation of the traditional exorcism narrative appears to function as a form of inoculation against societal uprising. Thus, any oppositional reception needs to be combined with the type of scrutiny that fully criticizes the ideological messages of these films. Only such critical reception will lead to the deconstruction of the metaphorical oppression inherent in the subgenre. Such criticism helped deconstruct the slasher, leading to the postmodern and neoslashers that reflected on this scrutiny. The exorcism cinema subgenre, currently consisting of 127 films produced around the world, needs such attention to determine the possibility of any revolutionary messages.

FUTURE DIRECTIONS WITH EXORCISM CINEMA

Our analysis reveals that some version of the traditional exorcism narrative recurs throughout the majority of exorcism films. The persistence of this narrative indicates a need to expand the study reported here. More in-depth and varied analyses of the all the exorcism films identified in the filmography—not to mention those that have yet to be produced—is necessary to determine whether subsequent research will confirm the conclusions presented in this book, or take the study of the exorcism cinema subgenre in an entirely different direction. Either way, the relationship between these films and their historical periods attests to the importance of further study.

Of course, this book offers only one way to read exorcism cinema, a reading heavily informed by psychoanalytical, critical, and cultural theories. These philosophies inform our understanding of how exorcism films and the traditional exorcism narrative appear to advance an oppressive ideology. We acknowledge that other approaches could potentially illustrate other meaningful metaphorical and ideological messages contained within the films. Indeed, other metaphorical readings are possible, such as in *Deliverance from Evil* (2012, Eduardo Quiroz and Jose Quiroz), which equates possession with grief, or *The Taking of Deborah Logan* (2014, Adam Robitel), which functions as an allegory for Alzheimer's. *High School Exorcism* (2014, Peter Sullivan), meanwhile, uses possession and exorcism to explore issues of bullying and slut-shaming among teenagers. Using different theoretical lenses to critique the subgenre might yield a variety of interpretations.

For example, the portrayal of possession also reflects the sort of body horror depicted in films featuring werewolves or other shapeshifting monstrosities, in which the human body suddenly changes and becomes capable of committing horrible acts. Andrew Tudor argues that the horror films of the 1970s and 1980s focused primarily on "the fear of one's own body."[39] Similarly, Barbara Creed argues that Regan in *The Exorcist* displays an "unsocialized body" that revolts against traditional norms of appropriateness for women through its grotesque appearance and behavior.[40] Others, meanwhile, argue that exorcism films comment on the threat of women's life-giving ability,[41] because such films often reflect prevailing sociocultural anxieties regarding rape, pregnancy, and abortion, particularly since women have little to no choice over their possession (e.g., rape and pregnancy) or the exorcism (e.g., abortion); in the case of the latter, the men in their lives exert this control.[42] In a sense, then, possession becomes a metaphor for a variety of social anxieties, particularly those regarding puberty, pregnancy, and the mysteries of the female body. Thus, exorcism primarily functions as a way to tame the unruly feminine body and make it more acceptable to society.

Conversely, a psychological and sociological analysis could consider how the rise of authoritarianism in the United States during the first two decades of the twenty-first century contributed to the exorcism cinema subgenre's resurgence. The psychological trait of authoritarianism involves the fear of others and of sociocultural change, and this fear is exacerbated during times of economic stress, such as the two time periods analyzed in this book.[43] The rise of this trait in the general populace could relate to the way that exorcism cinema portrays the empowerment and subsequent disempowerment of marginalized identities. Indeed, given that horror frequently deals with the fear of the Other, the periodic resurgence of authoritarian attitudes likely contributes to the genre's cyclical popularity, which increases and/or decreases depending on the overall social mood.

In addition, psychological, sociological, and even further cultural studies approaches should also be employed to consider how mainstream audiences and horror aficionados alike receive these films. Throughout this book we have discussed different possible readings of these films, but these readings reflect only our own critical interpretations. To truly understand if these films transmit the embedded ideologies we have identified as central to the traditional exorcism narrative, reception studies could ascertain how viewers make sense of these stories. Such studies could consider the socializing impacts that result from exposure to these films as predicted by cultivation theory, social cognitive theory, and perceived reality. Any encoding/decoding research could serve to demonstrate how people respond to these ideological messages, and if they read any other messages into these potentially polysemous texts. Such reception studies would then provide a better understanding of exorcism films, particularly with regard to how and why they continue to propagate, and how they relate to prevailing sociocultural anxieties regarding women, people of color, and non-heteronormative identities.

Further analysis could also account for why so few exorcism films feature women of color as the victims of possession. *Abby* remains the only American production to feature a non-white possessed woman. The homogeneity of the possessed-woman-as-threat figure also recurs in the doubting priest figure. Few films have positioned men of color in the role of the exorcist or holy man; black and Latino men only appear as exorcists in *Abby, The Unborn, Deliver Us, Deliverance from Evil,* and *The Vatican Tapes* (2015, Mark Neveldine). Furthermore, as previously discussed, only one woman of color has assumed the role of exorcist, in *Last Exor-*

cism II. Thus, exorcism cinema's lack of representation requires additional analysis. bell hooks has argued that feminist film theory often fails to account for women of color when it theorizes how the cinematic apparatus suppresses women.[44] Likewise, Jenny Korn suggests Western society in general (and the United States in particular) devalues women of color, and thus does not care if they succumb to possession.[45] Perhaps the scarcity of possessed women of color suggests a belief that exorcism cannot redeem such women. Similarly, the shortage of non-white exorcists possibly reflects a colonialist belief that people of color lack power within the context of traditional society and culture. At the same time, feminist film theorists have argued that black female sexuality represents an even greater unknown and thus a more immediate threat than white female sexuality.[46] If true, then more exorcism films should portray women of color becoming possessed. These hypotheses and others deserve further scrutiny to uncover more issues of intersectionality.[47]

Furthermore, exorcism films tend to reinforce dominant patriarchal ideologies, and this suggests that men represent the apparent target audience for this subgenre. Therefore, subsequent research could reveal more about how such films depict masculinity. Indeed, on the rare occasions when exorcism films depict possessed men, they seem to fall into one of two categories: either the men become queered (as in *Exorcist II: The Heretic, Dominion: Prequel to the Exorcist*, and *Possessed*) or they become more powerful and infectious (as in *The Exorcist III* and *Deliver Us*). In the first case, they represent an extension of the traditional exorcism narrative, because their queering aligns them with a non-dominant group that requires repression. In the second case, they reinforce the traditional exorcism narrative's central thematic concern because they compel women to carry out evil acts. However, some films have depicted such men as threatening, such as *The Possession of Joel Delaney* (1972, Waris Hussein), *Amityville II: The Possession, The Possession of Michael King*,[48] *Deliver Us from Evil*, and the Polish film *Demon* (2015, Marvin Wrona). In these films, possession appears to relate to the monstrous masculine concept discussed in chapter 7. These films and others like them require more in-depth examination to determine what causes them to deviate from the traditional exorcism narrative and how the monstrous masculine compares to the monstrous-feminine.

Furthermore, the doubting priest trope seems to have fallen out of favor during the exorcism resurgence period. The priests in *Emily Rose, Deliver Us, The Shrine* (2010, Jon Knautz), *The Devil Inside* (2012, William Brent Bell), and *The Vatican Tapes* (2015, Mark Neveldine) do not suffer the same lack of faith as others of their ilk. In these films, other people assume the role of the doubter, and these others may or may not have had any previous spiritual or religious identity to call into question. Indeed, as discussed in chapters 6 and 7, some exorcism films even cast doubt on religion's place in the world by suggesting that the priests ultimately caused the possession to occur. More research on the intersection of masculinity and religion could help explain the diminished representation of the doubting priest trope in more recent films.

Nevertheless, the presence of a male savior has remained consistent across these films, suggesting that patriarchal authority remains well represented. Some films even position the possessed woman's loved ones in the role of the male savior, as in *The Possession* (2012, Ole Bornedal) and *Inner Demons* (2014, Seth Grossman). Yet, even the depiction of the male savior trope necessitates further examination. The use of male violence to exorcize a demon represents perhaps the least effective means of dispelling the evil spirit, but several movies have relied on this masculine presentation of exorcism. In his discussion of *The Exorcist*, Woods contends that Father Karras's use of violence to drive the demon from Regan's body does not align with standard Catholic rituals, given that such aggression merely dislodges the demon to possess someone else (in this case, the demon exits Regan and enters Karras).[49] Moreover, such acts of masculine violence may actually promote the very feminist ideologies they seek to repress; witnessing such brutal acts of violence perpetrated against women in the name of "saving" them could lead some viewers to conclude that the possessed woman was better off without the exorcism. Considering that Nell's exorcists were content to kill her in *Last Exorcism II*, such readings may have merit.

This study also demonstrates a need for further examination of the parodies produced during the resurgence period, such as *The Disco Exorcist* (2011, Richard Griffin), *Hellbenders* (2012, J. T. Petty), *Hell Baby* (2013, Robert Ben Garant and Thomas Lennon), *Bad Exorcists* (2015, Kyle Steinbach), *Exorcistas* (2015, Aníbal Herrera), and *Shark Exorcist* (2016, Donald Famer). The fact that such films emerged during the height of the resurgence rather than a lull period could indicate that this subgenre reached a saturation point in popular culture due to the sheer number of films produced in the early part of the twenty-first century. More importantly, though, further analysis could consider how these parodies use the tropes and themes that recur throughout the films that comprise the exorcism cinema subgenre; such analysis could reveal whether these parodies offer increased challenges to the traditional exorcism narrative. An analysis of the humor in these parodies could provide valuable insight into how they react to the fear of the Other found in the majority of exorcism films.

This book focused on films that depict possession and exorcism, to the exclusion of the books, television shows, games, and other media that also feature such narratives. Thus, more work must be done to determine the extent to which the traditional exorcism narrative applies to stories told in other media, especially as current texts suggest that it does. For instance, Mark Ludens' novel *The Exorcist's Apprentice* (2015) features a young man studying to be an exorcist, while Paul G. Tremblay's novel *A*

Head Full of Ghosts (2015) tells the story of a Catholic priest's attempt to exorcize a young woman. Meanwhile, Robert Kirkman, creator of *The Walking Dead*, has been writing the comic book series *Outcast* since 2013; this series centers on a tortured young man who performs exorcisms on a variety of possessed individuals. The cable network Cinemax developed a television series based on this story, which premiered in June 2016. Most significantly, however, a television series based on *The Exorcist* premiered on the Fox Network in September 2016.[50] In the series, two Catholic priests investigate the troubling case of the Rance family, whose eldest daughter appears to have succumbed to demonic possession. These various media texts appear to perpetuate the traditional exorcism narrative. As such, further analysis could reveal how the narrative applies to similar texts produced in other media, and thus provide more insight into the full extent of this subgenre.

CONCLUSION

Thomas Schatz argues that the success of any genre—or in this case subgenre—depends on its thematic appeal, and in how it addresses sociocultural conflicts by adjusting to reflect audiences' and filmmakers' changing attitudes toward these conflicts.[51] The continuation of the traditional exorcism narrative, then, appears to indicate that these conflicts have not changed, nor have the audiences' or filmmakers' attitudes toward them. Indeed, exorcism films seemingly depend on the presence of the same sociocultural anxieties for their propagation. While challenges to the traditional exorcism narrative have arisen toward the end of this current cycle, such films seem to inspire fear mainly because they depict the marginalization and oppression of groups that threaten to upend tradition and stability within a society or culture. Perhaps exorcism cinema hinges on the oppression of non-dominant groups, because such oppression functions as part of the coping mechanism people rely on when confronting their own fear and uncertainty regarding their own lives and their place in the world. Indeed, those who seek to maintain control over a society or culture (e.g., the forces of the white, heteronormative patriarchy) utilize repression as a way of subjugating Others and thus maintaining tradition.[52]

Exorcism cinema's tendency to advance such oppressive ideology indicates that the subgenre generates fear in audiences primarily by portraying an Othering that reflects a non-dominant group's struggle against oppression. As Wood argues, horror films function as "collective nightmares,"[53] and they circulate within a society or culture only when the producer and audience of the film share a common ideology or way of seeing the world and—in exorcism cinema in particular—fearing the Other. As long as these individuals remain marginalized, they will continue to resurface in horror films as threatening monsters that require repression.[54] Indeed, the two prime eras for exorcism cinema seem to reflect the same sort of historically situated fears of Others. Until humanity can overcome its fear of the Other, the traditional exorcism narrative will likely continue to perpetuate and reify these fears and perhaps even exacerbate them in situations that involve widespread fears and tensions regarding the role of the marginalized in global society and culture.

Thus, films that depict possession and exorcism appear to utilize the repression of Others as a way of allaying the dominant group's fears; however, no "real victory" over evil can occur so long as these very real sociocultural problems exist.[55] Horror reveals where Othering and oppression take place, as well as where and how a dominant ideology manifests and exerts power in order to dictate the conditions that define normality. According to Barry Keith Grant, the best horror films serve to "interrogate the ways by which dominant ideology is internalized by individual subjects."[56] Such horror films can criticize the Othering of marginalized peoples and scrutinize how dominant ideological forces (i.e., patriarchy, heteronormativity, colonialism) work to maintain their positions of power. By metaphorically depicting this Othering, such films can enact change, progress, and revolution, and possibly undo the repression, suppression, and oppression of marginalized peoples. After all, the rebellious Satan challenged conservative structures that refused any innovation or change, and possessed individuals also represent the potential for such disruption.[57]

Reimagining and reworking definitions of normality first requires an ability to recognize the Othering that occurs in media texts, and *Possessed Women, Haunted States* uncovers where this Othering occurs in exorcism films. While this Othering appears to emerge as the subgenre's defining feature, some exorcism films nevertheless challenge these conventions and provide other metaphorical commentaries on the world, suggesting that the dual representation of possession and exorcism can serve to portray something other than the suppression of those who do not conform to some privileged identity or position in societies and cultures. We hope that this book assists others in identifying how this Othering occurs throughout the exorcism cinema subgenre, and suggests how such depictions could change going forward.

NOTES

1. For a more detailed discussion of the circulation of sociocultural power dynamics and its links to knowledge and sexuality, see Michel Foucault, *The History of Sexuality: An Introduction (Vol. 1)* (New York: Random House, 1978).

2. Andrew Tudor, "Excerpt from 'Why Horror? The Peculiar Pleasures of a Popular Genre' with a New Afterword by the Author" in *Horror Film and Psychoanalysis:*

Freud's Worst Nightmare, ed. Steven Jay Schneider (Boston: Cambridge University Press, 2009), 58.

3. As discussed in Chris Dumas, "Horror and psychoanalysis: An introductory primer," in *A Companion to the Horror Film*, ed. Harry M. Benshoff (Malden: John Wiley & Sons, Inc., 2014), 31.

4. Ania Loomba, *Colonialism/Postcolonialism* (New York: Routledge, 1998), 47.

5. For more, see Harry M. Benshoff, "'Way too Gay to Be Ignored': The Production and Reception of Queer Horror Cinema in the Twenty-First Century," in *Speaking of Monsters: A Teratological Anthology*, eds. Caroline Joan S. Picart and John Edgar Browning (New York: Palgrave, 2012), 133 and Harry M. Benshoff, "Blaxploitation Horror Films: Generic Reappropriation or Reinscription?," *Cinema Journal* 39, no. 2 (2000): 31.

6. Richard Nowell, *Blood Money: A History of the First Teen Slasher Film Cycle* (New York City: Continuum International Publishing Group. 2011), 46.

7. Ibid.

8. Ibid.

9. Ibid., 50.

10. Ibid., 47.

11. Ibid., 50.

12. Alexandra Heller-Nicholas, "'The Power of Christ Compels You': Moral Spectacle and The Exorcist Universe," in *Roman Catholicism in Fantastic Film: Essays on Belief, Spectacle, Ritual and Imagery*, ed. Regina Hansen (Jefferson: McFarland & Company, Inc., 2011), 65–80.

13. Steven P. Miller, *The Age of Evangelicalism: America's Born-again Years* (New York: Oxford University Press, 2014), 78–86.

14. For more on the rhetorical construction of masculinity in the action films of the 1980s and 1990s, see Susan Jeffords, *Hardbodies: Hollywood Masculinity in the Reagan Era* (New Brunswick: Rutgers University Press, 1994) and Susan Jeffords, "Can Masculinity Be Terminated?," in *Screening the Male: Exploring Masculinities in Hollywood Cinema*, eds. Steven Cohan and Ina Rae Hark (New York: Routledge, 1993), 230–244.

15. Kevin J. Wetmore, *Post-9/11 Horror in American Cinema* (New York: Continuum, 2012), 142.

16. Richard Woods, *The Devil* (Merrimack: The Thomas More Press, 1973), 112–13.

17. Anthony Faiola, "A Modern Pope Gets Old School on the Devil," *The Washington Post*, last modified May 10, 2014, https://www.washingtonpost.com/world/a-modern-pope-gets-old-school-on-the-devil/2014/05/10/f56a9354-1b93-4662-abbb-d877e49f15ea_story.html.

18. Ibid.

19. Ibid.

20. Ibid.

21. Ibid.

22. Ibid.

23. For instance, in 2015, a South Korean family traveled to Germany to exorcize a female family member who had seemingly become possessed. For more on this story, see David Boroff, "Five People from South Korea Family Arrested After Relative, 41, Dies During Exorcism in Germany: Authorities," *New York Daily News*, last modified December 11, 2015, http://www.nydailynews.com/news/crime/arrested-relative-dies-exorcism-article-1.2462848.

24. Graham Thompson, *American Culture in the 1980s* (Edinburgh: Edinburgh University Press, 2007), 31.

25. Wetmore, *Post-9/11 Horror*, 193.

26. Stephen King, *Danse Macabre* (New York: Pocket Books, 1982/2010), 29.

27. King, *Danse*, 4.

28. Daniel Humphrey, "Gender and Sexuality Haunts the Horror Film," in *A Companion to the Horror Film*, ed. Harry M. Benshoff (Malden: John Wiley & Sons, Inc., 2014), 39.

29. In reality, exorcisms often require numerous sessions to reach a conclusion, whereas cinematic depictions routinely feature much speedier resolutions. Thus, in exorcism films, the act of overcoming a lack of faith renders the man much more powerful, since he gains the spiritual strength and vitality to vanquish the demon and restore order so quickly.

30. Christine Spines, "Horror Films . . . and the Women Who Love Them!," *Entertainment Weekly*, July 31, 2009.

31. Andrew Scahill, "Demons Are a Girl's Best Friend: Queering the Revolting Child in *The Exorcist*," *Red Feather Journal* 1, no. 1 (2010): 39–55.

32. Michael Calia, "Hollywood Moves Back to Demonic Possession Stories," *The Wall Street Journal*, last modified October 28, 2015, http://www.wsj.com/articles/hollywood-moves-back-to-demonic-possession-stories-1446048013.

33. According to Harry M. Benshoff (1997), "the liberating identificatory pleasures that the movie monster provides are frequently accessed by non-white, as well as non-straight, spectators" (205).

34. Harry M. Benshoff, *Monsters in the Closet: Homosexuality and the Horror Film* (New York: Manchester University Press, 1997), 11.

35. Brigid Cherry, "Refusing to Refuse to Look: Female Viewers of the Horror Film," in *Horror, The Film Reader*, ed. Mark Jancovich (New York: Routledge, 2002), 180.

36. For more, see Benshoff, "Blaxploitation Horror," 32.

37. Loomba, *Colonialism*, 35.

38. Cherry, "Refusing to Refuse to Look," 169.

39. Andrew Tudor, "Unruly Bodies, Unquiet Minds," *Body & Society* 1, no. 1 (1995): 26.

40. Barbara Creed, *The Monstrous-Feminine: Film, Feminism, and Psychoanalysis* (New York: Routledge, 1993), 40.

41. Kelly Oliver, *Knock Me Up, Knock Me Down: Images of Pregnancy in Hollywood Films* (New York: Columbia University Press, 2012), 144.

42. Rebecca Munford and Melanie Waters, *Feminism and Popular Culture: Investigating the Postfeminist Mystique* (New Brunswick: Rutgers University Press, 2013), 153.

43. Amanda Taub, "The Rise of American Authoritarianism," *Vox*, last modified March 1, 2016, http://www.vox.com/2016/3/1/11127424/trump-authoritarianism.

44. bell hooks, "The Oppositional Gaze: Black Female Spectators," in *The Feminism and Visual Culture Reader*, ed. Amelia Jones (New York: Routledge, 2010), 112.

45. Jenny Korn, "The Devil Makes White Girls Do Backbends: 150 Words on Horror Films," *Jennykorn.com*, last modified February 23, 2013, http://jennykorn.com/2013/02/23/devil-backbends/.

46. Anneke Smelik, "Feminist Film Theory," in *The Cinema Book* (3rd Ed.), ed. Pam Cook (London: British Film Institute, 2007), 499.

47. Indeed, this analysis does not consider the portrayal of class in these films. For the majority of films, the possessed person appears to hail from a middle or lower socioeconomic class, with Regan and Gul representing the few upper class possessed people. Further interrogation is needed to understand how this aspect of identity informs the portrayal of possession and exorcism.

48. Interestingly, Michael King becomes both the possessed and the doubting person who regains his faith through his confrontation with exorcism. More importantly, however, Michael King displays quite a bit of agency in this film—more so than Casey Beldon in *Unborn* or even Nell in *Last Exorcism II*—likely as a result of his male nature, which allows him to exorcise himself, a feat apparently off limits to possessed women.

49. Woods, *The Devil*, 33–34.

50. For more, see Denise Petski, "Tracy Ifeachor Joins ABC Pilot 'Spark'; Brianne Howey In Fox's 'The Exorcist'," *Deadline Hollywood*, last modified February 24, 2016, http://deadline.com/2016/02/tracy-ifeachor-cast-abc-pilot-spark-brianne-howey-the-exorcist-1201708583/ and David Crow, "The Exorcist TV Series Picks Up Planet of the Apes Director," *Den of Geek!*, last modified February 2, 2016, http://

www.denofgeek.us/movies/the-exorcist/252247/the-exorcist-tv-series-picks-up-planet-of-the-apes-director.

51. Thomas Schatz, "Film Genre and the Genre Film," in *Film Theory and Criticism* (6th Ed.), eds. Leo Braudy and Marshall Cohen (New York: Oxford University Press, 1991/2004), 700.

52. Benshoff, *Monsters*, 8.

53. Robin Wood, *Hollywood from Vietnam to Reagan . . . and Beyond* (New York: Columbia University Press, 2003), 70.

54. Benshoff, *Monsters*, 8–9.

55. Woods (1973) considers this idea in regards to actual possessions, stating that focusing on possessions as an individual problem elides over the attention needed to resolve social and cultural dilemmas, and allows for the drama of exorcisms to offer the (false) hope that evil has been vanquished. However, such victories are illusory unless society at large confronts the underlying problems.

56. Barry Keith Grant, "'When the Woman Looks': *Haute Tension* (2003) and the Horrors of Heteronormativity," in *Feminism at the Movies: Understanding Gender in Contemporary Popular Cinema*, eds. Hilary Radner and Rebecca Stringer (New York: Routledge, 2003), 284.

57. Woods, *The Devil*, 125–26.

Filmography

The list below contains all of the exorcism films we have identified during the course of this project. The films are listed in chronological order according to their release date, and appear under their original titles, followed by English translations and alternate titles.

1. *Der Dibuk* (aka *The Dybbuk*). Poland: Michal Waszynski, 1937.
2. *Matka Joanna od aniołów* (aka *Mother Joan of the Angels*, aka *The Devil and the Nun*). Poland: Jerzy Kawalerowicz, 1961.
3. *Il demonio* (aka *The Demon*). Italy: Brunello Rondi, 1963.
4. *Naked Evil* (aka *Exorcism at Midnight*). UK: Stanley Goulder, 1966.
5. *Las melancólicas* (aka *Exorcism's Daughter*, aka *The House of Insane Women*). Spain: Rafael Moreno Alba, 1971.
6. *The Devils*. USA: Ken Russell, 1971.
7. *The Possession of Joel Delaney*. USA: Waris Hussein, 1972.
8. *The Exorcist*. USA: William Friedkin, 1973.
9. *Abby*. USA: William Gidler, 1974.
10. *Chi sei?* (*Beyond the Door*, aka *The Devil Within Her*). Italy/USA: Ovidio G. Assonitis and Robert Barrett, 1974.
11. *L'éventreur de Notre-Dame* (aka *Exorcisms*, aka *Demoniac*, aka *Exorcism and Black Masses*, aka *Exorcisme et messes noires*). France: Jesús Franco, 1974.
12. *Magdalena, vom Teufel besessen* (aka *Magdalena, Possessed by the Devil*, aka *Magdelena: The Devil Inside the Female*, aka *Beyond the Darkness*, aka *Devil's Female*). Germany: Walter Boos, 1974.
13. *Şeytan*. Turkey: Metin Erksan, 1974.
14. *L'anticristo* (aka *The Antichrist*, aka *The Tempter*). Italy: Alberto De Martino, 1974.
15. *O Exorcismo Negro* (aka *Exorcisme noir*, aka *The Black Exorcism*, aka *The Bloody Exorcism of Coffin Joe*). Brazil: José Mojica Marins, 1974.
16. *Lisa e il diavolo* (aka *Lisa and the Devil*, aka *The House of Exorcism*). Italy: Mario Bava and Alfredo Leone, 1974.
17. *L'ossessa* (aka *Enter the Devil*, aka *The Devil Obsession*, aka *The Eerie Midnight Horror Show*, aka *The Sexorcist*, aka *The Tormented*). Italy: Mario Gariazzo, 1974.
18. *La endemoniada* (aka *The Possessed*, aka *Demon Witch Child*). Spain: Amando de Ossorio, 1975.
19. *Exorcismo*. Spain: Juan Bosch, 1975.

20. *L'esorciccio* (aka *The Exorcist: Italian Style*). Italy: Ciccio Ingrassia, 1975.
21. *Un urlo dalla tenebre* (aka *The Return of the Exorcist*, aka *The Possessor*). Italy: Franco Lo Cascio and Angelo Pannacciò, 1975.
22. *I Don't Want to Be Born* (aka *Sharon's Baby*). UK: Peter Sasdy, 1975.
23. *Exorcist II: The Heretic*. USA: John Boorman, 1977.
24. *Alucarda, la hija de las tinieblas* (aka *Alucarda*). Mexico: Juan López Moctezuma, 1977.
25. *Good Against Evil*. USA: Paul Wendkos, 1977.
26. *The Possessed*. USA: Jerry Thorpe, 1977.
27. *Nurse Sherri* (aka *The Possession of Nurse Sherri*, aka *Beyond the Living*). USA: Al Adamson, 1978.
28. *The Manitou*. USA: William Girdler, 1978.
29. *Malabimba* (aka *The Malicious Whore*, aka *Possession of a Teenager*). Italy: Andrea Bianchi, 1979.
30. *Amityville II: The Possession*. USA: Damiano Damiani, 1982.
31. *Jing hun feng yu ye* (aka *Devil Returns*). Hong Kong: Yao-Chi Chen, 1982.
32. *La bimba di satana* (aka *Satan's Baby Doll*). Italy: Mario Bianchi, 1982.
33. *Mo Tai* (aka *The Devil Fetus*). Hong Kong: Hung-Chuen Lau, 1983.
34. *The Demon Murder Case*. USA: William Hale, 1983.
35. *Ninja III: The Domination*. USA: Sam Firstenberg, 1984.
36. *Beetlejuice*. USA: Tim Burton, 1988.
37. *The Exorcist III*. USA: William Peter Blatty, 1990.
38. *Repossessed*. USA: Bob Logan, 1990.
39. *Teenage Exorcist*. USA: Grant Austin Waldman, 1991.
40. *The Possession of Michael D.* (aka *Legacy of Evil*). Canada: Michael Kennedy, 1995.
41. *The Mangler*. USA: Tobe Hooper, 1995.
42. *Stigmata*. USA: Rupert Wainwright, 1999.
43. *Possessed*. USA: Steven E. de Souza, 2000.
44. *Lost Souls*. USA: Janusz Kaminski, 2000.
45. *Scary Movie 2*. USA: Keenan Ivory Wayans, 2001.
46. *Exorcism*. USA: William A. Baker, 2003.
47. *Exorcist: The Beginning*. USA: Renny Harlin, 2004.
48. *Constantine*. USA: Francis Lawrence, 2005.
49. *Dominion: Prequel to the Exorcist*. USA: Paul Schrader, 2005.
50. *The Exorcism of Emily Rose*. USA: Scott Derrickson, 2005.
51. *Exorcism: The Possession of Gail Bowers*. USA: Leigh Scott, 2006.
52. *Requiem*. Germany: Hans-Christian Schmid, 2006.
53. *Blackwater Valley Exorcism*. USA: Ethan Wiley, 2006.
54. *Costa Chica: Confession of an Exorcist* (aka *Legion: The Final Exorcism*). USA: David Heavener, 2006.
55. *The Exorcist Chronicles*. USA: Will Raee, 2007.
56. *Chronicles of an Exorcism*. USA: Nick G. Miller, 2008.

57. *Semum*. Turkey: Hasan Karacadag, 2008.

58. *1920*. India: Vikram Bhatt, 2008.

59. *Home Movie*. USA: Christopher Denham, 2008.

60. *[Rec]²*. Spain: Jaume Balagueró and Paco Plaza, 2009.

61. *The Unborn*. USA: David S. Goyer, 2009.

62. *The Grudge 3*. USA: Toby Wilkins, 2009.

63. *La Posesion de Emma Evans* (aka *The Possession of Emma Evans*, aka *Exorcismus*). Spain: Manuel Carballo, 2010.

64. *The Shrine*. USA: Jon Knautz, 2010.

65. *The Last Exorcism*. USA: Daniel Stamm, 2010.

66. *The Rite*. USA: Mikael Håfström, 2011.

67. *Season of the Witch*. USA: Dominic Sena, 2011.

68. *The Disco Exorcist*. USA: Richard Griffin, 2011.

69. *Devil Seed* (aka *The Devil in Me*). Canada: Greg A. Sager, 2012.

70. *[Rec]³: Génesis* (aka *[REC]³: Genesis*). Spain: Paco Plaza, 2012.

71. *The Devil Inside*. USA: William Brent Bell, 2012.

72. *The Possession*. USA: Ole Bornedal, 2012.

73. *Deliverance from Evil*. USA: Eduardo Quiroz and Jose Quiroz, 2012.

74. *Dupa dealuri* (aka *Beyond the Hills*). Romania: Cristian Mungiu, 2012.

75. *This is the End*. USA: Seth Rogen and Evan Goldberg, 2013.

76. *Demon Equation* (aka *Demon Exorcism: The Devil Inside Maxwell Bastas*). USA: Richard G. James, 2013.

77. *Exorcist Chronicles*. USA: Philip Gardiner, 2013.

78. *An Irish Exorcism* (aka *The Exorcism Diary*). Ireland: Eric Courtney, 2013.

79. *The Vatican Exorcisms*. Italy: Joe Marino, 2013.

80. *Karuto* (aka *Cult*). Japan: Kôji Shiraishi, 2013.

81. *Amy*. USA: Patnaik R. P., 2013.

82. *The Conjuring*. USA: James Wan, 2013.

83. *Hell Baby*. USA: Robert Ben Garant and Thomas Lennon, 2013.

84. *The Last Exorcism Part II*. USA: Ed Gass-Donnelly, 2013.

85. *The Cloth*. USA: Justin Price, 2013.

86. *Hellbenders*. USA: J. T. Perry, 2014.

87. *The Diabolical*. USA: Ryan Callaway, 2014.

88. *Exorcism*. UK: Lance Patrick, 2014.

89. *High School Exorcism*. USA: Peter Sullivan, 2014.

90. *Inner Demons*. USA: Seth Grossman, 2014.

91. *The Taking of Deborah Logan*. USA: Adam Robitel, 2014.

92. *Deliver Us from Evil*. USA: Scott Derrickson, 2014.

93. *Grace: The Possession*. USA: Jeff Chan, 2014.

94. *The Possession of Michael King*. USA: David Jung, 2014.

95. *Asmodexia*. Spain: Marc Carreté, 2014.

96. *Proof of the Devil*. USA: Paul Catalanotto, 2014.

97. *Bad Exorcists*. USA: Kyle Steinbach, 2015.

98. *Exorcistas*. Chile: Anibal Herrera, 2015.

99. *The Exorcism of Molly Hartley*. USA/Canada: Steven R. Monroe, 2015.

100. *The Vatican Tapes*. USA: Mark Neveldine, 2015.

101. *Incarnate*. USA: Brad Peyton, 2015.

102. *Exeter*. USA: Marcus Nispel, 2015.

103. *Paranormal Activity: The Ghost Dimension*. USA: Gregory Plotkin, 2015.

104. *The Wicked Within*. USA: Jay Alaimo, 2015.

105. *February* (aka *The Blackcoat's Daughter*). USA: Oz Perkins, 2015.

106. *The Ouija Exorcism*. USA: Nick Slatkin, 2015.

107. *Ava's Possessions*. USA: Jordan Galland, 2015.

108. *The Atticus Institute*. USA: Chris Sparling, 2015.

109. *Toema: Munyeokul* (aka *Exorcist*, aka *The Chosen: Forbidden Cave*). South Korea: Kim Hwi, 2015.

110. *Demon*. Poland: Marcin Wrona, 2015.

111. *The Possession Experiment*. USA: Scott B. Hansen, 2015.

112. *Exorcist: House of Evil* (aka *The Nameless*). USA: David Trotti, 2016.

113. *The Exorcism of Anna Ecklund*. UK: Andrew Jones, 2016.

114. *The Offering* (aka *The Faith of Anna Waters*). USA/Singapore: Kelvin Tong, 2016.

115. *Shark Exorcist*. USA: Donald Farmer, 2016.

116. *Accidental Exorcist*. USA: Daniel Falicki, 2016.

117. *Diário de um exorcista - zero*. Brazil: Renato Siqueira, 2016.

118. *No Hiding Place*. Nigeria: Joseph Yemi Adepoju, 2016.

119. *The Conjuring 2*. USA: James Wan, 2016.

120. *Goksung* (aka *The Wailing*). South Korea: Hong-jin Na, 2016.

121. *Ghostbusters*. USA: Paul Feig, 2016.

122. *Victoria's Exorcism* (aka *Exorcist: The Fallen*). USA: Garrett Benach, 2016.

123. *Dark Exorcism*. USA: David Spaltro, 2016.

124. *The Secrets of Emily Blair*. USA: Joseph P. Genier, 2016.

125. *The Crucifixion*. USA/Romania: Xavier Gens, 2017.

126. *American Exorcist*. USA: Tony Trov and Johnny Zito, 2017.

127. *American Exorcism*. USA: Tripp Weathers, 2017.

Bibliography

Allen, Tracy. "This Week in Horror Movie History—*Amityville II: The Possession* (1982)." *Cryptic Rock.* Last modified September 26, 2014. http://crypticrock.com/this-week-in-horror-movie-history-amityville-ii-the-possession-1982/.

Allyn, David. *Make Love, Not War: The Sexual Revolution, an Unfettered History.* Boston: Little, Brown, 2000.

"Amityville." *Warrens.net.* Accessed August 10, 2005. http://www.warrens.net/Amityville.html.

Baker, Charles A. "The Exorcist Revisited." *Film Criticism,* 1, no. 2 (1976): 21–24.

Ballon, Bruce and Molyn Leszcz. "Horror Films: Tales to Master Terror or Shapers of Trauma?" *American Journal of Psychotherapy* 61, no. 2 (2007): 211–30.

Bandura, Albert. "Social Cognitive Theory of Mass Communication." In *Media Effects: Advances in Theory and Research* (2nd Ed.), edited by Jennings Bryant and Dolf Zillmann, 121–53. Hillsdale: Lawrence Erlbaum Associates, 2002.

Baudrillard, Jean. *Simulacra and Simulation.* Ann Arbor: University of Michigan Press, 1981.

Benshoff, Harry M. *Monsters in the Closet: Homosexuality and the Horror Film.* New York: Manchester University Press, 1997.

———. "Blaxploitation Horror Films: Generic Reappropriation or Reinscription?," *Cinema Journal* 39, no. 2 (2000): 31–50.

———. "'Way too Gay to Be Ignored': The Production and Reception of Queer Horror Cinema in the Twenty-First Century." In *Speaking of Monsters: A Teratological Anthology,* edited by Caroline Joan S. Picart and John Edgar Browning, 131–44. New York: Palgrave, 2012.

Bishop, Kyle. "The Sub-Subaltern Monster: Imperialist Hegemony and the Cinematic Voodoo Zombie." *The Journal of American Culture* 31, no. 2 (2008): 141–52.

Biskind, Peter. *Easy Riders, Raging Bulls: How the Sex-Drugs-and-Rock 'N' Roll Generation Saved Hollywood.* New York: Simon & Schuster, 1998.

Bivins, Jason C. "By Demons Driven: Religious Teratologies." In *Speaking of Monsters: A Teratological Anthology,* edited by Caroline Joan S. Picart and John Edgar Browning, 105–15. New York: Palgrave-MacMillan, 2012.

"The Blair Witch Project (1999)." Box Office Mojo. Accessed August 10, 2015. http://www.boxofficemojo.com/movies/?id=blairwitchproject.htm.

Boeskool, Chris. "'When You're Accustomed to Privilege, Equality Feels Like Oppression.'" *Huffpost Politics.* Last modified March 14, 2016. http://www.huffingtonpost.com/chris-boeskool/when-youre-accustomed-to-privilege_b_9460662.html.

Boroff, David. "Five People from South Korea Family Arrested After Relative, 41, Dies During Exorcism in Germany: Authorities." *New York Daily News.* Last modified December 11, 2015. http://www.nydailynews.com/news/crime/arrested-relative-dies-exorcism-article-1.2462848.

Brandum, Dean. "Abby Ho'ed." *Filmbunnies* (blog). August 13, 2008. https://filmbunnies.wordpress.com/2008/08/13/abby-hoed-william-girdlers-abby-1974/.

Briggs, Katharine M. *The Fairies in English Tradition and Literature.* New York: Routledge, 1967.

———. *An Encyclopedia of Fairies, Hobgoblins, Brownies, Bogies, and Other Supernatural Creatures.* New York: Pantheon Books, 1976.

189

Britton, Andrew. "The Exorcist." In *American Nightmare: Essays on the Horror Film*, edited by Andrew Britton, Richard Lippe, Tony Williams, and Robin Wood, 50–53. Toronto: Festival of Festivals, 1979.

Bruckheimer, Jerry. "Illuminating Evil: Making *Deliver Us from Evil.*" *Deliver Us from Evil*. Blu-ray. Directed by Scott Derrickson. Culver City: Screen Gems, 2014.

Brummett, Barry. "What Popular Films Teach Us About Values: Locked Inside with the Rage Virus." *Journal of Popular Film and Television*, 41, no 2 (2013): 61–67.

Caciola, Nancy. *Discerning Spirits: Divine and Demonic Possession in the Middle Ages*. Ithaca: Cornell University Press, 2003.

Calia, Michael. "Hollywood Moves Back to Demonic Possession Stories." *The Wall Street Journal*. Last modified October 28, 2015. http://www.wsj.com/articles/hollywood-moves-back-to-demonic-possession-stories-1446048013.

Campbell, Jan. *Film and Cinema Spectatorship: Melodrama and Mimesis*. Malden: Polity Press, 2005.

Cantor, Joanne. "Fright Reactions to Mass Media." In *Media Effects: Advances in Theory and Research*, edited by Jennings Bryant and Dolf Zillman, 213–41. Hillsdale: Lawrence Erlbaum Associates, 1994.

———. "'I'll Never Have a Clown in My House'—Why Movie Horror Lives On." *Poetics Today* 25, no. 2 (2004): 283–304.

Carroll, Noël. *The Philosophy of Horror, Or, Paradoxes of the Heart*. New York: Routledge, 1990.

Chattaway, Peter T. "Devil in the Details?: Horror-Flick Director Seeks to Confront Postmodern Culture With Ultimate Issues." *Christianity Today*, 49 no. 11 (2005): 102.

Cheirif, Samantha. "Former NYPD Officer Ralph Sarchie Talks DELIVER US FROM EVIL, Having His Life Story Made into a Movie, and His Experiences with the Paranormal." *Collider.com*. Last modified July 2, 2014. http://collider.com/ralph-sarchie-deliver-us-from-evil-interview/.

Cherry, Brigid. "Refusing to Refuse to Look: Female Viewers of the Horror Film." In *Horror, The Film Reader*, edited by Mark Jancovich, 169–78. New York: Routledge, 2002.

Church, David. "Review: *The Exorcism of Emily Rose.*" *Disability Studies Quarterly* 26, No. 2 (2006): 1–3.

———. "From Exhibition to Genre: The Case of Grind-House Films." *Cinema Journal* 50, no. 4 (2011): 1-25.

Clover, Carol J. *Men, Women, and Chain Saws: Gender in the Modern Horror Film*. Princeton: Princeton University Press, 1992.

Collins, Brian. "*Lisa and the Devil* and (Later) Some Pea Soup." *Birth. Movies. Death.* Last modified July 10, 2015. http://birthmoviesdeath.com/2015/07/10/lisa-and-the-devil-and-later-some-pea-soup.

Connell, R. W. and James W. Messerschmidt. "Hegemonic Masculinity: Rethinking the Concept." *Gender & Society* 19, no. 6 (2005): 829–59.

Conterio, Martyn. "Films That Time Forgot: *The Exorcist III* (1990)." *New Empress Magazine*. Last modified January 22, 2013. http://newempressmagazine.com/2013/01/films-that-time-forgot-the-exorcist-iii-1990/.

Cooper, Davina. *Power in Struggle: Feminism, Sexuality and the State*. Buckingham: Open University Press, 1995.

Cortés, Juan B. and Florence M. Gatti. *The Case Against Possessions and Exorcisms: A Historical, Biblical, and Psychological Analysis of Demons, Devils, and Demoniacs*. New York: Vantage Press, 1975.

Coupland, Douglas. *Generation X: Tales for an Accelerated Culture*. New York: St. Martin's Press, 1991.

Cowan, Douglas E. "Horror and the Demonic." In *The Routledge Companion to Religion and Film*, edited by John Lyden, 403–19. New York: Routledge, 2009.

———. "Religion and Cinema Horror." In *Understanding Religion and Popular Culture: Theories, Themes, Products and Practices*, edited by Terry Ray Clark and Dan W. Clanton, Jr., 56–71. New York: Routledge, 2012.

Crane, Jonathan L. "'It was a Dark and Stormy Night . . . ': Horror Films and the Problem of Irony." In *Horror Film and Psychoanalysis: Freud's Worst Nightmare*, edited by Steven Jay Schneider, 142–56. Boston: Cambridge University Press, 2004.

Creed, Barbara. *The Monstrous-Feminine: Film, Feminism, and Psychoanalysis*. New York: Routledge, 1993.

———. "Horror and the Monstrous-Feminine: An Imaginary Abjection." In *Feminist Film Theory: A Reader*, edited by Sue Thornham, 251–66. Edinburgh: Edinburgh University Press, 1999.

———. "Kristeva, Femininity, Abjection." In *The Horror Reader*, edited by Ken Gelder, 64–70. New York: Routledge, 2000.

Crow, David. "The Exorcist TV Series Picks Up Planet of the Apes Director," *Den of Geek!*. Last modified February 2, 2016. http://www.denofgeek.us/movies/the-exorcist/252247/the-exorcist-tv-series-picks-up-planet-of-the-apes-director.

Derrickson, Scott. "Illuminating Evil: Making *Deliver Us from Evil*." *Deliver Us from Evil*. Blu-ray. Directed by Scott Derrickson. Culver City: Screen Gems, 2014.

Deutch, Richard. *Exorcism: Possession or Obsession?* London: Bachman & Turner, 1975.

Deutsch, Nathaniel. *The Maiden of Ludmir: A Jewish Holy Woman and Her World*. Los Angeles: University of California Press, 2003.

Dolan, Jill. *The Feminist Spectator as Critic*. Ann Arbor: UMI Research Press, 1988.

Dumas, Chris. "Horror and Psychoanalysis: An Introductory Primer." In *A Companion to the Horror Film*, edited by Harry M. Benshoff, 21–37. Malden: John Wiley & Sons, Inc., 2014.

Edwards, Justin D. and Rune Graulund. *Grotesque*. New York: Routledge, 2013.

Eggertson, Chris. "From 'Blair Witch' to 'Project Almanac': A History of the Found Footage Genre." *Hitfix*. Last modified February 2, 2015. http://www.hitfix.com/news/from-cannibal-holocaust-to-project-almanac-a-history-of-the-found-footage-genre.

Erickson, Daniel. *Ghosts, Metaphor, and History in Tony Morrison's* Beloved *and Gabriel Garcia Marquez's* One Hundred Years of Solitude. New York: Palgrave MacMillan, 2009.

"The Exorcist." *Box Office Mojo*. Accessed July 27, 2015. http://www.boxofficemojo.com/movies/?id=exorcist.htm.

"'The Exorcist' fairly close to the mark." *National Catholic Reporter*, Sept. 1, 2000.

"The Exorcist III." *Box Office Mojo*. Accessed August 7, 2015. http://www.boxofficemojo.com/movies/?page=main&id=exorcist3.htm.

"The Exorcist III (1990)." *Rotten Tomatoes*. Accessed August 7, 2015. http://www.rottentomatoes.com/m/exorcist_3/.

Fahy, Thomas. "Introduction." In *The Philosophy of Horror*, edited by Thomas Fahy, 1–13. Lexington: The University of Kentucky Press, 2010.

Faiola, Anthony. "A Modern Pope Gets Old School on the Devil." *The Washington Post*. Last modified May 10, 2014. https://www.washingtonpost.com/world/a-modern-pope-gets-old-school-on-the-devil/2014/05/10/f56a9354–1b93–4662-abbb-d877e49f15ea_story.html.

Falconer, Pete. "Fresh Meat? Dissecting the Horror Movie Virgin" in *Virgin Territory: Representing Sexual Inexperience in Film*, edited by Tamar Jeffers McDonald, 123–37. Detroit: Wayne State University Press, 2010.

Fitch, Alex. "Light in the Darkness: William Peter Blatty's Faith Trilogy." *Electric Sheep Magazine*. Last modified February 25, 2011. http://www.electricsheepmagazine.co.uk/features/2011/02/25/light-in-the-darkness-william-peter-blattys-faith-trilogy/comment-page-1/

Foucault, Michel. *The History of Sexuality: An Introduction (Vol. 1)*. New York: Random House, 1978.

Freeland, Cynthia A. *The Naked and the Undead: Evil and the Appeal of Horror*. Boulder: Westview Press, 2000.

Friedman, Lester D. "'Canyons of Nightmare': The Jewish Horror Film," in *Planks of Reason: Essays on the Horror Film*, edited by Barry Keith Grant and Christopher Sharrett, 82–106. Lanham: Scarecrow press, Inc., 2004.

Fry, Carrol L. *Cinema of the Occult: New Age, Satanism, Wicca and Spirituality in Film*. Bethlehem: Lehigh University Press, 2000.

Gerbner, George, Larry Gross, Michael Morgan, Nancy Signorielli, and James Shanahan. "Growing Up with Television: Cultivation Processes," *in Media Effects: Advances in Theory and Research* (2nd Ed.), edited by Jennings Bryant and Dolf Zillmann, 43–66. Hillsdale: Lawrence Erlbaum Associates, 2002.

Gelder, Ken. "Global/Postcolonial Horror: Introduction." *Postcolonial Studies* 3, no. 1 (2000): 35–38.

Grant, Barry Keith, ed. *The Dread of Difference: Gender and the Horror Film*. Austin: University of Texas Press, 1996.

———. "'When the Woman Looks': *Haute Tension* (2003) and the Horrors of Heteronormativity." In *Feminism at the Movies: Understanding Gender in Contemporary Popular Cinema*, edited by Hilary Radner and Rebecca Stringer, 283–95. New York: Routledge, 2011.

Grimes, William. "Hans Holzer, Ghost Hunter, Dies at 89." *The New York Times*. Last modified April 29, 2009. http://www.nytimes.com/2009/04/30/books/30holzer.html?_r=2&.

Hall, Stuart. "Culture, the Media, and the 'Ideological Effect.'" In *Mass Communication and Society*, edited by James Curran, Michael Gurevitch, and Janet Woollacott, 315–47. London: Edward Arnold, 1977.

———. "Encoding, Decoding." In *The Cultural Studies Reader*, edited by Simon During, 90–103. New York City: Routledge, 1993.

Hantke, Steffan. "Academic Film Criticism, the Rhetoric of Crisis, and the Current State of American Horror Cinema: Thoughts on Canonicity and Academic Anxiety." *College Literature* 34, no. 4 (2007): 191–202.

Harisson, Kristen and Joanne Cantor. "Tales from the Screen: Enduring Fright Reactions to Scary Media." *Media Psychology* 1, no. 2 (1999): 97–116.

Hart, Adam Charles. "Millennial Fears: Abject Horror in a Transnational Context." In *A Companion to the Horror Film*, edited by Harry M. Benshoff, 329–44. Malden: John Wiley & Sons, Inc., 2014.

Heffernan, Kevin. "Art House or House of Exorcism? The Changing Distribution and Reception Contexts of Mario Bava's *Lisa and the Devil*." In *Sleaze Artists: Cinema at the Margins of Taste, Style, and Politics*, edited by Jeffrey Sconce, 144–63. Durham, NC: Duke University Press, 2007.

Hefner, Brooks E. "Rethinking *Blacula*: Ideological Critique at the Intersection of Genres." *Journal of Popular Film and Television* 40, no. 2 (2012): 62–74.

Heller-Nicholas, Alexandra. "'The Power of Christ Compels You': Moral Spectacle and The Exorcist Universe." In *Roman Catholicism in Fantastic Film: Essays on Belief, Spectacle, Ritual and Imagery*, edited by Regina Hansen, 65–80. Jefferson: McFarland & Company, Inc., 2011.

———. *Found Footage Horror Films: Fear and the Appearance of Reality*. Jefferson: McFarland & Company, Inc., 2014.

Hewitt, Simon. "I'm Not Sure I Like the Sound of That: Palliative Effects of the 'Synchronous Monster' in Cinema." Presentation at Fear, Horror, & Terror at the Interface, 7th Global Conference, Oxford, United Kingdom, September 5–7, 2013.

hooks, bell. "The Oppositional Gaze: Black Female Spectators." In *The Feminism and Visual Culture Reader*, edited by Amelia Jones, 107–18. New York: Routledge, 2010.

Humphrey, Daniel. "Gender and Sexuality Haunts the Horror Film." In *A Companion to the Horror Film*, edited by Harry M. Benshoff, 38–55. Maldwn: Wiley Blackwell, 2014.

Hunter, I. Q. "Trash Horror and the Cult of the Bad Film." In *A Companion to the Horror Film*, edited by Harry M. Benshoff, 482–500. Malden: John Wily & Sons, Inc., 2014.

Hutchings, Peter. "Masculinity and the Horror Film." In *You Tarzan: Masculinity, Movies and Men*, edited by Pat Kirkham and Janet Thumim, 84–94. New York: St. Martin's Press, 1993.

———. "International Horror in the 1970s." In *A Companion to the Horror Film*, edited by Harry M. Benshoff, 293-309. Malden: John Wiley & Sons, Inc., 2014.

Jancovich, Mark, ed. *Horror, The Film Reader*. New York: Routledge, 2002.

Jackson, Rosemary. *Fantasy: The Literature of Subversion*. London: Methuen, 1981.

Jeffords, Susan. "Can Masculinity Be Terminated?" In *Screening the Male: Exploring Masculinities in Hollywood Cinema*, edited by Steven Cohan and Ina Rae Hark, 230–44. New York: Routledge, 1993.

———. *Hardbodies: Hollywood Masculinity in the Reagan Era*. New Brunswick: Rutgers University Press, 1994.

Kapacinskas, Thomas J. "'The Exorcist' and the Spiritual Problem of Modern Woman." *Psychological Perspectives: A Quarterly Journal of Jungian Thought* 6, no. 2 (1975): 176–83.

Karademir, Burcu Sari. "Turkey as a 'Willing Receiver' of American Soft Power: Hollywood Movies in Turkey during the Cold War." *Turkish Studies* 13, no. 4 (2012): 633–45.

Kermode, Mark. *The Exorcist: Revised 2nd Edition*. London: British Film Institute, 2003.

———. "Better the Devil You Know." *The Guardian*. Last modified January 24, 2004. http://www.theguardian.com/film/2004/jan/25/features.review.

King, Cynthia M. and Nora Hourani. "Don't Tease Me: Effects of Ending Type on Horror Film Enjoyment." *Media Psychology* 9, no. 3 (2007): 473–92.

King, Stephen. *Danse Macabre*. New York: Pocket Books, 1982/2010.

Konow, David. *Reel Terror: The Scary, Bloody, Gory, Hundred-Year History of Classic Horror Films*. New York: Thomas Dunne Books, 2012.

Korn, Jenny. "The Devil Makes White Girls Do Backbends: 150 Words on Horror Films." *Jennykorn.com*. Last modified February 23, 2013. http://jennykorn.com/2013/02/23/devil-backbends/.

Krzywinska, Tanya. "Demon Daddies: Gender, Ecstasy and Terror in the Possession Film." In *The Horror Film Reader*, edited by Alain Silver and James Ursini, 247–67. New York: Limelight Editions, 2000.

"The Last Exorcism." *Box Office Mojo*. Accessed August 10, 2015. http://www.rottentomatoes.com/m/last_exorcism/.

"The Last Exorcism (2010)." *Rotten Tomatoes*. Accessed August 10, 2015. http://www.rottentomatoes.com/m/last_exorcism/.

"The Last Exorcism Part II." *Box Office Mojo*. Accessed August 10, 2015. http://www.boxofficemojo.com/movies/?id=lastexorcism2.htm.

"The Last Exorcism Part II (2013)." *Rotten Tomatoes*. Accessed August 10, 2015. http://www.rottentomatoes.com/m/the_last_exorcism_part_ii_2013/.

Lawrence, Novotny. *Blaxploitation Films of the 1970s: Blackness and Genre*. New York: Routledge, 2008.

Listverse staff. "25 Fascinating Facts About The Exorcist." *Listverse*. Last modified October 30, 2009. http://listverse.com/2009/10/30/25-fascinating-facts-about-the-exorcist/.

Loomba, Ania. *Colonialism/Postcolonialism*. New York: Routledge, 1998.

Marcus, Bianca. "A Single Woman: Rebellion Against and Reinforcement of Traditional Gender Roles in *The Exorcist*." *Kino: The Western Undergraduate Journal of Film Studies* 2, no. 1 (2011): 1–3.

Massanari, Adrienne L. *Participatory Culture, Community, and Play: Learning from reddit*. New York: Peter Lang, 2015.

McCabe, Bob. *The Exorcist: Out of the Shadows*. New York: Omnibus Press, 1999.

Medhurst, Martin J. "Image and Ambiguity: A Rhetorical Approach to *The Exorcist*." *The Southern Speech Communication Journal* 44, no. 1 (1978): 73–92.

Messner, Michael A. "'Changing Men' and Feminist Politics in the United States," *Theory and Society* 22, no. 5 (1993): 723–37.

Miller, Steven P. *The Age of Evangelicalism: America's Born-again Years.* New York: Oxford University Press, 2014.

Mitchell, Juliet. *Psychoanalysis and Feminism.* New York: Vintage Books, 1974.

Mulvey, Laura. "Visual Pleasure and Narrative Cinema." In *Film Theory and Criticism* (6th Ed.), edited by Leo Braudy and Marshall Cohen, 837–48. New York: Oxford University Press, 1975/2004.

Munford, Rebecca and Melanie Waters. *Feminism and Popular Culture: Investigating the Postfeminist Mystique.* New Brunswick: Rutgers University Press, 2013.

Nicolini, Kim. "Chasing Hell: The Films of William Friedkin." *CounterPunch* 20, no. 5 (2013): 25–26.

Nowell, Richard. *Blood Money: A History of the First Teen Slasher Film Cycle.* New York City: Continuum International Publishing Group. 2011.

O'Grady, Lorraine. "Olympia's Maid: Reclaiming Black Female Subjectivity." In *The Feminism and Visual Culture Reader* (2nd Ed.), edited by Amelia Jones, 208–20. New York: Routledge, 2010.

Ogunfolabi, Kayode Omoniyi. "History, Horror, Reality: The Idea of the Marvelous in Postcolonial Fiction." PhD diss., Michigan State University, 2008.

Oliver, Kelly. *Knock Me Up, Knock Me Down: Images of Pregnancy in Hollywood Films.* New York: Columbia University Press, 2012.

Olney, Ian. "Spanish Horror Cinema." In *A Companion to the Horror Film*, edited by Harry M. Benshoff, 365–89. Malden: John Wiley & Sons, Inc., 2014.

———. "Unmanning *The Exorcist*: Sex, Gender and Excess in the 1970s Euro-Horror Possession Film." *Quarterly Review of Film and Video* 31, no. 6 (2014): 561–71.

Opsasnik, Mark. "The Haunted Boy of Cottage City: The Cold Hard Facts Behind the Story That Inspired 'The Exorcist.'" *Strangemag.* Accessed August 8, 2015. http://www.strangemag.com/exorcistpage1.html.

Overstreet, Jeffrey. *Through a Screen Darkly: Looking Closer at Beauty, Truth and Evil in the Movies.* Ventura: Regal Books, 2007.

Özkaracalar, Kaya. "Horror Films in Turkish Cinema: To Use or Not to Use Local Cultural Motifs, That is the Question." In *European Nightmares: Horror Cinema in Europe Since 1945*, edited by Patricia Allmer, Emily Brick, and David Huxley, 249–60. New York: Columbia University Press, 2012.

"Paranormal Activity (2009)." *Box Office Mojo.* Accessed August 10, 2015. http://www.boxofficemojo.com/movies/?id=paranormalactivity.htm.

Paul, William. *Laughing Screaming: Modern Hollywood Horror and Comedy.* New York: Columbia University Press, 1994.

Petridis, Sotiris. "A Historical Approach to the Slasher Film." *Film International* 12, no. 1 (2014): 76–84.

Petski, Denise. "Tracy Ifeachor Joins ABC Pilot 'Spark'; Brianne Howey In Fox's 'The Exorcist.'" *Deadline Hollywood.* Last modified February 24, 2016. http://deadline.com/2016/02/tracy-ifeachor-cast-abc-pilot-spark-brianne-howey-the-exorcist-1201708583/.

Phipps, Keith and Scott Tobias. "The Present and Future of Found-footage Horror." *The Dissolve.* Last modified October 30, 2014. https://thedissolve.com/features/movie-of-the-week/804-the-present-and-future-of-found-footage-horror/.

Pieto, Rick. "'The Devil Made Me Do It': Catholicism, Verisimilitude and the Reception of Horror Films." In *Roman Catholicism in Fantastic Film: Essays on Belief, Spectacle, Ritual and Imagery*, edited by Regina Hansen, 52–64. Jefferson: McFarland & Company, Inc., 2011.

Pinedo, Isabel. "Recreational Terror: Postmodern Elements of the Contemporary Horror Film." *Journal of Film and Video* 48, no. 1/2 (1996): 17–31.

Potter, W. James. "Perceived Reality in Television Effects Research." *Journal of Broadcasting and Electronic Media* 32, no. 1. (1988): 23–41.

Qayum, Seemin, and Raka Ray. "Male Servants and the Failure of Patriarchy in Kolkata (Calcutta)." *Men and Masculinities* 13, no. 1 (2010): 111–25.

Richardson, Niall, Clarissa Smith, and Angela Werndly. *Studying Sexualities: Theories, Representations, Cultures.* New York: Palgrave Macmillan, 2013.

Robinson, Tasha. "The Theme That Ties All of Guillermo del Toro's Movies Together." *io9.* Last modified October 20, 2015. http://io9.gizmodo.com/the-theme-that-ties-all-of-guillermo-del-toros-movies-t-1737615770.

Rogers, Nicholas. *Halloween: From Pagan Ritual to Party Night.* Oxford: Oxford University Press, 2002.

Scahill, Andrew. "Demons Are a Girl's Best Friend: Queering the Revolting Child in *The Exorcist.*" *Red Feather Journal* 1, no. 1 (2010): 39–55.

Schatz, Thomas. "Film Genre and the Genre Film." In *Film Theory and Criticism* (6th Ed.), edited by Leo Braudy and Marshall Cohen, 691–702. New York: Oxford University Press, 2004.

Schober, Adrian. *Possessed Child Narratives in Literature and Film: Contrary States.* New York: Palgrave, 2004.

"Şeytan (1974)." *And You Call Yourself a Scientist!* (blog). March 2, 2008. http://www.aycyas.com/turkishexorcist.htm.

Sharrett, Christopher. "The Horror Film as Social Allegory (and How It Comes Undone)." In *A Companion to the Horror Film,* edited by Harry M. Benshoff, 56–72. Malden: John Wiley & Sons, Inc., 2014.

Shipka, Danny. *Perverse Titillation: The Exploitation Cinema of Italy, Spain and France, 1960–1980.* Jefferson: McFarland & Company, Inc., 2011.

Slovick, Matt. "The Exorcist." *The Washington Post,* 1996. At http://www.washingtonpost.com/wp-srv/style/longterm/movies/features/dcmovies/exorcist.htm. Accessed February 13, 2016.

Smelik, Anneke. "Feminist Film Theory." In *The Cinema Book* (3rd Ed.), edited by Pam Cook, 491–501. London: British Film Institute, 2007.

Smith, Iain Robert. "The Exorcist in Istanbul: Processes of Transcultural Appropriation Within Turkish Popular Cinema." *PORTAL Journal of Multidisciplinary International Studies* 5, no. 1 (2008): 1–12.

Smith, Jonathan. "'The Visitor' is All of 70s Horror Shoved into One Film." *Vice.* Last modified October 31, 2013. http://www.vice.com/read/the-visitor-is-the-entirety-of-70s-horror-shoved-into-one-film.

Sobchack, Vivian. "Bringing it All Back Home: Family Economy and Generic Exchange." In *The Dread of Difference: Gender and the Horror Film,* edited by Barry Keith Grant, 143–63. Austin: University of Texas Press, 1996.

Spines, Christine. "Horror Films . . . and the Women Who Love Them!" *Entertainment Weekly,* no. 1058, July 31, 2009, 30–33.

Stone, Bryan. "The Sanctification of Fear: Images of the Religious in Horror Films." *The Journal of Religion and Film* 5, no. 2 (2001): Online.

"Story Notes for *The Exorcism of Emily Rose.*" *AMC.com.* Accessed February 19, 2016, http://www.amc.com/talk/2011/10/story-notes-trivia-the-exorcism-of-emily-rose.

Strayer, Kirsten. "Art, Horror, and International Identity in 1970s Exploitation Films." In *Transnational Horror Across Visual Media: Fragmented Bodies,* edited by Dana Och and Kirsten Strayer, 109–25. New York: Routledge, 2013.

Taub, Amanda. "The Rise of American Authoritarianism." *Vox.* Last modified March 1, 2016. http://www.vox.com/2016/3/1/11127424/trump-authoritarianism.

"Teenage Exorcist" (1991). *buried.com.* Last modified February 16, 2008. http://www.buried.com/horrormovies/teenage-exorcist-1991/4373/.

Telotte, J. P. "Faith and Idolatry in the Horror Film." In *Planks of Reason: Essays on the Horror Film,* edited by Barry Keith Grant and Christopher Sharrett, 20–35. Lanham, MD: Scarecrow press, Inc., 2004.

Thompson, Graham. *American Culture in the 1980s.* Edinburgh: Edinburgh University Press, 2007.

Tomlinson, Simon. "The Devil in Roland Doe: How the 1973 Horror Film *The Exorcist* was Based on a Real-life Possession in Missouri." *Daily Mail.* Last modified October

8, 2013. http://www.dailymail.co.uk/news/article-2449423/Devil-Roland-Doe-The-Exorcist-based-real-life-Missouri-possession.html.

Tudor, Andrew. *Monsters and Mad Scientists: A Cultural History of the Horror Movie.* Cambridge: Basil Blackwell Ltd., 1989.

———. "Unruly Bodies, Unquiet Minds." *Body & Society,* 1, no. 1 (1995): 25–41.

———. "Excerpt from 'Why Horror? The Peculiar Pleasures of a Popular Genre' with a New Afterword by the Author." In *Horror Film and Psychoanalysis: Freud's Worst Nightmare,* edited by Steven Jay Schneider, 55–67. Boston: Cambridge University Press, 2009.

Ward, Graham. *True Religion.* Malden: Blackwell Publishing, 2003.

Wetmore, Kevin J. *Post-9/11 Horror in American Cinema.* New York: Continuum, 2012.

White, Jacquelyn W., Barrie Bondurant and Cheryl Brown Travis, "Social Constructions of Sexuality: Unpacking Hidden Meanings." In *Sexuality, Society, and Feminism,* edited by Cheryl Brown Travis and Jacquelyn W. White, 11–33. Washington, DC: American Psychological Association, 2000.

White, Patricia. *Uninvited: Classical Hollywood Cinema and Lesbian Representability.* Indianapolis: Indiana University Press, 1999.

Willis, Andy. "Paul Naschy, *Exorcismo* and the Reactionary Horrors of Spanish Popular Cinema in the Early 1970s." In *European Nightmares: Horror Cinema in Europe Since 1945,* edited by Patricia Allmer, Emily Brick, and David Huxley, 121–29. New York: Columbia University Press, 2012.

Willson, Jr., Robert F. "*The Exorcist* and Multicinema Aesthetics." *The Journal of Popular Film* 3, no. 2 (1974): 183–87.

Wilmington, Michael. "San Diego Movie Reviews: 'Repossessed': Devil Made Them Do It." *Los Angeles Times.* 1990. http://articles.latimes.com/1990–09–25/entertainment/ca-1326_1_san-diego-movie-reviews. Accessed September 24, 2015.

Wood, Robin. "The American Nightmare: Horror in the 70s." In *Horror, The Film Reader,* edited by Mark Jancovich, 25–32. New York: Routledge, 2002.

———. *Hollywood from Vietnam to Reagan . . . and Beyond.* New York: Columbia University Press, 2003.

Woods, Richard. *The Devil.* Merrimack: The Thomas More Press, 1973.

Index

9/11, 15, 90, 103, 122, 125–126, 136, 143, 149, 170–171; post-9/11 period, 127–128, 137, 144–145, 162, 171–172, 174

Abby, 15, 45, 49, 51–56, 60–62, 65n61, 65n66, 70–72, 81, 83, 113, 133, 154, 177
abjection, 5–6, 22, 24–33, 37, 41n94, 75, 76, 80, 83, 99, 111, 131, 141–142, 154, 163, 174, 175
adolescence, 22, 26–27
agency, 16, 25, 28, 30–31, 33–37, 40n54, 49, 52, 53, 56, 70, 71, 75, 83, 111, 113, 117, 119, 130–131, 135, 142, 150, 155–156, 158–164, 174, 183n48
AIDS, 15, 88–89, 91, 101, 125, 170
Alucarda, la hija de las tinieblas, 49
American Exorcist, 174
Amityville II: The Possession, 15, 94, 108, 112–117, 120–122, 135, 144, 178
The Amityville Horror, 114–115, 162
Anneliese: The Exorcist Tapes, 129
The Antichrist. See L'anticristo

L'anticristo, 49, 64n44

appropriation, 13, 35, 56–57, 59–60
Assonitis, Ovidio G., 48, 64n38
authoritarianism, 177
authority, 13–14, 21, 50, 97, 118, 157; authority, paternal, 5, 25–26, 29–30, 32–33, 35, 98, 100, 103, 117; authority, patriarchal, 5, 16, 25, 30, 33, 36, 55, 62, 96, 98, 100–101, 119–120, 142–143, 159, 163, 179

Bad Exorcists, 179
Beetlejuice, 94

Benshoff, Harry M., 13, 52, 61, 65n54, 65n58, 71
Beyond the Darkness. See Magdalena, vom Teufel besessen
Beyond the Door. See Chi sei?
Bishop, Kyle, 61, 82
Black Devil Doll from Hell, 92
Blacula, 51
The Blaxorcist. See Abby
Blair, Linda, 2, 24, 44, 69, 90, 94–95, 128
The Blair Witch Project, 128, 137
Blatty, William Peter, 22, 62n1, 67, 73, 107–108, 110, 122, 126–129
The Bloody Exorcism of Coffin Joe. See O Exorcism Negro
Boorman, John, 67, 84n1

Carroll, Noël, 4–5
Catholic Church, 9, 21, 26, 32, 40n70–41n71, 53, 58, 70, 72, 79, 109–110, 113, 117–122, 130, 131, 137, 139, 142–144, 147n42, 147n43, 158, 169
Catholicism, 10, 22, 59, 71, 94, 98, 120, 134
Chi sei?, 48
Christianity, 31, 52–53, 56, 66n82, 72, 81, 119; Christianity, black, 52–53
civil rights, 88, 169
Clover, Carol J., 8, 22, 27, 30, 32, 34, 36–37, 89
colonialism, 3, 13, 14, 52, 53, 55, 57, 61–62, 65n61, 66n82, 71, 73, 81–83, 167–168, 178, 181
The Conjuring, 129, 162, 174
The Conjuring 2, 129, 162
conservative, 15, 46–47, 49, 55, 60, 62, 64n44, 88, 91–92, 101–103, 105n22, 150, 170, 174, 181; neoconservative, 88–89

Constantine, 156
countercultural, 3, 92, 117, 173–174
Cowan, Douglas E., 4, 6, 117
Creed, Barbara, 5, 22, 24–27, 31, 33, 41n94, 176
cultivation theory, 11, 145, 177

damsel in distress, 3, 8, 30–31, 154, 156, 159
Deliver Us from Evil, 112, 129, 132–136, 143, 173, 177, 178
Deezen, Eddie, 98–99
Demon , 178
Demon Witch Child. See La endemoniada
Demoniac. See L'éventreur de Notre-Dame
demonic possession, 3, 9, 26, 32–33, 35–36, 48, 75, 99, 113, 133, 135, 161, 171
Il Demonio, 30
Derrickson, Scott, 129–132
The Devil, 8, 9–10, 21, 32–33, 38n15, 40n70, 44, 53, 70, 71, 92, 95, 97–98, 103, 108, 169, 171–172, 181
The Devil and the Nun. See Matka Joanna od aniolów
The Devil Fetus. See Mo Tai
The Devil Inside, 136, 178
The Devil Obsession. See L'ossessa
Devil Returns. See Jing hun feng yu ye
Devil's Due, 156
The Devil's Exorcist. See El juego del diablo
Devil's Female. See Magdalena, vom Teufel besessen
The Devil's Gift, 92
The Devils, 16n1, 30
Der Dibuk, 1–2, 16n1, 29
The Disco Exorcist, 179
disempowerment, 3, 28, 36, 49, 62, 90–91, 97, 168, 177
djinn, 58, 66n82
documentary, 15, 127, 136–137, 140, 151–152, 154
Dolan, Jill, 61, 83
Dominion: Prequel to the Exorcist, 68, 78, 80–83, 108, 178
doubting priest, 34, 37, 53, 70, 76, 79–80, 97–98, 111, 113, 116, 120–121, 131, 134–135, 138–139, 142–143, 153,

157, 160–162, 167, 173–175, 177–179
Dracula, 40n69, 50
The Duxorcist, 94
dybbuk, 2, 9, 27, 165n25
The Dybbuk. See Der Dibuk

The Eerie Midnight Horror Show. See L'ossessa
empowerment, 3, 5, 8, 14, 35–36, 56, 61, 75, 79, 81, 82, 131, 143, 150, 154, 157, 159–164, 167–168, 175, 177; empowerment, female 7, 22–23, 25, 28, 34, 36–37, 46, 94, 96–100, 145, 149–150, 154, 156–157, 161–164
La endemoniada, 49
Enter the Devil. See L'ossessa
Erksan, Metin, 56, 65n73
Eshu, 51–56, 65n54
L'esorciccio, 48, 94
Esu-Elegbara. *See* Eshu
L'éventreur de Notre-Dame, 47
O Exorcism Negro, 48
Exorcism and Black Masses. See L'éventreur de Notre-Dame
The Exorcism of Emily Rose, 129–131, 143, 155, 160, 169, 178
Exorcism at Midnight. See Naked Evil
The Exorcism of Molly Hartley, 147n43, 162–163
Exorcism's Daughter. See Las melancólicas
exorcism ritual, 3, 8–9, 29, 37, 79, 93, 139, 161–162
Exorcisms. See L'éventreur de Notre-Dame
Exorcismo, 48
Exorcist: The Beginning, 68, 77–81, 111
The Exorcist, 1–3, 6, 9–11, 14–15, 21–38, 38n5, 38n15, 40n70, 41n79, 41n91, 43–49, 51, 53, 55–60, 62, 66n82, 66n90, 67–71, 73, 77–78, 82–83, 84n1, 84n15, 87, 92, 94–97, 100, 102–103, 107–110, 113–114, 117, 120–122, 125–128, 132–133, 135, 142, 144, 150, 153–154, 156, 165n20, 167, 169, 173, 176, 179; *The Exorcist* (TV series), 84n11, 180
Exorcist II: The Heretic, 38n15, 67–73, 76–78, 80–83, 84n15, 108, 111, 113,

131, 162, 178

The Exorcist III, 68–69, 73–76, 82, 89–90, 113, 127, 132–135, 144, 178

The Exorcist: Italian Style. See L'esorciccio

The Exorcist's Apprentice, 179

Exorcistas, 179

exploitation cinema, 15, 45–47, 60, 63n33, 93; Blaxploitation, 46, 49–53, 56, 65n58; nunsploitation, 30, 49; sexploitation, 47, 49

feminism, 5, 12, 14, 23–25, 30, 38n5, 45, 47, 60–61, 73, 91, 102, 145, 149, 150, 158, 162, 164, 168, 172, 178–179; feminism, second-wave, 21–23, 25, 28–29, 59, 103, 145

feminist theory. *See* feminism

Final Girl, 30, 90–92, 101–102

Foucault, Michel, 13–14, 175

found footage, 127–128, 136–137, 140, 144, 146n15, 150, 152, 165n10

Friedkin, William, 1, 22, 38n5, 43, 67, 126–127

gay rights, 23, 172

The Gemini Killer, 68–75

genre, 4–7, 17n37, 32, 44–45, 50, 87, 90, 94, 95, 103, 137, 157, 172, 174, 177, 180; subgenre, 1, 4, 8–11, 14, 31, 36–37, 46, 48, 62, 69, 84, 87–91, 94–96, 101–104, 122, 127, 137, 146n15, 169, 174, 178, 180; subgenre, exorcism cinema, 3, 9, 11, 15–16, 23, 30, 32, 34, 35, 44, 87–88, 90, 91, 94, 104, 108, 109, 127, 134, 153, 157, 160, 161, 170, 172–173, 176, 177, 179, 181

generation gap, 21–22

ghosts, 112, 123n20

Girdler, William, 51–52

globalization, 29, 45–47, 49, 60

Grace: The Possession, 123n23, 136, 140–144, 147n47, 155

Harlin, Renny, 77–78, 80

A Head Full of Ghosts, 180

hegemony, 46, 62, 83

Hell Baby, 179

Hellbenders, 179

Heller-Nicholas, Alexandra, 10, 107, 137

heteronormativity, 3, 12–14, 37, 52–53, 72, 74, 82, 88, 97, 133, 167, 168, 173, 180–181; non-heteronormative, 3, 12, 38, 61, 62, 65n69, 72, 75, 81, 83, 88, 89, 97, 111, 167, 177

Hewitt, Simon, 26–28

Hollywood, 7, 9, 45–46, 56, 60–62, 64n38, 137. *See also* globalization

homosexuality, 13, 14, 27, 65n69, 71, 82, 89, 97, 100

horror, 3–4, 7, 10, 17n18, 26, 45, 66n90, 72–73, 87, 91, 94, 112, 125–126, 144, 177, 181; horror films, 1, 2, 4–7, 8, 10, 11–12, 14, 17n18, 22, 25, 30–31, 33–34, 44–47, 50, 52, 59–62, 64n34, 72, 92, 94, 125, 127–128, 143, 145, 147n33, 149, 156, 168, 171–176, 180–181; horror, genre, 17n37, 32, 90, 95, 103, 137, 172, 174; horror, pleasure, 5, 7, 24, 37, 128, 131, 175; horror, post-9/11, 93, 94, 103, 125–126, 128, 137, 143–145, 149, 150, 157, 171, 174

The House of Exorcism. See Lisa e il diavolo

Hutchings, Peter, 22, 40n69, 64n42

I Don't Want to Be Born, 161

ideology, 3–4, 6, 9, 11–14, 25, 31, 37, 39n40, 45–47, 49–50, 52, 55, 56, 60–62, 71–72, 82, 83, 88, 91, 92, 101, 104, 113, 126, 128, 143, 144, 145, 149–150, 164, 167, 168, 170, 173–181

invasion, 8, 25, 27–28

Islam, 9, 38n6, 49, 58–60, 62, 66n78, 66n82, 66n90, 170

Jesuit, 24, 109, 117, 132

Jing hun feng yu ye, 93

Judaism, 9, 10

El juego del diablo, 47

Karras, Fr. Damien, 24, 26, 27, 29–30, 33–35, 40n54, 57, 68, 73, 74–75, 76, 83, 92, 98, 113, 127, 134, 135, 142, 144, 153, 156, 157, 173, 179

Kermode, Mark, 21, 22, 28–29, 38n5, 38n14, 40n53, 43, 67, 68, 77, 84n10, 123n17, 127
Kinderman, Lt. William, 68, 73–74, 75, 76, 82, 113, 127
King, Stephen, 6, 22, 33, 93, 172
Kristeva, Julia, 5, 131

The Last Exorcism, 16, 98, 102, 123n23, 136, 149–164, 165n23, 165n25
The Last Exorcism Part II, 16, 149–164, 165n23, 174, 179, 183n48
lesbian, 19n92, 25, 27; lesbianism, 27, 49
liminal, 4, 26, 27, 54, 71, 75, 83, 84n16
Lisa and the Devil. See Lisa e il diavolo
Lisa e il diavolo, 48, 64n35
Lorna the Exorcist. See Les possédées du diable

MacNeil, Chris, 23–25, 28, 57, 59, 108, 127
MacNeil, Regan, 2, 22, 24–30, 32, 34–35, 39n40, 40n70–41n71, 44, 57, 62n1, 68, 69–71, 73, 83, 94, 95, 96, 100, 108, 112–113, 122, 127, 131, 154, 176, 179, 183n47
Magdalena, Possessed by the Devil. See Magdalena, vom Teufel besessen
Magdalena, vom Teufel besessen, 49
male savior, 3, 34, 37, 143, 157, 161, 162, 163, 179
The Mangler, 93
The Manitou, 49
Marcus, Rev. Cotton, 98, 150–152, 153–154, 155, 156–157, 158, 164
marginalization, 3, 5, 12, 14–16, 38, 49–50, 55, 61, 62, 69, 72, 81, 82, 97, 113, 119, 122, 143–145, 149, 159, 167–168, 173–175, 177, 180–181
Marshall, William, 51, 52
masculinity, 12, 14, 19n80, 22, 27–28, 33–36, 41n79, 46, 50–55, 62, 70–72, 74–76, 82, 83, 91–92, 97, 98, 101, 103, 108, 111, 112, 116, 117, 133–135, 144, 147n33, 149–150, 157, 173, 174, 178–179; masculinize, 27, 35, 91
Matka Joanna od aniołów, 29
McCambridge, Mercedes, 27, 44, 83
Las melancólicas, 16n1, 30, 47

Merrin, Fr Lankester, 23–24, 26, 29, 33, 58, 68, 69, 70–71, 77, 78–81, 83, 92, 98, 108, 111, 127, 157
metaphor, 3–4, 6, 14, 23, 25–26, 29–30, 34–37, 49, 52, 62, 72, 82–83, 92, 101, 112, 116–117, 120, 126, 133, 134, 144, 152, 154–156, 161–164, 171, 173–177, 181. *See also* traditional exorcism narrative
Michel, Anneliese, 129
Mo Tai, 93
morality, 3, 5, 7, 8, 23, 37, 51–53, 55, 71, 91, 125, 143–144, 168
monstrous-feminine, 31, 70, 72, 178
monstrous masculine, 135, 178
Mother Joan of the Angels. See Matka Joanna od aniołów

Naked Evil, 16n1, 30, 48
New Millennium, 90, 104, 127, 172
Ninja III: The Domination, 93

occult, 22, 90, 112, 151; occult film, 8, 22, 25, 30, 36, 63n33, 90, 93
oppression, 3, 5, 12–16, 25, 29, 30, 35–38, 39n18, 39n40, 49–50, 56, 61–62, 71, 75, 81–84, 91, 104, 113, 117, 119–120, 122, 133, 136, 141–145, 150, 154, 155, 160–164, 167–168, 173–176, 180–181
L'ossessa, 49, 124n34

Other, 6, 12, 14, 30–31, 50, 55, 56, 60–62, 66n82, 71, 74, 75, 81, 82, 92, 103, 111, 113, 115, 144, 167, 168, 171, 173–175, 177, 179, 180–181
Outcast, 180
Özkaracalar, Kaya, 58, 59

Paranormal Activity, 137
Paranormal Activity: The Ghost Dimension, 136
parody, 15, 48, 68, 84, 87, 90, 93–97, 102–103, 105n26, 113, 121, 179
paternal law. *See* authority, paternal
paternal order. *See* authority, paternal
patriarchy, 12, 14, 19n80, 26, 29, 33, 35–37, 49, 52, 62, 63n33, 64n42, 74–76, 81, 91, 98, 103, 116, 131,

134–136, 143, 150, 158–159, 160, 162, 167–168, 180–181

patriarchal, 3, 13, 26–27, 30–31, 33, 35–37, 39n18, 41n79, 46, 55, 91, 119, 135, 142, 144, 160, 168; patriarchal figure, 24, 70, 98, 100, 103, 159, 163; patriarchal ideology, 31, 52, 72, 92, 101, 144, 173, 178; patriarchal institution, 12, 19n80, 28, 32–35, 70, 72, 76, 82, 92, 115, 117, 120, 134, 139, 156; patriarchal oppression, 75, 91, 160; patriarchal order. *See also* authority, patriarchal 24–25, 27–29, 31–32, 34–37, 41n78, 51, 60, 70, 75, 79–81, 91, 93, 96, 97, 98, 111, 113, 116, 119, 120, 121–122, 131, 133, 134, 139, 147n33, 153, 154, 156, 159, 163, 174; patriarchal stability, 27, 111, 117, 120, 122; patriarchal values, 33, 37, 52, 56, 60, 72, 79, 81, 88, 91, 92, 109, 120, 134, 144, 157, 159–161, 164

Pazuzu, 23–24, 27, 29, 38n15, 39n40, 44, 53, 55, 57, 66n82, 68–72, 74, 77, 80–81, 84n15, 108

perceived reality, 11, 145, 177

Petridis, Sotiris, 87, 90, 101, 103, 104n16

phallus, 31, 55, 160

Pieto, Rick, 6, 10

Pope Paul VI, 21, 169

Les possédées du diable, 47

Possessed, 108, 110–113, 116, 120–122, 128, 135–136, 155, 178, 181

The Possessed. See La endemoniada

possessed-woman-as-threat, 34, 36, 61, 103, 121, 122, 143, 161, 162, 167, 173, 177; possessed-Other-as-threat, 61, 121–122, 145

The Possession of Michael King, 136, 178

The Possessor. See Un urlo dalla tenebre

postcolonialism, 13, 39n40, 45, 52, 56, 60–62, 66n82, 71–72, 168

postmodern, 89, 90, 94, 101–103, 127, 145, 163, 170, 176

power, 9, 12–14, 29, 31, 33, 35–37, 50, 54, 60–61, 73, 83, 84n14, 92, 96, 99–100, 113, 118–119, 131, 136, 142, 150, 152, 154–164, 165n24, 167–168, 175, 178, 181. *See also* empowerment; power dynamics,

16, 61, 81, 126, 181n1; power, feminine, 35, 150, 162, 163; power, masculine, 71, 75, 82, 120, 133, 135, 159, 183n29

pregnancy, 151, 154, 156, 165n25, 176–177

puberty, 26, 177. *See also* adolescence

psychoanalysis, 4–5, 17n18, 23, 25, 45, 176

Quarantine, 137

queer identity, 14, 26, 65n54, 71–72, 75, 83, 91

queer theory, 13, 81–83, 93, 97, 98, 100, 113, 115–116, 122, 168, 178

racism, 3, 13, 50, 52, 61, 65n54, 84, 103, 167. *See also* colonialism

Reagan, Ronald, 88, 103

realism, 7, 103–104, 113–114, 122, 125, 126, 128, 129, 132, 136, 143, 145

[Rec], 137

[Rec]², 136, 137–140, 143, 156, 161

[REC]³: Génesis , 136, 138

recontextualization, 60, 66n90. *See also* appropriation

Repossessed, 15, 90, 95–100, 103

repression, 3, 5, 12–13, 28, 29, 33, 35–37, 40n70, 55, 56, 60, 61, 62, 64n53, 66n82, 72, 91, 92, 96, 100–101, 113, 119, 122, 131, 133, 141, 145, 150, 153, 155, 158–161, 163, 167–168, 174–175, 178–181

Requiem, 129

The Return of the Exorcist. See Un urlo dalla tenebre

revolting child, 22, 26

rhetoric, 41n79, 52, 71, 72–73, 83, 88, 103, 113, 126, 157, 162, 168, 182n14

Ripper of Notre Dame. See L'éventreur de Notre-Dame

Rosemary's Baby, 48, 156

Sarchie, Ralph, 132–135, 146n30, 173

Satan. *See* The devil

satanism, 8, 22, 48, 49, 90, 152, 156

satanic film. *See* occult film

satanic panic. *See* occult

Scahill, Andrew, 26, 38n6, 39n30, 174

Scary Movie 2 , 94

Schrader, Paul, 77–78, 80

The Sexorcist. See L'ossessa

sexual revolution, 22, 46

sexuality, 6, 13, 15, 21, 27, 28, 39n18, 40n70, 41n78, 43, 46, 51–52, 83, 88, 91, 92, 97, 99, 101, 102, 103, 113, 115–116; sexuality, black, 55–56, 62, 65n54, 178; sexuality, burgeoning, 26, 29, 33, 36, 41n71, 142, 155–158; sexuality, female, 12–13, 16, 22, 25, 26, 29–30, 32–37, 40n54, 46, 49–50, 52–57, 60, 64n34, 80, 83, 87, 91–92, 96–99, 101, 103, 105n22, 111, 113, 115, 119–122, 133, 141, 150, 153–155, 158–161, 165n25, 178; sexuality, teenage, 15, 27, 88, 101–102, 170; sexuality, transgressive, 46, 63n33, 83

Şeytan, 15, 45, 50, 56–62, 66n82

Shark Exorcist, 179

Shipka, Danny, 46, 49, 60, 64n35, 64n44

The Shrine, 178

slasher films, 10, 15, 30, 73, 88–93, 94, 101–103, 104n15, 104n16, 125, 143, 169, 175; neoslashers, 90, 103, 176; slashers, postmodern, 90, 101–103

Smith, Iain Robert, 56–57, 59

social cognitive theory, 11, 177

sociocultural, 4, 9, 11–13, 15, 25, 29, 31–33, 43, 83, 91, 95, 101–102, 104, 111, 113, 122, 125–127, 144, 168–172, 174, 177, 181, 181n1; sociocultural anxieties, 3, 6–8, 15, 22–23, 26, 33, 87–88, 90, 103, 125–126, 144, 169, 171, 172, 176, 177, 180; sociocultural tensions, 3, 5–6, 9, 12, 22, 36, 56, 60, 92, 149, 167; sociocultural values, 19n80, 88, 113

Stamm, Daniel, 40n66, 102, 156–157

Stigmata, 15, 94, 109, 113, 117–122, 139, 142, 144

suppression, 12, 16, 27, 29, 36, 37, 61, 81, 89, 112, 167, 168, 181

symbolic father, 29, 81, 92

symbolic order, 5, 10, 25, 26, 31, 33, 39n30, 52, 55, 58, 61, 65n69, 70, 70–71, 83, 96, 112, 117, 130, 133, 142, 161. *See also* patriarchal order

Teenage Exorcist, 15, 95, 98–101, 103

terrorism, 103, 125, 126, 143, 170–171

The Tormented. See L'ossessa

torture porn, 10, 93

traditional exorcism narrative, 3, 9, 14–16, 23, 30, 34, 36–37, 45, 47, 49, 56, 59–62, 68–71, 74–76, 78–84, 91, 93–96, 98, 100–102, 104, 109, 111, 113, 115–122, 127–130, 133, 136, 138–140, 142–145, 150, 153, 156–158, 160–164, 167–168, 173–181. *See also* metaphor

transcultural, 45, 56, 60. *See also* appropriation

transgression, 5, 26, 27, 30, 35, 46, 49, 54, 71, 72, 75, 81, 83, 91, 97, 112, 115, 122

tropes, 4, 10, 14, 16, 23, 26, 30, 34, 36–37, 44, 48, 59, 61, 64n34, 66n90, 78, 82, 90, 94, 96, 103, 120–121, 127, 132, 133, 137, 143, 145, 161–164, 167, 173, 178–179

Tudor, Andrew, 4, 6, 8, 44, 117, 168, 176

Turkification. *See* appropriation.

The Unborn, 162–163, 174, 177, 183n48

Undershorts, 94

Un urlo dalla tenebre, 49

vampire, 3–4, 10

The Vatican Tapes, 41n91, 177, 178

verisimilitude, 127, 137, 140. *See also* realism

virgin/whore dichotomy, 31–34, 36, 49, 80, 99, 102, 119, 141, 143

violence, 7, 9, 28–29, 35, 37, 43, 46, 76, 90–91, 103, 116, 134–135, 144, 154; violence, masculine, 27–28, 76, 91, 112, 116–117, 120, 134, 179

voice, 6, 27–28, 35–36, 53–55, 61–62, 65n66, 71, 74–75, 81, 84, 91, 96, 111, 118–120, 130–131, 138, 143, 144, 150, 154–159, 161, 173–174

Warren, Ed, 146n30, 162

Warren, Lorraine, 146n30, 162

Waszynski, Michal, 1, 128

werewolf, 4, 50, 176

Wetmore, Kevin J., 8, 12, 125–126, 137, 143–144, 149–150, 157, 171
witches, 3, 49; witchcraft, 8, 22, 75
women's liberation, 23, 46, 119, 172. *See also* feminism
Wood, Robin, 6, 12–13, 168, 180
Woods, Richard, 9, 64n40, 171, 179, 184n55

Yoruba religion, 51–52, 55–56, 65n54, 84n16
youth culture, 22, 46, 48, 117, 169. *See also* generation gap

zombies, 4, 10, 82, 99, 137

About the Authors

Christopher J. Olson received his MA in media and cinema studies from DePaul University in Chicago, Illinois, in 2014. He currently works as an adjunct professor at Dominican University in River Forest, Illinois, where he teaches classes on masculinity and interracial communication. He also teaches a class on film as art at Harry S. Truman College in downtown Chicago, and an online class on game studies at Governors State University in Chicago's Southland. Since 2014, he has served as co-host of *The Pop Culture Lens* podcast, which he co-created with his partner, Dr. CarrieLynn Reinhard of Dominican University. Together, they co-edited the book *Making Sense of Cinema: Empirical Studies into Film Spectators and Spectatorship* (Bloomsbury Academic, 2016), as well as a forthcoming collection of essays that examine depictions of gender and sexuality in children's entertainment.

CarrieLynn D. Reinhard received her PhD in communication from the Ohio State University in Columbus, Ohio, in 2008; she received her MA in communication from the same university in 2005. She served as a postdoctoral researcher in virtual worlds and reception studies at Roskilde University in Roskilde, Denmark, from 2008 through 2010. She currently works as an associate professor at Dominican University in River Forest, Illinois, where she teaches classes in digital communication technologies, game design, communication research methods, and persuasion. She has published numerous articles and book chapters on reception studies, primarily concerning digital communication technologies. Along with her partner, Christopher J. Olson of Dominican University, she is co-editor of *Making Sense of Cinema: Empirical Studies into Film Spectators and Spectatorship* (Bloomsbury Academic, 2016), co-host and co-creator of *The Pop Culture Lens* podcast, and co-editor of a forthcoming collection of essays that examine depictions of gender and sexuality in children's entertainment.

CPSIA information can be obtained
at www.ICGtesting.com
Printed in the USA
BVOW01*0332291016

466342BV00001B/5/P